Signs of Cleopatra

For two thousand years images of Cleopatra have been implicated in the fantasies of European cultures. The name of Cleopatra identifies not so much a person as the place where power and desire intersect. Across different periods and cultures this has borne widely diverse meanings. Images of Cleopatra are structured not by her own history but by the traces of specific past struggles for authority.

Mary Hamer recovers those traces. *Signs of Cleopatra* is a set of Cleopatra puzzles, using the Bakhtinian argument that a contest of meanings based around a figure indicates that issues of the widest importance are being organized and grounded through it. Taking particular images of Cleopatra from history, classics, film, literary studies, art history and the history of science, the author explores the social and historical formations which produced them, questioning the processes of representation as she does so.

Mary Hamer is a cultural historian, working on the politics of representation. She has most recently held fellowships at the Commonwealth Center for Literary and Cultural Change, University of Virginia, and at the Bunting Institute, Radcliffe College, Harvard.

Gender, Culture, Difference
General editor: Catherine Belsey

Signs of Cleopatra

History, politics, representation

Mary Hamer

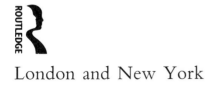

London and New York

First published 1993
by Routledge
11 New Fetter Lane, London EC4P 4EE

Simultaneously published in the USA and Canada
by Routledge
a division of Routledge, Chapman and Hall, Inc.
29 West 35th Street, New York, NY 10001

Typeset in 10/12pt Bembo by
Intype, London
Printed and bound in Great Britain by
Butler & Tanner Ltd, Frome

British Library Cataloguing in Publication Data
Hamer, Mary
  Signs of Cleopatra: History, Politics, Representation. – (Gender, Culture,
Difference Series)
  I. Title II. Series
  932.021092

Library of Congress Cataloging in Publication Data
Hamer, Mary
    Signs of Cleopatra: history, politics, representation / Mary Hamer.
      p.   cm. — (Gender, culture, difference)
    Includes bibliographical references and index.
    1. Cleopatra, Queen of Egypt, d. 30 BC, in fiction, drama, poetry, etc.
  2.   Queens in literature. 3.   Women – Mythology. 4.   Cleopatra, Queen
  of Egypt, d. 30 BC.   5. Arts.   I. Title.   II. Series.
  PN57.C55H36   1993
  809'.93351–dc20   92–10396

ISBN 0–415–04871–0
        0–415–04872–9 (pbk)

For Emily and Camilla, my daughters

Contents

Gender, Culture, Difference
General editor's preface

Feminism has now reached a point where it is possible to produce a series of books written with the explicit aim of bringing together the politics of gender, cultural analysis, and theoretically informed ways of reading. *Gender, Culture, Difference* offers a new kind of cultural history, which investigates the topics feminism has foregrounded and takes the full range of cultural documents as its material.

GENDER

Feminism attends to the power relations inscribed in the areas patriarchal history treats as incidental: sexuality, private life and personal relations, cultural difference itself. At the same time, it also recognizes transgression of the existing conventions as a mode of resistance, and therefore takes an interest in behaviour traditionally classified as perverse or dangerous. Above all, it is able to identify the differences within the relationships and practices it explores, treating them not as unified and homogeneous, but as contradictory to the degree that they participate in the uncertainties, incoherences, and instabilities of the cultures where they are found. The series addresses the topics politicized by feminism, analysing them as sites where power is contested.

CULTURE

It is in culture that hierarchies of power are defined and specified. Recent theory urges that the material of cultural analysis is always textual. We have no access to 'experience', past or present, but only to the differential meanings in circulation within a culture. And these meanings reside in the existing documents, which can be read in order to make a history that refuses the injustices perpetrated by conventional patriarchal histories.

The documents of culture include, of course, every kind of material that it is possible to interpret: images, design and fashion, maps and domestic architecture, as well as philosophy, law, medicine . . . But the project also involves attention, perhaps special attention, to fiction, since it is in stories, legends, plays, and poems that many cultures have tended to treat most freely and most precisely the relations between the sexes. (This in itself is a matter of some interest to feminism: fiction is what a patriarchal culture identified as 'not true', not serious, not real and important. But, to the extent that life follows art, in practice fiction returns to haunt the 'real' history which marginalizes it.)

DIFFERENCE

Cultural contradictions, incoherences, and instabilities are pressure points for feminism, because they constitute evidence that existing power relations are always precarious. In this respect the interests of feminism coincide with recent modes of interpretation which specifically seek out instances of uncertainty, of difference within the text. For this reason, the series takes advantage of a range of theoretical developments which promote a differential practice of reading.

At the same time, feminism avoids the closed mode of address which sets out to deflect criticism and forestall debate. *Gender, Culture, Difference* is a speculative series that sets out to enlist readers in the process of discussion, and does not hesitate to engage with questions to which it has no final answers.

A NEW DIRECTION

The series brings together a differential reading practice and the construction of a cultural history which celebrates difference. In this respect *Gender, Culture, Difference* also offers a new model for literary studies. The epoch of the Author is over; few teachers and virtually no students now want to hear about maturity and the organic society, or about ambiguity and balance; and Elizabethan and other world pictures are totally played out. Meanwhile, English departments are looking for a way forward. It would not be at all surprising if feminism proved itself to be responsible for identifying one of the most exciting among the possible new directions.

Catherine Belsey

Plates

Acknowledgements

The debts incurred in writing this book have been many. I was dependent on the generosity of scholars and experts in disciplines of which I was ignorant and it rarely failed. Many individual acts of enlightenment are acknowledged in the footnotes but they still do not give an adequate sense of the enthusiastic interest and co-operation I encountered.

Ted Kenney, John Ray, and Dorothy Thompson were particularly mindful of contacts and information that might be of value. The continuing interest of Gillian Beer, Martin Bernal, and Kate Belsey was a source of steady encouragement. Above all, Kate briskly urged me forward through moments of anxiety: I owe the successful completion of the project to her support.

I am grateful, too to Janice Price, who encouraged steadily, without interfering. I constantly exchanged work-in-progress with Suzanne Raitt over the time that this book was being written: her intellectual companionship has been one of the great pleasures of the journey.

The final tasks connected with producing the book were performed in the United States, at the Bunting Institute and at the Commonwealth Center, University of Virginia: I want to offer the warmest thanks to my colleagues in both places.

Grants towards research visits for this book were received from the Hort Fund, the Thomas Mulvey Fund, and the Judith B. Wilson Fund, all of Cambridge University, and from the Twenty-Seven Foundation of London University.

The assistance given by my husband has been extensive and practical, in this as in so many undertakings.

An earlier version of chapter 2 appeared under the same title in *Textual Practice*, Summer 1988.

Introduction

It was the baffling opacity of pictures that propelled me into this study. Leafing through the files of the Photographic Collection of the Warburg Institute, with rather a different project (about Shakespeare's women) in mind, I was brought up short by the images I found under the heading of Cleopatra. In the first place, they were so unfamiliar. They did not reflect or match my own sense of what Cleopatra was about. That sense, as I was to realize some time later, was overwhelmingly determined by Shakespeare's presentation. The pictures I found did not address the narrative of *Antony and Cleopatra* or share its tragic vision. The difference of focus was bewildering. One of the principal themes of the images, Cleopatra's banquet, I had to look up in a reference dictionary. When the topos was familiar, as in the case of Cleopatra's death, the treatment surprised me with its emphasis on the erotic. I could scarcely recognize Cleopatra in these guises.

Among the Warburg filing cabinets I learned to stop using Shakespeare as a norm and to ask what Cleopatra had meant before he wrote. My work as a teacher of literature had shaped my notion of Cleopatra: people with different backgrounds would base theirs on different sources. At the Renaissance it would have been the Roman poets or Plutarch, while for many people in the later twentieth century Elizabeth Taylor has defined the meaning of Cleopatra. Recognizing this was a step in the right direction. It meant giving up the fantasy that there was an accurate original to which subsequent versions could be referred. But it did not explain the pictures, which often seemed to contradict each other by implication. Some early woodcuts and engravings that bore the name of Cleopatra, for instance, might show her as naked and seductive, with a snake, like Eve: there were several of these, by different artists, made in Italy and Germany. One by Veneziano showed her with flowing hair, a tree in the background, and a cupid, complete with bow, at her side. On the other hand, her body, flattened into the confined space under a masonry arch in a book frontispiece by Holbein, might speak of pain and constraint. I was often surprised by the strength and amplitude of the naked bodies depicted. There was no single or predictable meaning to be read from them. Some were quite simply mysterious: a sixteenth-century roundel showed a naked woman, the moon on her head and the sun at her genitals, in a sailing ship coming into a harbour whose quay was lined with solid, well-dressed female citizens.

Because these images were filed in a library, they did bear labels with their attribution, in most cases. But their meanings remained inaccessible. Rarely had many of the images been the subject of sustained critical attention in themselves. At that time, Lucy Hughes-Hallett's work on the image of Cleopatra had not been published: when it did come out, it offered an admirable and encyclopaedic assembly of materials but it was not setting out to question the mechanisms that supported the creation of meaning in individual examples. Before that, images of Cleopatra had usually been subsumed in wider discussions of the separate artist's *oeuvre*. When images of Cleopatra were addressed directly, it was assumed that they were sufficiently 'explained' by relating them to the particular version of a classical text where the incident depicted was described or to the virtuosity of the artist. Peter Walch, for instance, has shown how in the eighteenth century a frontispiece engraved by Gravelot for Rollin's *Ancient History* established a model for a whole series of pictures of Cleopatra in the presence of Octavian. Valuable as it was, such information did nothing to dispel the confusion of a viewer faced with the restless variety of the visual signs produced under the name of Cleopatra.

Even when some individual information about the conditions in which an image had been produced had been made available by scholarship, the problem did not go away – as I found when I read that a seventeenth-century Dutch version of Cleopatra's banquet was painted as a memorial portrait of the family the artist had lost in the plague: it showed his dead father as Antony and his dead mother as Cleopatra (Plate 2.2). At that point, beside myself with a curiosity that I justify as intellectual, I was hooked. If the image of Cleopatra could, with decorum, be mapped on to the memory of a deceased mother, I wanted to know how.

Issues of politics and desire are at stake in representing Cleopatra. In this figure they are fascinatingly entwined and collapsed into each other. That is one reason why the figure of Cleopatra has survived so strongly as a term in cultural exchange and been reworked so often. Its power to generate and sustain fantasy is exceptional. More than eroticism is involved: it is a question of the status of Cleopatra as a founding myth in Western culture.

This is not too strong a way to put it. Cleopatra lived and more importantly died at a moment from which our era has often traced its origin. Augustan Rome, with its architecture, law, literature, and history, has been acknowledged as the source of an ideal of civic order. It has been bound together in the Western mind with another originary moment, the lifetime of the founder of Christianity. It was the decree of Augustus that all the world should be enrolled, you remember, and that was why Jesus was born in Bethlehem, away from his home town of Nazareth. Privileged secular texts had supported the same identification. Scholars commenting on Virgil's fourth *Eclogue*, in which he writes of the birth of a new age, used readily to see in it an intuitive acknowledgement that the world was being transformed not only by the rule of Augustus but by the advent of a divine being, Jesus. Milton opens his *Ode on the Morning of Christ's Nativity* by affirming this dual identification.

All this would only associate Cleopatra contingently with the moment of origin but there is reason to connect her with it more intrinsically. It was upon the defeat of Cleopatra that Augustus founded his own rule. From the year he broke her power and indirectly brought about her death, in 30 BC, he established a new authority for himself in Rome. To mark it he took a new name, Augustus: he had been called Octavian before. It would have been usual to have September, the month of his birth, renamed to match. Instead, he ordered that the month renamed in his honour should be the one in which he brought down Cleopatra, which is why we still call the eighth month August. Other gestures, as my first chapter explains, reinforced the implication that the rule of Augustus was predicated on the defeat of Cleopatra.

This leads me to argue that Cleopatra and her story have the weight of originary myth in Western culture: and, used in metaphor, they are specially disposed to illumine the place of women in the social order. They are charged with the power to generate fantasy as a function of their historical positioning. Stories that account for the status quo are spun out of them. My second chapter shows how some versions of Cleopatra made at the Renaissance and the Reformation were inflected by the moves to subordinate women within the household and within marriage. In these examples the figure is shaped and perceived in relation to current attempts to institute a particular regime of domestic power. Later chapters examine Cleopatra being shaped by different struggles: around the place of women in intellectual debate in the eighteenth century (Chapter 3) or the creation of women as dreamers and shoppers in the nineteenth (Chapter 4).

By its status as originary myth the figure of Cleopatra is also aligned with an important component of the individual unconscious. As a female figure, situated at the opening of the constituting narrative of a culture, Cleopatra's meaning in representation inevitably overlaps with the figure of the mother in individual history. Both are found at the beginning of memory itself, at the point of the foundation of identity. The term 'Cleopatra' locates the notion of a woman's body and the notion of authority together. This combination readily maps on to the figure of the mother in the unconscious, the trace of early experience when the mother's power is supreme and her body is the horizon of desire. It is usual to consider the pleasure of Cleopatra's body in terms of the adult sexuality with which it is conventionally associated. I am arguing that it is also helpful to think of it in terms of the multiple desires of the child, which find their satisfaction and their emblem in the mother's body.

This does not mean that Cleopatra is often represented literally as a mother. Quite the reverse. Not until some twentieth-century works does the fact that Cleopatra actually gave birth to four children receive much attention. When I relate the figure of Cleopatra in representation with the figure of the mother in the unconscious I am addressing the question of desire as Cleopatra has been used to represent it. My point is that by no means all the desires with which Cleopatra is associated in representation are sexual. Historical and political analysis, which opens out the local and specific meanings brought into play in images of Cleopatra, also makes it plain that the issue of sexual desire, however variously conceived, does not necessarily govern or orchestrate the way the figure is represented. In Venice, for instance, in the eighteenth century, Tiepolo made use of the figure of Cleopatra as a sign of Newtonian looking, while in Paris a hundred years later it is made both by Gautier and Delacroix into the sign of the Revolutionary past, suppressed under the current regime.

There are indeed matters of desire at issue here, though it is not sexual desire that is primarily at stake in these examples. Conflicting attempts to satisfy the drive to understand, to represent, and to interpret appearances animate Tiepolo's usage. In Paris it was the urge to restore the memory of a shared past with its hope for a new political order. These are desires which are social, relating to the bonds of the community, its organization, and the exchange of meanings that goes on within it. The figure of Cleopatra has been appropriated in representations as a site where attempts at cultural self-understanding can take place.

In September 1991 the popular American journal *Newsweek* wanted to air some issues associated with Afrocentrism and its reinterpretation of the past. They did it under the byline 'Was Cleopatra black?' The front cover showed the head of an Egyptian queen from a temple relief with a bright modern ear-ring fixed to the stone ear. The figure of Cleopatra was invoked to bring into focus the challenge, if not the threat, implied by rethinking Western culture from an Afro-American perspective. The ear-ring hung on it was carefully selected: shaped like a map of Africa and striped with the red, black, and green of black nationalism in America, it is one that black Americans can buy and wear today.

This move is in decided contrast with earlier treatments of Cleopatra, where the question of her non-European ethnicity is rarely foregrounded. Notions of the oriental or the exotic are brought into play by Boccaccio at the Renaissance and Gautier in the nineteenth century, for example, but Tiepolo's eighteenth-century Cleopatra is created as a blonde Venetian, waited on by blacks. The question 'Is Cleopatra black?' is actually formulated and uttered in de Mille's 1934 *Cleopatra* but is put into the mouth of an *ingénue*, who is laughed to scorn. The dynamic of ethnicity as it interacts with gender in the representation of Cleopatra and its work in maintaining Eurocentrism deserves a book of its own.

The name and image of Cleopatra are still appropriated for political and cultural debate. These debates, even if apparently indifferent to questions of gender politics, implicitly engage in these politics by their very use of Cleopatra as metaphor. Another example, from the *Economist* of the same week of 1991, may make this clearer. The *Economist* opened its account of the market struggle between Pepsi and Coca Cola by reporting that Coke had made a startling new choice of advertising agency. It had appointed Creative Artists Agency, which deals with publicity for top film stars, as its media adviser. The *Economist* article put it like this:

> She is the world's best known brand, a venerable star beginning to fret that age might be withering, and custom staling, her infinite variety. He is Hollywood's most powerful talent agency, a dashing leading man who promises to return to her the full bloom of youth.[1]

The tacit quotation from Shakespeare's *Antony and Cleopatra* does more than offer a stylish take on the current problems of international marketing. In its closely textured evocation of high and low culture – which takes in Elizabeth Taylor, Shakespeare, Plutarch, and Cecil B. de Mille – it assumes and plays on a universal knowledge. This 'knowledge', which it both repeats and constitutes, is the understanding of what ageing 'must' mean to women. The authority implicit in the name of Cleopatra is elegantly compromised and reformulated into 'best known brand' and 'venerable star'. Cleopatra is translated into just another commodity, valued at the market price, which drops with the passage of time, even for Elizabeth Taylor.

The literal meaning of the name of Cleopatra is 'glory of her father'. But the connotations of the name do not endorse patriarchal authority. The term 'Cleopatra' speaks of the combination of public authority and responsibility with an active female sexuality. It locates political power in a body that cannot be coded as male. In any patriarchal system, it speaks of the transgression of the law. The act of evoking Cleopatra through representation calls that law into question and highlights the position of women within the social order. Current attempts to define women and limit their scope within the local social order inevitably shape the terms in which Cleopatra is conceived.

In this book I have selected a small number of examples from the history of Cleopatra's representation in the West for close investigation. They consist of visual images as well as texts and were chosen from different periods and various sites, ranging from pre-Reformation Augsburg to pre-war Hollywood. My aim has been to restore each of them to the context of time and place in which they were produced and to situate them in relation to the complex of contemporary debate and struggle for different forms of power. Although the theme may be one that has been reworked many times, like the story of Cleopatra's banquet first told by Pliny, as the text or image elaborates the theme it begins to speak of its own historical moment and the concerns of that moment. Picking up those signals and making them the basis of rereadings of the changing cultural force of the term Cleopatra constitute the work of this book. This makes each chapter a new detective enterprise in itself and each image an enigmatic challenge.

Critical theory provided a number of basic positions and pointed towards a methodology. I shall discuss the theoretical framework first. In 1987, when I was starting this work, the full impact of post-modernism had already made itself felt. The practice of criticism had been radically altered by the infusion of a highly sophisticated body of theory, originating principally in France. The theories had not been developed to serve the needs of literary criticism or art history but in the course of work in linguistics, anthropology, philosophy, sociology, psychoanalysis, semiotics, and history. They were very diverse and by no means unified or monolithic but they did share some common emphases. In broad terms, they addressed the way community life imposes the acceptance of particular structurings of experience on its subjects. The object of enquiry was not the individual author but the mechanisms by which the social order and its institutions are set in place. This approach understood culture as the workings of a particular social formation and studied its traces in the ways of thinking and seeing as well as in the material objects, institutions, and practices produced by it. Possibilities for the criticism of texts and images were transformed. Political analysis and historical interpretation of text and image displaced aesthetic judgement as the controlling interest. This approach offered to formulate a set of questions which could be used to investigate the images of Cleopatra that challenged me so strongly.

Among the theorists who particularly influenced my own work were Michel Foucault and Jacques Lacan. Initially a historian of science, Foucault developed a series of historical analyses of his society, the hospital, the prison, and the madhouse. Crucially, he also brought this methodology to bear on the classification systems of knowledge itself, emphasizing the changes they went through over time; instead of presenting this evidence to suggest a coherent natural development, his work brought home the discontinuities in the past. Foucault's enterprise was dedicated to denaturalizing the institutions of social and intellectual life, by making their arbitrary and temporal character apparent. He threw the whole notion of tradition into question. This suited my own set of disparate images very well: it suggested that it would be appropriate to focus on the differences between them, even to discount the apparent continuities. There was something to be learned by highlighting the features which could not be assimilated into a coherent tradition and interrogating them. Most important of all was Foucault's relentless focus on the question of power and the ways it had been created and articulated within social arrangements. This encouraged me to formulate my key question: what interests were served, at discrete historical moments, by summoning up the image of a dead Egyptian queen in periods and cultures to which the living woman never had access?

The work of the Freudian psychoanalyst, Jacques Lacan, offered terms for addressing a completely different set of questions. Lacan provided a new way of theorizing the individual. Interest had been directed away, as I have indicated, from examining the unique character of the person who produced the text or image. There was more than one reason for this. The new, almost anthropological, perspective wanted to understand how whole systems worked and tried to see the single object as it was embedded in the ways of living where it was produced. And Roland Barthes, the semiotician, had declared, as a corollary of this emphasis on the collective, that it was restrictive to attribute a text to a single name as its source: the notion of the author was dead. Language, the primary form of social symbol-making, was not dependent for its meanings on the will of a single user or writer and those meanings would always be in excess of her intentions. In this highly theorized enquiry into the life of the collective, Lacan's rereading of Freud offered terms for addressing the perceptions and motivations of the unit.

Lacan's work rehabilitated the discussion of the individual. Particularly as it was elaborated by others, it also provided terms for discussing the reception rather than the making of texts and images and for attempting to theorize the difference between male and female response. This was what I needed in order to ask how unconscious response might differ between male and female members of the audience. Although images of Cleopatra made by women do exist, all the examples I discuss in this book were made by men. They are shaped by male fantasy but they are received and made powerful by the way they interlock with the fantasies of women as well as with those of men. Lacan offered an account of how those fantasies might be distinguished from each other and of the mechanisms of identification which might bind viewer and image.

In distinction from Foucault's work, the theory Lacan proposed was transhistorical: it held good for all periods. Like other theorists, he grounded his enquiry on the price that was paid for admission to the social order, which he identified with the capacity to make and exchange symbolic meanings. He argued that fantasy and desire received their characteristic structures in the process of admission to language (which he called the symbolic order), when the child assumed a gendered identity.

This identity was determined by the way the child's Oedipal desire became organized by the rules of society, in the form of the incest taboo. This process he identified with learning to recognize and take up a place within a world ruled by what he called the law of the father: a world ordered by reference to the symbolized male organ, the phallus. Lacan's theory proposes a model of primary structures in the human psyche and allows questions of individual response to be more rigorously formulated in relation to the central founding fact of human culture, the authority of the male and subordination of the female.

If symbol-making was intimately connected with maintaining the structure of society, and if that structure was grounded in representing women as inferior or secondary to men, images of Cleopatra took on a whole new resonance. How could a woman with supreme political power be represented at all? What acts of qualification or diminution would have to be performed on the figure in order for it to be allowed visibility? How would male fantasy shape and respond to such images? How would female fantasy engage with them? And what about the differing issues at stake at specific historical moments, in representing Cleopatra? Would the detail of an image point so firmly towards a local and temporary crisis that an observer would be able to reconstruct the crisis and construe the image? Were the issues worked over by means of the figure of Cleopatra confined to matters of gender politics? Would the historical figure of Cleopatra, the woman who really did rule over Egypt, turn out to have any connection at all with the images made in her name?

The fascination of struggling with the images and their history then took over. This book gives an account of a few selected examples, opened up to examine the way politics and history intersect in the act of representation and to ask a further question. What part have images of Cleopatra played in regulating the lives and perceptions of nameless women who lived after her?

Chapter 1

Looking like a queen

It wasn't until 1933 that the Vatican realized they'd got their hands on Cleopatra. The only way of seeing her before had been through the ambiguous and unsatisfactory texts of poets and the slightly daunting profile on the coinage she issued. Now, a yellowish marble head, stuck to an alien body and its nose repaired in a programme of restoration, was declared a portrait of Cleopatra VII, last queen of Egypt (Plate 1.1). At last there was a chance of getting a proper look.

Curiosity and the desire for possession are forms of response to the mystery of Cleopatra's power. By reducing that power to a matter of personal appearance, it is made less challenging and its subversive force is undermined. It appears to endorse the familiar structures of desire and it becomes something that can be controlled and above all made legible. It is a response to Cleopatra as heritage, an established component of Western culture. It divides the twentieth century sharply from times closer to those in which she herself lived. Plutarch, who wrote in the greatest detail about Cleopatra and was said to have drawn his information from the tales of a relative who had lived in the palace at Alexandria, claimed that her looks were not exceptional. According to Plutarch, Cleopatra's power was not something that impressed itself primarily through its effect on the vision, as physical beauty does.

> For her actual beauty, it is said, was not in itself so remarkable that none compared with her, or that no-one could see her without being struck by it, but the contract of her presence, if you lived with her, was irresistible; the attraction of her person . . . and the character that attended all she said or did, was something bewitching.[1]

Plutarch, at least, was clear that Cleopatra's secret was not to be plumbed merely by looking at her.

Our own age feels differently. Two more marble heads have been identified since 1933: of all the visual images of Cleopatra that date from antiquity, and the range includes coin portraits and stone reliefs as well as sculptured heads, there is no doubt that the three marble heads have

Plate 1.1 Vatican head. Reproduced from 'Ikonographische Beiträge', Curtius, 1933.

special status.[2] Perhaps this is self-evident: they approximate most closely to the appearance of a living body and allow her to be seen in the round. (This is because the heads are Hellenistic rather than Egyptian: they are produced in the Greek tradition, as it was developed by the rulers who inherited Alexander's empire; native Egyptian sculpture did not, in general, produce realistic individual portraiture.) There is a sense in which the figure from the past is brought close to the viewer, presented in a form that can be assimilated: the heads have no unfamiliar details to be decoded; they present themselves as 'simply' the head of a beautiful woman, to be enjoyed.

There is of course nothing simple about it. The means by which ancient portrait heads are identified, the money for which they change hands, and the way their meaning changes as they move about the world all qualify the 'simple' experience of looking.

There is no intrinsic reason why anyone should believe that any of the three heads currently authenticated in fact represents Cleopatra.[3] They all owe their identification to circumstantial evidence, the comparison with coin types that is the basis of identification of most ancient sculptured heads. It is on the evidence of hair-style, nose, and mouth that the Vatican, Berlin, and Chercel heads are named. A number of coin issues with Cleopatra's name on show a woman with what is known as a melon hair-do – the hair tied back in a sort of bun – and a prominent nose, in some cases rather heavily hooked. The further work of scholarship which goes into speculating whether the heads are 'originals' or 'copies', and whether there is any relation between them, depends more on the skills of a visual connoisseur than on any other evidence. A web of the most highly educated guesswork has been woven to secure the image of Cleopatra. If the methodology is not in itself exceptional – it is standard practice – there are one or two features which emphasize the fragility of any conclusions. In the first place, for instance, the Vatican head has no nose. Perhaps the single most characteristic feature is missing. And the hair-do, advanced as a significant feature in all three heads, is admitted to be part of a recognized style of female royal image found over the two preceding centuries. Add to this the really quite close similarity between these and heads identified as those of earlier queens, Arsinoe II and Arsinoe III, for instance, and the confident sense that it is indeed an ancient image of Cleopatra we are looking at must weaken.

The head in the Berlin museum – the third is in Algeria – must be the image of Cleopatra to achieve the widest circulation in any period. The Germans put it on a stamp.[4] And yet its credentials are by no means the most impeccable of the three. It was bought by the museum in 1976 for what is usually called an undisclosed sum and is quoted as being of unknown provenance. Not all scholars have accepted it as ancient. Yet it is the most completely satisfying of the heads from a certain perspective. The Vatican head has no nose; the Chercel head is less accessible, blanker, and more stylized. The Berlin head gives the most gratifying illusion of an individual woman whom we should call beautiful without having to make allowances for difference of period or culture (Plate 1.2). By it we are permitted to reinvest Cleopatra in the visible, in spite of Plutarch's warning.

But the reinvestment is not, emphatically, on her terms. On the German stamp, Cleopatra, or what is called Cleopatra, no longer has reference to a woman who lived in a place and time remote in history. What she means is now. And on the stamp her image is the sign not of herself and her own political and cultural context but of Germany, whose economic power has allowed the purchase of this treasure of undisclosed value and whose cultural authority brings Cleopatra to the German people of the West, offering her guaranteed image for their consumption and use.[5]

But stamps, once in use, are receipts. They signify that payment for mail delivery has been made, so that Cleopatra's head becomes enlisted as one more way of endorsing the contract between administration and the citizen, or rulers and ruled, in Germany. Once Cleopatra's image was taken up by nations and cultures not her own, its meaning, inevitably, changed. That one might predict. But some patterns recur. If, for instance, the Romans who conquered her used her image as a sign of their own military and cultural superiority, the example of the German postage stamp shows they were not the last to do so. For a long time Cleopatra has been the sign of *someone else's victory, the witness of the acceptance of rule.*

Getting this meaning out of Cleopatra reverses, in fact, the force of her own representations of herself in first-century Egypt. The images of her coinage, on the south wall of the temple at Dendera, and in the public spaces where she displayed herself in ceremonial were all designed in the service of promoting her own political authority and in appealing to a divine endorsement of her power. The forms available to her were juggled, using both the native Egyptian tradition and the iconography of Greek culture, to address both communities within her kingdom and to reach well beyond it.

Astute as this manipulation of cultural diversity may have been, Cleopatra could not ensure a favourable reception for the early images, which we assume were put into circulation on her own authority. The visibility

Plate 1.2 Berlin head, Antikenmuseum SMPK, Berlin.

these images were designed to achieve transgressed the cultural codes of Rome, provoking a hostile reception from the first. This was true of many features of Egyptian culture. It gave rise to the problem of interpreting display, a grounding practice of Hellenistic culture but repudiated, at least in theory, by Romans as alien to their founding values. More radically, sexual difference itself and how it should be marked and maintained was at issue. Rome favoured a severe discrimination between the sexes: in Egypt, as we shall see, this was not the case.

This chapter will take some of the earliest images of Cleopatra and situate them in relation to the clash between Roman and Egyptian culture. It will mean developing a new position for viewing the Egyptian, in order to avoid reduplicating the perspective which defines what is Egyptian as exotic and mysterious. Close analysis of the detail of contemporary representational codes will help to do this, combined with attention to the political force of religious practice in Egypt. In the process, some familiar notions of gender distinction and family organization, inherited from the classical tradition, will be historicized and called into question. The argument will close by highlighting Octavian's attempt to take over the representational space of Cleopatra and use it as a foundation for his own enhanced authority.

First, Cleopatra must be placed in terms of her own ethnicity and the chronology of world political history. Cleopatra VII was not in fact Egyptian but Greek by extraction: a descendant of Alexander's Macedonian general Ptolemy who had inherited the greater part of Alexander's empire. She was probably the first of her line to speak Egyptian, among the seven or eight languages attributed to her. With her brother Ptolemy XIII she inherited the throne in 51 BC at the age of seventeen. Julius Caesar settled a feud between the two heirs, leaving Cleopatra on the throne with her younger brother Ptolemy XIV. In 47 BC she bore a son, whom she called Caesarion, naming Caesar as the father. She spent the following two years until Caesar's assassination living in Rome as his mistress. In 41 BC she again became involved in Rome's internal affairs when she met Mark Antony. Although Antony married Octavia, the sister of Octavian, in 40 BC and had two children by her, in 37 BC he rejected her for Cleopatra. Antony and Cleopatra had three children, twins, Cleopatra Selene and Alexander Helios, born in 40 BC, and Ptolemy, born in 36 BC after their marriage in 37 BC. In 34 BC Antony declared Cleopatra a Hellenistic monarch and distributed provinces to their children. In 32 BC he divorced Octavia, and his will, recognizing Caesarion as the son of Julius Caesar and leaving eastern provinces largely to Cleopatra, became known in Rome. Octavian declared war on Cleopatra, and in 31 BC the joint forces of Antony and Cleopatra were defeated at the battle of Actium. Pursued by Octavian to Egypt, first Antony and then Cleopatra committed suicide, in August, 30 BC.

In Egypt, where Cleopatra was born into the reigning house, there were two principal ethnic groups and two cultures reflecting the history of its conquest by Alexander in 332 BC. The ruler, the court, and the administration were Greek. The mass of the population were farmers, holding land from the king. These peasants were Egyptian, as were the priests who maintained the ancient religion and with it the very focus of Egyptian civilization. But the two groups were not as clearly divided as this definition might suggest. Scholars continue to argue over the precise relation between the cultures in practice but in one area it is clear how the ruling Greeks had adapted to local conditions. The Ptolemies had been careful from early in their rule to avoid challenging the native religion: they adopted its forms and took part in its ceremonies to support their own tenure of the throne. The text of the Rosetta Stone, for instance, is a record of the gratitude of the priests for special favours granted by Ptolemy V. And there is evidence that some families of the administrative class used Greek names for official purposes and Egyptian ones for private. Egyptian culture, however, seems to have been relatively impervious to Greek influence. Its religious practices were unmodified by external sources right up to the point of their extinction well after the advent of Christianity in Late Antiquity. It is sometimes claimed that, although the written language, Demotic, made use of the Greek alphabet, it was controlled by the priests and shows only very limited borrowings from Greek.[6]

Yet the way the country was run could not but be affected by the foreign presence. And among the administrative changes brought by the Greeks was the more generalized use of coinage. This is important because it was in the forms of coin portraits that the visual image of Cleopatra was to achieve its widest circulation in the ancient world. Egyptians had had a problem with the notion of minting: gold, it was held, was the flesh of the gods and not to be put to base practical applications. This belief understandably delayed the development and use of a local coinage so that it was not until about 360 BC, that is, only thirty years before Alexander's conquest, that the first native coin was struck. A gold coin with a hieroglyphic legend and the image of a rearing horse was issued, at the insistence of a Greek and to pay Greek mercenaries. It has been recently demonstrated, however, that the Egyptians were minting Athenian-style silver tetradrachms, a currency copied and accepted in many places outside Athens, in considerable quantities at this time. Before this discovery it had been agreed that the use of coins within Egypt itself had been confined to trafficking Greeks or the Persian colonial administration.[7]

So coins are not a native Egyptian artefact but a Hellenistic one, although it is true that under the Ptolemies Egypt moved towards a new market economy and the use of coin became more widespread. Ptolemaic coins were issued not only from Alexandria but from Egyptian-controlled

Phoenicia and Cyprus. By the time Cleopatra came to strike her own, a number of conventions were established. They involved a repetition of motifs, such as the phrase 'of Ptolemy the King' found on all Ptolemaic issues and the head of Ptolemy Soter, founder of the dynasty, displayed on most of them. There was a recurring female model, too. Arsinoe II, the most prominent of the Ptolemaic queens before Cleopatra VII, became in some ways a prototype for royal female portraiture. But the most important thing about the coinage developed under the Ptolemies was that, following the practice of Alexander, it showed the monarch's head.

This was something that Athenian coinage, say, or republican coinage from Rome necessarily did not. And the force of putting a portrait head on a coin was, in direct consequence, considerable. When Julius Caesar did so it was read as a sign of his wish to be king. The coins issued in the name of Cleopatra can be decoded too. There are fifteen or so separate coin issues bearing Cleopatra's head.[8] Between them they repeat only four different images, however, and these belong to distinct phases of her reign: one bears only her own head, one is said to represent her with the infant Caesarion, and the others are issued by Cleopatra in conjunction with Mark Antony.

Plate 1.3 Coin from the Alexandria mint, British Museum.

Of these, only one portrait type was current in Egypt itself (Plate 1.3). It is found right through: on silver drachms and bronzes from Alexandria from early in Cleopatra's reign and on tetradrachms from Askalon dating from its end. (It is also found on clay portrait sealings found at Edfu.) It is the portrait on which identification of the marble heads chiefly depends. Sympathetic, smooth, and Hellenistic in style, it is very reminiscent of portraits of earlier queens, particularly Arsinoe III. The hair is tied back in a sort of bun and a diadem, the sign of rule, is bound about the head and tied at the nape. The unusual width of the diadem favoured here has been remarked: it was not to be confused with a mere fillet. The head is not veiled, as some earlier heads of queens had been: the assertion of rule is not qualified by any particular emphasis on gender.

On the reverse is shown an eagle standing on a thunderbolt, with the twin cornucopias, symbols found on Egyptian coins since the time of the second or third Ptolemies. The double cornucopia was particularly associated with Arsinoe II. Continuity with tradition is reiterated. Similarly, if in Greek letters it is written 'of Cleopatra the queen', the legend is exactly parallel to what was written on other monarchs' coins.

Plate 1.4 Coin from Cyprus, British Museum.

A much less common image of Cleopatra occurs on a bronze coin, possibly from Cyprus (Plate 1.4). It might be said to offer an image of the queen to validate the exceptional conditions of her rule, lacking an adult male co-regent. Not that she was the first Ptolemaic queen to take such a role, for in the previous century there had been instances of sole rule by women.[9] With the legend, 'Kleopatras basileis' (of Queen Cleopatra), it bears the double cornucopia on one side. What can be read from the other is more obscure: scholars have argued that it was issued on the birth of Caesarion and shows Cleopatra as Aphrodite with the infant Eros. Attractive as the thesis is, and it may be recalled when the iconography of the Dendera temple is discussed, caution is indicated: although the head and the sceptre clearly indicate royal status, it is not beyond contention that the smaller mass to the lower right should be interpreted as a baby's head.

It is in the coins issued with Mark Antony that Cleopatra's image is most strikingly redefined. The new type first appeared in 37 BC at the time when, in exchange for putting the resources of Egypt at Antony's disposal, Cleopatra received from him, as triumvir, the grant of new territories outside Egypt, parts of Coele, Syria, Phoenicia, and Cilicia. She was to hold these as a Roman client-ruler. The portrait of Cleopatra, its conjunction with that of Mark Antony, and other iconographic features produce a new version of the queen.

Plate 1.5 Tetradrachm from Antioch, *c.* 36 BC.

It is a revision that relates itself specifically to the Roman rather than the Ptolemaic tradition. The graceful profile of the Alexandrian coins is replaced by an unflattering waist-deep portrait of an older woman wearing a big necklace (Plate 1.5). The nose is big, the lower jaw sticks out. The image appeals not to past images of Hellenistic queens but to the Roman present. In fact, to the portrait tradition displayed in the image of Mark Antony on the reverse of the coin: Cleopatra looks like Mark Antony in a wig.[10]

As a triumvir, it would have been perfectly normal for Mark Antony to make use of a travelling mint to strike his own coins, away from Rome, to pay his troops. It is the standard form of Antony's portrait that is shown: bareheaded, surrounded by the Greek words 'Antony, Commander-in-Chief for the third time, Triumvir'. The obverse, however, can be read as an elaborate compilation of the insignia of Cleopatra's power: the necklace supplements the sign of the diadem and the words 'Queen Cleopatra, *Thea Neotera*' have a certain asperity as they are forced into conjunction with the honorifics of a Roman republic which had repudiated queens. The meaning of the title Thea Neotera (literally, the younger/newer goddess) is still disputed: scholars argue over the exact source of the political advantage it might confer through association with a divine or a merely human predecessor. It has been variously interpreted as identifying the queen with Aphrodite-Hathor or with another Cleopatra, Cleopatra Thea, an earlier Seleucid queen who had ruled over the territory in which Cleopatra VII's present issue was to circulate. (This woman's reputation for ruthlessness in the pursuit of power may have helped to shape early responses to her Egyptian namesake.)

Similar coin images are repeated on another issue of Mark Antony, bronzes from the kingdom of Chalcis in Lebanon, which Antony had given to Cleopatra. Here both figures are shown together on the same side, an arrangement used in Ptolemaic coinage to represent joint monarchs, married to each other.[11] Manipulating the emblems of authority is the aim of these representations, not portraiture: the resemblance between the heads of male and female rulers already noted is emphasized by showing them side by side.

These coins give some idea of the fine nuancing of convention available in the striking of images for public circulation and establish that those conventions could include the use of imagery derived from the worship of divine or deified women. At the same time there were representational norms: for a queen at least the nominal presence of a male co-ruler was usual. But within Egypt there was evident care to assert continuity with the dynasty by a careful echoing of established iconography.

This caution about disrupting culturally endorsed patterns had been a prime feature in the Ptolemies' tenure of Egypt. They took particular care to preserve the close association between spiritual and temporal authority that was established in Egypt. This identification of political power with religious authority is a principal factor in accounting for Cleopatra's representation as both royal and divine. Her ancestors had kept that possibility open for her. To emphasize his commitment to native forms Ptolemy V, for instance, had had himself crowned at Memphis, the ancient Egyptian capital, with pharaonic rites, probably following his acclamation in Macedonian style at Alexandria, the new Greek city built by Alexander. A substantial programme of temple-building and repair was undertaken by the Ptolemies: they were responsible for the construction of major temples at Philae, Dendera, Edfu, Karnak, and Kom Ombo as well as minor works elsewhere. But more crucially, when they took over the throne, the Ptolemies maintained the close identification of the monarchy with the native religion. The Pharaohs had been perceived as the ideal priests. The Ptolemaic kings, though they were Greek and not Egyptian, continued to fill this role.

It was a political choice. Under the native religion the Pharaoh not only performed acts of worship but was himself the object of cult: it has even been claimed that the Pharaoh's statue was itself more sacred than his person.[12] Egyptian religion, in providing for the worship of both current monarchs and their predecessors, established the monarchy as a sacred institution at the heart of life. The Greeks, in taking cognizance of this, were acting no more cynically than the Roman emperors were later to do in encouraging their own cults in Asia Minor; notions of private religious sensibility derived from the northern European experience of reformed Christianity are not much help in interpreting the religious practices of antiquity. Ruler cult, it has been effectively argued, particularly the cult of a ruler coming from outside, offered a form in which alien modes of authority could be assimilated to local ways of life. This made for stability under foreign rule.[13]

Ptolemaic queens took from the first a more substantial role than queens in other kingdoms in the public representation of the dynasty. They played a special part in ruler cult too. The case of Arsinoe II, the first to be deified, offers a useful demonstration of the political returns from this system.[14] She was worshipped during her lifetime and, when she died, her husband – who was also her brother – the son of the dynasty's founder, defined her personal cult in these terms:

> His Majesty decreed that her statue be set up in all the temples. This pleased their priests, for they were aware of her noble attitude toward the gods and of her excellent deeds to the benefit of all the people . . . Her name was proclaimed as the beloved of the ram, the goddess Philadelphos, Arsinoe.[15]

The queen has become a symbol of the benevolence of the dynasty, endorsed by the priests in recognition of her services to the native population. She is renamed to make her into a symbol of the continuity between the native pharaonic past and the present Hellenized rule of the Ptolemies too, or rather into a focus where its loyalties meet. One title, 'beloved of the ram', associates her with the chief Egyptian god, Amun, the other, 'Philadelphos', which means brother/sister-loving, identifies her in relation to her brother, husband, and former co-regent, Ptolemy II, the contemporary ruler of Egypt.

At the same time, the queen's place in the historical sequence of monarchs was preserved. On the Mendes stela where this deification is recorded, the queen is shown both as a recipient of worship, one of the company of local gods, and as worshipping at the side of her husband. Rather than as individuals, royal couples were divinized as ancestors, and even as reigning monarchs. The Ptolemaic line itself was established as divine.

There is a third aspect: if Arsinoe was to some extent exceptional, as the first Ptolemaic queen to be accepted as a divinity and deeply assimilated in her own right into native religious life, she was also a prototype. Although Ptolemaic queens were to be associated with a number of goddesses from the native religion, she was the first of them to be identified with Isis. This was a connection that Cleopatra would turn to advantage.

The veneration of Isis went back two thousand years already when the Ptolemies first came to Egypt. Although she was to have many attributes in later cults, the first stories and images are of a mother and child. The stories written down in the Ramesside period were already ancient. They told of Isis hiding her child, Horus, in the swamps of Khemmis, where he was to wait in safety till he was strong enough to avenge his murdered father, Osiris. The rise, early in Dynasty XXI, about 1000 BC, of numerous cults of child-gods and what has been called a 'veritable theology of birth' led to further refinements, among them the first sculptures in the round of Isis with the child Horus. Images of goddesses suckling kings had been made since at least Dynasty VI, a thousand years earlier. The Isis/Horus dyads, which were still being produced in the time of Cleopatra, represented Isis, like the later figures of the Virgin in Western art, as the nursing mother. But they are associated, unlike images of Mary, with an active sexuality. When the Greeks came to Egypt, they recognized Isis: their own name for her had been Aphrodite. And it was chiefly under that name that Arsinoe II was worshipped as Isis, the woman in whom the erotic and the nurturing aspects are found together.

This splendid, erotic generative force, charged with warmth and tenderness, is often seen, perhaps wishfully, as quite free from those destructive aspects that often make mother-goddesses particularly fearsome. Elements in the sources which hint at unreliable, terrifying, or lethal aspects are not much dwelt on. While the professional literature on the Hellenistic cult of Isis is vast, the myth and cult of Isis have also excited keen interest and been written about extensively by non-specialists. Isis and her cult have engaged both male historians – J. Stevens Curl's enthusiasm is most striking – and feminists.[16] I propose to restrict my own discussion to a brief outline of the stories associated with Isis and of the extent of her cult.

Any explanation can hardly avoid over-systematizing. The conventional source for this material is Plutarch's account, *On Isis and Osiris*, written in the early part of the second century AD. This gathers together and offers in a more coherent narrative fragments that had existed in discrete and unstable form in the religious practice of the previous two and a half thousand years. In these Isis did not come to prominence till quite late, and was not initially known as the wife of Osiris. From her earliest appearance, however, she had been associated with the tending of the dead body and responsibility for the rites that would revive or renew life in it. The cult had come to assume a commanding position inside Egypt and had been carried abroad by seafarers, so that small local temples of Isis were found at many ports round the eastern Mediterranean and the Aegean during the Ptolemaic period. Isis was also worshipped in Rome itself.

According to Plutarch, Isis was both sister and wife to Osiris: it was said that they had intercourse even before they were born, in the darkness of the womb. In maturity, she watched over his well-being but was unable to protect him against the enemies who trapped him in a chest which they sealed and cast adrift. Grieving, she wandered the world till she found the chest, opened it, and mourned. Later, her husband's enemy found the chest, which she had put aside to concentrate on her child, Horus, dismembered the body, and scattered the remains throughout the marshes. It was Isis who sought and retrieved these fragments. (Plutarch claims that the phallus was lost but no Egyptian source has been found to corroborate this.) This familiar outline, however, is only achieved at the expense of omitting references in Plutarch's text which are more ambiguous: there was a child Isis suckled and subsequently set on fire. Her cry of grief killed one boy and a second died at the sight of her angry face; she displeased her son by releasing his enemy instead of killing him; she gave birth prematurely to the weakly Harpocrates. Isis was certainly a figure of maternal and erotic power: identification with her involved, however, beyond mere benevolence, taking up a position of authority in a social order. And this is where the identification with queens becomes relevant.

Cleopatra VII exercised her role as queen in a culture where authority and power were demonstrated and preserved by signifying practices of the kind I have described as well as by the conduct of war and pursuit of conquest. European understanding of the use she made of these forms has been shaped by the perspective of Roman writers hostile to her political ends. Her documented involvement with the cult of the Apis bull, the wall-relief at Dendera, the pageantry of Cleopatra's meeting with Antony at Tarsus, their self-representation as Isis and Osiris, and the tableau of her death need to be read as acts selected or created from the repertoire of Hellenistic political display. A context of spectacle at once religious and political in nature supported Cleopatra's use of public display. As the examples of Cleopatra's own deployment of spectacle are discussed in the following pages, it is their meaning within Hellenistic culture that will be emphasized.

Not that the purest republican intentions could have redeemed the animal cults of the Egyptians for Roman taste. Though they were found to some extent in other societies, and Plutarch later claimed that they were merely a concession to popular fancy, while the true focus of Egyptian spirituality lay elsewhere, the Romans fastened on this feature of Egyptian religion as both typical and debased. Cleopatra, however, went out of her way to be associated with the worship of the Apis bull, a living animal sought out and identified by special signs and kept throughout its lifetime in conditions of ritualized splendour.[17] When it died, the Apis bull went through a formalized and lengthy process of mummification before it was buried in great state and the search for its successor began.

In 51 BC, within a month of Cleopatra's accession, a new Buchis bull was installed at Armant in Upper Egypt where another bull cult was also observed: some scholars have translated the stele – an upright slab bearing sculptured designs or inscriptions – on which this is recorded as saying that the queen was present in person and 'all the people saw her'. A stele from Saqqara records that the following year Cleopatra made a substantial contribution to the maintenance of the recently deceased Apis bull and of its cult at Memphis, providing 412 silver coins to establish a table of offerings; she also paid for a daily allowance of wine, milk, and bread for those involved in the worship and work connected with the bull, with further measures of beans, two different oils, and an allowance of meat. Cleopatra is inscribed in the terms used to define a powerful female ruler from the pharaonic past, Hatshepsut: she is 'the queen himself', the female Pharaoh. The male term, ruler, is qualified by its female holder. Hatshepsut, for state functions, had assumed the full regalia of power, even to the ceremonial beard. If Cleopatra ever went this far, out of sight of Alexandria and committed to satisfying the pharaonic traditions of Memphis, no account of it survives.

But it is through the wall-relief at Dendera, the most permanent of her large-scale gestures – for there is also the public ceremonial she stage-managed to consider – that Cleopatra was inscribed most prominently on the country she ruled.[18] She is shown, with her son Caesarion, making an offering to the divinities of the temple, Hathor, in this period often identified with Isis, and her son Harsomtus (Plate 1.6).

As a visual statement it is literally monumental and reminiscent of the giant reliefs of her father, Ptolemy XII, incised in temple walls at Kom Ombo and Philae. The temple interior and its rituals were not accessible to ordinary people but they could see the massive reliefs the Ptolemies cut into the exterior walls. While her father was, rather optimistically, shown vanquishing his enemies, Cleopatra is represented in an act of worship. The relief takes up a wall over 100 feet in length, at the rear of the temple whose foundation ceremony took place while her father, Ptolemy XII, still ruled. It follows the conventions of Ptolemaic representation by disposing its elements with regard both to the layout of the shrine – the 'grammaire du temple' – and to the codes of pharaonic art. This produces two paired sequences of figures, backing on to each other at a central point, where they are separated by a large head of Hathor, the temple goddess. In each sequence, the outer pair of figures represents the human rulers, making their offering. Facing them stand the row of gods who are being worshipped.

Cleopatra stands outermost, behind her son, Caesarion, represented as the Pharaoh. (Although the date of this relief is not known it was certainly created before Cleopatra's death; Caesarion would then have been only 14.) She carries both the sistrum and the mnet, objects with a special relevance to the goddess and which were rattled to excite her. There is a small figure between herself and her son, representing his ka: Caesarion

Plate 1.6 Relief from the rear wall of the temple of Hathor at Dendera.

himself offers incense. Although they are faced by one small and five full-size figures of gods, a number of these are duplicate or alternative forms of the same deities with varying attributes, Hathor and her son Horus. Hathor is also represented in the form of Isis, while Horus is shown in the form of Harsomtus. Osiris, the father, is represented only once. Thus the line-up on the left would go: small Harsomtus (Horus), Isis (Hathor), Harsomtus (Horus), Osiris-Onnophris, Horus, and Isis (Hathor) – repeating the image of Hathor and Horus, mother and son, under variant names.

These details can be expanded to reveal how closely the images identify Cleopatra with the gods to whom she is making offering. Cleopatra's crown includes the falcon tail-feathers sacred to Horus and Isis. It also duplicates elements, the sun disc and the cow horns sacred to Hathor and Isis, that are in fact worn by the figure of Hathor/Isis closest to Cleopatra in the relief. The goddess, however, wears the vulture head-dress as a mark of her divinity and Cleopatra is distinguished by the cobra modius, the diadem with uraeus which is the mark of a queen. The diminished role allotted to Osiris, the spouse of Hathor/Isis, is important. He occurs only in one of the two sequences and then he is shown standing not in front of Hathor but well to her rear, behind Harsomtus/Horus.

At Dendera emphasis is shifted on to the relation between mother and son.[19] The two mother–son pairs stand facing each other, inviting comparison, the legitimacy of the divine dyad being invoked in order to endorse the authority of the royal one. The fact that Cleopatra was only following tradition in aligning herself as queen with the goddess Hathor/Isis offered further support to the implicit claim made by the image. And the political implications went further still, if the local cult practices are borne in mind. Every year, as the reliefs in the temple at Edfu a few miles further south on the Nile illustrate, the image of the goddess Hathor was taken from the Dendera temple by river to be reunited with the image of the god at Edfu. Hathor and Horus are represented on the walls of Edfu temple in company with their son Harsomtus. So the annual rituals of the Dendera temple supported the notion of a mother/goddess who lived in separation from the god who was the father of her son, just as Cleopatra lived divided from Caesar, whom she claimed as the father of her son Caesarion. Queen and goddess alike ruled without benefit of a consort's presence: the need for the validation of a male co-regent is confronted and set aside by appeal to divine precedent; the absence of Caesarion's father is transformed into a positive asset, since it confirms the parallel between the divine pair and the royal one.

Coins, stele, and wall-reliefs give tangible demonstration of images in circulation within Cleopatra's lifetime. But, when it comes to discussing the public ceremonial by which the queen staged herself, we are no longer in direct contact with the evidence. It is only through reports written after her death by authors who did not share her culture that we know anything about the public events she stage-managed: the dressing as Isis, which Plutarch asserts took place on many occasions; or presenting herself in splendour – 'The barge she sat in, like a burnished throne, Burned on the water' – to Mark Antony at Tarsus; even the tableau she is said to have created out of her own death.

There was a tradition of public celebration through procession and spectacle already well established in Egypt before the Ptolemies arrived. The hardship of everyday life was alleviated by a regular programme of festivals throughout the year and the statues of gods, usually shut away in temples to which only priests had access, were carried through the street. In addition to these regular epiphanies, the street could be turned into a theatre of national and international politics.

An account has survived of one of these occasions, the grand procession of Ptolemy Philadelphus, the second Macedonian ruler of Egypt. Unlike the festivals associated with the native religion, this occasion was entirely Greek in iconography and significance. Its audience lay mainly outside Egypt. Elaborate enough to have probably needed more than a single day to wind its way through Alexandria, it established the primacy of what was then the new Greek capital, displacing Memphis; at the same time, by its great splendour it celebrated the wealth of Egypt and the triumph of the Ptolemaic dynasty. The inclusion of 80,000 armed troops ensured that the other Hellenistic monarchies were warned off. An important feature was the celebration of Dionysus, staged on vehicles moving as part of the procession.

Some idea of the magnificence and ingenuity of the display, suggesting a fusion of the spectacle of the court masque and the parades of Holy Week, can be obtained:

> a four-wheeled cart was led along by sixty men . . . 12 feet wide, on which there was a seated statue of Nysa [probably the nurse of Dionysus] twelve feet tall, wearing a yellow chiton woven with gold thread, and wrapped in a Laconian himation. This statue stood up mechanically without anyone laying a hand on it, and it sat back down again after pouring a libation of milk from a gold phiale.[20]

It was followed by a winepress, 36 feet long, where sixty satyrs were treading the ripe grapes as they sang, accompanied by flutes; after that again came a vast wineskin, covered with leopard skins, from which wine flowed continually as it went. These tributes to Dionysus as the god of wine were accompanied by the staging of scenes from his life, including his 'Return from India', where his 18-foot image was carried on an elephant.

The representation of Dionysus had a role to play in the justification of Greek rule in Egypt, for the images emphasized continuity between

Ptolemy, as Alexander's general, and Alexander himself. For propaganda purposes, Alexander's journey of conquest into the East had been likened in his own lifetime to the civilizing mission credited to Dionysus, as described, for instance, in *The Bacchae*. Identification with Dionysus, revived and claimed by Cleopatra's own father Ptolemy XII, was also claimed by Mark Antony: its potential political force was considerable. It could validate the future as well as the past. If it endorsed the Ptolemies' tenure of Egypt, it might also endorse an attempt by Antony and Cleopatra to establish a unified Eastern power to vanquish and obliterate the strength of Rome.[21]

In spite of the contemporary political thrust of such spectacles, Cleopatra's identification with a legendary erotic opulence starts here in the images, nearly always recounted and not actually available now for our inspection, of public display. I take the manipulation of cultural difference to be crucial in this transfer. Display was licensed in Egypt but not in Rome. The tombs of New Kingdom nobles at Qurneh flaunt the splendour that their owners could command. This tradition was not modified under the Greek rulers who followed the Pharaohs. The Romans did not subscribe to the Hellenistic concept of *tryphe*, which included the demonstration of power through the display of luxury. It meant that the wealth of Egypt, already the envy of other nations, was not discreet but flaunted.

This was completely at odds with Roman ideals. The story of an encounter between Egypt and Rome that took place long before Cleopatra's time may help to make this difference clear. When around 140 BC Ptolemy VIII, who was grossly overweight, received his Roman visitors, Scipio Aemilianus and the Stoic philosopher Panaetius, in a transparent garment, they recoiled with embarrassment. The public meaning of the act as a display of wealth and power failed to register successfully and, stripped of referents, the exhibition swiftly produced shame in its foreign viewers.[22] Cleopatra's displays of herself also to some extent failed of their mark, both in the period and for later historians. Cultural difference continues to blur how they are read, fading the political force of the display. At the same time attention remains focused on the body of the queen. This makes her presentation of herself, in Plutarch's account, as Aphrodite, for later readers an almost exclusively erotic demonstration and invitation; what it asserted in her own day of the majesty of the dynasty and its ancient right grounded in the native religion is overlooked.

The misreading occurs because it was possible, using the signifying practices of Egyptian public life, for a woman to be the sign and locus of political power. The public depiction of queens noted earlier makes that quite plain. But the provision for queens to take a part, like men, in the public representation of the dynasty was not an isolated phenomenon. It seems to be accompanied – I can argue the connection in no more detail – by a number of practices which suggest that polarity between the sexes was not heavily emphasized in Ptolemaic Egypt. Here we begin to touch on the questions of gender distinction and family organization noted earlier. Roman notions of these are familiar to us to some degree because in many ways we are still governed by them in the West. Egyptian practice, however, diverged from the Roman. Even though the rights of women under the law had been eroded under the Greek administration, in Egypt there was less discrimination between the rights of male and female than was known elsewhere in the ancient world, with regard, in particular, to marriage legislation and the inheritance of property. (We are not in a position to compare the marriage practices of the Macedonians, as they are unknown.)

Roman women, though not so confined as Greek ones were, like them, disadvantaged under the law in comparison with men. Under both Greek and Roman law women were defined in terms of male relatives, their inheritance rights were restricted, and their freedom to engage in marriage or public contracts was subjected to the guidance or agency of a male. In Egypt daughters inherited equally with sons and women were at liberty to choose their own husbands – a freedom, incidentally, which made them a scandal to the men of Rome. And it has been argued, though not without provoking some resistance, that marriage contracts of the Ptolemaic period imply reciprocal moral obligations and community of property.[23]

Connected, surely, with this gender proximity, as it were, is the practice of what we call incest. Keith Hopkins argues, from a study of the census returns collected in Roman Egypt, that brothers married their sisters.[24] The practice was not confined to the royal house and it was not merely a matter of form. The marriages were consummated and produced children. They were lawfully and publicly celebrated. Hopkins has estimated that under the Romans about one-third of all brothers with marriageable sisters married inside the family.

Before this, the Ptolemies had followed the practice of the Pharaohs in permitting brother/sister marriage in the royal house. The example of Ptolemy II and Arsinoe II has already been quoted; Cleopatra herself had been married to two of her younger brothers in succession before she ruled with Caesarion.

Apart from its interest as the only known example in world ethnography, the absence of incest prohibition in Roman Egypt and the admission of incest within the royal house in earlier periods have a particular resonance for a study of representation there. Freud, reread by Lacan, makes a direct connection between seeing, sexual difference, the incest taboo, and representation. According to Lacan, it is by recognition of both sexual difference and the incest taboo that the child gains access to the symbols by which meaning is communicated. In a culture where such a taboo is not significant, or its significance is reduced, we look to see if representation is affected. Clearly, the symbolic order in Egypt has not collapsed. Nor is the phallus without importance: there was a golden one measuring 180 feet in length with a gold star at the end in the procession of Ptolemy Philadelphus. But the culture is, as we have noted, unusual in the way it allows near overlap between some important male and female rights and capacities. And here we return to the role allotted to Ptolemaic queens in public representation of the dynasty.

Like the freedom women had in choosing marriage partners, the Romans were not happy with it. Among the restrictions on women's scope in Rome was a veto on public visibility. There was almost no way in which an individual woman could be identified without bringing her sexual probity into question. The slippage between visibility and notoriety was instantaneous. When Gaia Afrania, a contemporary of Caesar, insisted on representing herself in the courts, her name became a byword for any woman of low character.[25] The Romans had no language or signifying practice in which a woman could be publicly uttered or produced without shame, let alone represent the state. Women were excluded from the work of public signification. For Romans, the woman on display as head of state, as Cleopatra put herself, was therefore in itself transgressive and untranslatable, except in terms of sexual availability.

But it was Octavian himself who most decisively and repeatedly transformed Cleopatra and the symbols of her country. The propaganda campaign that he orchestrated from 33 BC onwards is well documented: the tenor of its influence can be recognized in the texts of the Roman poets, as the following chapter will indicate. But he made use of a range of representational practices beyond the written for his interventions. In the first place, when he judged the moment had come for Rome to rally itself to declare war against the Eastern threat and the struggle with Mark Antony ceased to be understood as internal, Octavian had managed things so that formally the war was against Cleopatra only. She was constructed as the enemy without. To lend resonance to this identification, Octavian resurrected an archaic ceremony from the Roman past. The public declaration of war was accompanied and indeed constituted by a ritual act: he hurled a spear into a piece of waste ground.[26] This gesture, with its conscious atavism, called on Romans to stand firm in the ways of their fathers, the 'mos maiorum'. It was at the same time specifically a renewal of the law of *the* father, by the way it identified its other in the woman to which it was opposed and to whose dispossession it vowed itself.

After Actium, although he could not lead Cleopatra in person as Caesar had led her sister Arsinoe through Rome at his triumph, because she had escaped by killing herself, it is recorded that Octavian was not defeated.

He had an image made of her with the asp, and that was borne through the city.[27]

Roman triumphs were the formalized celebration of slaughter and pillage. For a general to qualify for a triumph the conditions were in theory strict.[28] In the first place, the general had to be of consular rank and to have had supreme responsibility for the campaign in question. And triumphs were not granted in case of civil war: it was the defeat of Cleopatra, not the defeat of Antony, that qualified in this case. The war must have been fought not to recover possessions but to extend Roman rule into entirely new territory. At least 5,000 of the enemy must have been killed and the conquest must be so secure that Roman forces could be withdrawn, to take part in the triumph.

Both persons and objects could feature. Any manifestation of captured wealth could be incorporated, and even the inclusion of exotic trees is recorded. The important prisoners – like Alexander Helios, the elder son of Mark Antony and Cleopatra, who did walk in Octavian's triumph but was not seen again afterwards – were usually killed subsequently, the others made into slaves. The play of meaning about the image of Cleopatra commissioned by Octavian was constrained by these conditions. Like other captured objects, the image bore witness to the bloodshed that had passed, and was itself a surrogate for the wealth of conquered Egypt and the irresistible force of Rome in the person of Octavian. The visible female body opened and eroticized by the snakebite guaranteed the absent male bodies, opened by weapons, of the enemies of Rome. If in Egypt the body of Cleopatra had been the site of the royal and political power of Egypt, the simulacrum of her female body penetrated by the snake reallocated that power to the male: the part the image played in the procession marked the transition of power not only from Egypt to Rome but from female to male.

A contradictory reading, one that was suppressed, was, however, also available. It is possible to argue, and not a few have done so, that the tableau of Cleopatra's death, set up by herself, which Plutarch describes and Shakespeare dramatizes, makes a bold appeal to the traditional association of the queen with the goddess Isis.[29] Dressed in her robes of state and wearing her crown, Cleopatra reasserted her royalty and her godhead. Even the fact of her dying is purged of finality: it has already been pointed out that Isis was associated with the rituals of death that guaranteed the after-life. Death by snakebite, too, could be read as an embrace by the sacred. Looked at like that, in the very scene of Cleopatra's death, the victory of Octavian is boldly denied. It is Cleopatra who conquers. And the formal celebration of the Roman state in the triumph may be reread as momentarily subverted, while the image of the woman with the snake on her arm passed through the street, into a procession of the Egyptian goddess Isis, the participants transformed, by implication, into her worshippers.

There was intended to be no ambiguity in subsequent demonstrations of the power of Octavian over the land and the queen he had defeated. When he added to his name, in 27 BC, three years after the death of Cleopatra, as part of the sequence by which he established a new order in Rome, including the terms on which he himself held power, he took 'Augustus' – an honorific with many positive associations, such as 'noble' and 'good auguries'.[30] Instead of bestowing this new name on the month of his birth, as his adoptive uncle, Julius Caesar, had done when a month was to be named after him, Augustus chose the month in which Egypt had fallen to him and Cleopatra had died in 30 BC. It was also the month which he had chosen for the celebration of his triumph in Rome in 29 BC.

He took over the signs of Egypt as he had taken the image of Cleopatra, producing them as the signs of an authority that was Roman and vested in his own particular person. The characteristic emblems of Egypt he made his own, from its ancient monuments to its Nilotic fauna. He took the sphinx for his seal and used it to sign, literally, himself.[31] He issued silver coins which showed a crocodile with opened mouth enclosed by the legend 'Aegypta capta'.

His grandest gesture, however, was to take down an obelisk that stood in Egypt and have it brought to Rome to act as the gnomon for what has been called the biggest clock of all time.[32] On the Campus Martius, an open space to the north-west of the ancient city, where citizens met to conduct elections, the obelisk was set up. Intended to create both sundial and calendar in one, the dial consisted of Greek letters and marks, all in bronze, which were set into slabs of travertine marble. The scale was vast: the dial was 100 yards across. The base of the obelisk was inscribed with the name of Augustus and his titles and the explanation that it was dedicated to the sun on the occasion of Egypt's being brought under the power of the Roman people.

Not just a marker for the time of Rome – perhaps some consolation for the fact that the Julian calendar had been calculated using Egyptian rather than Roman skills, when Cleopatra had been in Rome with Julius Caesar – the obelisk was also to draw attention to the achievements of Augustus by a spectacular public display enacted twice a year. It was set up so that on his birthday, 23 September, the autumn equinox (and, with inevitable symmetry, on 21 March, the spring one), towards sunset its shadow fell straight across the dial to mount the steps of and finally to enter the Ara Pacis Augustae, the altar of the peace of Augustus. This structure was a monument, voted by the senate to commemorate the order Augustus had imposed and maintained through his conquests. By the time it had been completed and dedicated, in 9 BC, the dial was also in place.

As for Egypt, Octavian kept it to himself. Unique arrangements were made for the governing of Egypt. From 27 BC onwards, other major Roman provinces had senators to govern them, with either a direct accountability to the senate and people of Rome or an indirect one, via the emperor. For Egypt, however, an equestrian, not a senator, was chosen: the appointment was made directly by the emperor, and the prefect, as this governor was known, was responsible to the emperor. There was no provision for accountability to the senate. Access to the country was also restricted for Romans: senators and well-known knights might not enter Egypt without imperial permission.[33]

And inside Egypt, Augustus took up some of the space in native religious life that the Ptolemies and, in particular, Cleopatra, had filled. He too inserted himself in the tradition. On his visit as conqueror, though he had inspected the remains of Alexander (breaking off a bit of the nose), he had drawn the line at investigating the Apis bull.[34] Sacred animals apart, however, the Roman emperor was prepared to take his place in the line of Pharaoh-priests. He had himself represented, according to the traditional canons of pharaonic art, offering the sun on its horizon to Hathor.[35] But it is no coincidence that this offering is made to the goddess with whom Cleopatra caused herself to be compared and at Dendera, the very site of the most lasting of those comparisons. By representing Augustus as the priest of Hathor the break with what has gone before is denied. The female ruler, offering cult to the female goddess, a tradition extending back well before the time of Cleopatra, is displaced. The importance of these acts of substitution may be gauged from the fact that Augustus did not disdain to be represented elsewhere as in the act of making offering to the Buchis bull.[36]

What is installed through the interventions of Augustus is nothing so simple as a crude colonization of Egyptian culture, nor is it enough to note the recourse in public imagery, both in Rome and Egypt, to phallic and male-identified symbols, like the sun. It seems clear that fantasies of the body played their part. What has been lost or changed is the assertion of the relation between masculine and feminine. At Memphis, the Apis bulls were kept stalled next to their mother, the cow Isis. When the representational space allocated to royal women in Egyptian culture was absorbed into male territory, the possibility of showing women as powerful in their own right, and in co-regency with men, was discarded.[37] A wider distance was opened between the sexes.

Chapter 2

Cleopatra: housewife

In 1669 the Dutch painter Jan de Braij of Haarlem memorialized the parents and four siblings he had lost in the plague of 1663–4 in a family portrait. Set in an interior furnished with some opulence, the picture would seem to record and mourn a vanished era of domestic harmony and fulfilment. Only one detail jars: the parents are represented as Antony and Cleopatra (Plate 2.2).

Accounts of contemporary practice offer no immediate resource to the bewildered spectator. In *Gods, Saints and Heroes: Dutch Painting in the Age of Rembrandt*, Albert Blankert and others address the relation between Dutch sitters and patrons and the classical and biblical themes invoked by their painters.[1] Comparison with Roman heroes or a great Israelite queen like Esther is shown to be a regular method of idealizing and endorsing the public position of contemporary figures, and, by the same token, of idealizing and endorsing both the republican political structure they supported and represented and the reformed church of which they were members. When it comes, however, to the de Braij portrait, Blankert is at a loss. Abandoning his previous exegetical model, Blankert suggests that they might have been to a fancy dress party. Apparently he can devise no other means of resolving the disturbing conflict between filial loyalty and the comparison of one's mother to Cleopatra. There is, however, a way in which to read this comparison positively, to recognize in the allusion to Antony and Cleopatra the assertion of the idealized exercise of the rule of patriarchal authority within marriage, and in consequence to see de Braij as paying the highest tribute to his parents and their relationship.[2]

Such a reading of the picture depends on an appreciation of the very specific signifier into which Cleopatra has been made by our culture.[3] She has been appropriated and transformed in the service of patriarchal ideology from a woman in history[4] into a cultural artefact, a signifier. It is on a critical point in the process of Cleopatra's inscription in the culture of early modern Europe, as demonstrated in two printed and illustrated texts, that this chapter will focus. In these texts, Boccaccio's *De Claris*

Mulieribus and Petrarch's *De Remediis utriusque Fortunae*, visual representations of Cleopatra are offered in close association with verbal definitions and evaluations. Word and image work independently and in conjunction to define Cleopatra by means of her relationship to male figures; it is a confrontation which problematizes power relations between the sexes, inflecting itself variously to encompass issues of domestic, sexual, and political power.

The pair of woodcuts illustrating the Ulm Boccaccio of 1473 represents Cleopatra in the two situations which would come to epitomize her in Western art: at the banquet where she won her bet with Antony by dissolving her pearl ear-ring and drinking it, and with the asp. The former image, in Boccaccio, is very clearly the emblem of a scandal: Cleopatra is shocking the men of her household. The accompanying text elaborates the terms in which her conduct is to be condemned. By what means, then, can it be open to de Braij, 200 years later in post-Reformation Holland, to use Cleopatra at her banquet as a signifier of domestic concord? Close reading of Boccaccio's text and an investigation of a somewhat later figure of Cleopatra, drawn for the translation of Petrarch's text published in Augsburg in 1532, lead me to argue that all three representations of Cleopatra are determined by attempts to construct gender relations. The local and temporal contingency of specific social groupings, as the attempt to assign power between the sexes takes its latest form, has determined the way in which Cleopatra is presented: her power and independence offered a challenge to patriarchy that had to be recuperated. The reinforcing of gender difference at the Renaissance and the Reformation's later enforcement and idealization of marriage each produced modifications in the way in which she was shown and valorized. In Reformation Augsburg it is her sexual and political power that is emphasized and deplored. It is a specific inflection of the ideology of gender in seventeenth-century Haarlem, I shall argue, that makes it possible for de Braij to honour his mother by representing her as Cleopatra.

The strategy of Cleopatra's inscription is one example of the reinforcing and renegotiation of gender difference that took place in early modern Europe. In 'Early feminism and the querelle des femmes', Joan Kelly-Gadol argues that women like Christine de Pisan were protesting against what they perceived as a recent redefinition of the role and scope of women and the erosion of their liberty and dignity.[5] The change from feudalism to capitalism was accompanied by a limiting and subordination of women generally. Recent analyses of the effect of the changed organization of production, such as Judith Brown's work on Renaissance Tuscany and Merry Wiesner's investigation of the German textile industry, help to identify the pressures which resulted in women's gradual exclusion from the skilled trades and the diverse effects of this exclusion.[6] Among these pressures, the confinement of women within the home and their subordination to a male head of household were particularly powerful. These did not act just as a practical measure of social control: Lawrence Stone has argued that during the period between 1450 and 1630 'both Church and state provided powerful new theoretical and practical support' for a reinforcement of 'the despotic authority of the husband and father – that is to say, of patriarchy'.[7] By a process of mystification the cultural prestige of women was enhanced within the same period. The new ideology of marriage conceived at the Reformation also contributed to an accompanying reassessment of women's sexuality: woman was 'no longer a vessel of sin, a whore of Babylon whose sexuality was fearful and deadly, but a "helpmeet" for men, secondary in authority and yet primary as an embodiment of domestic purity'.[8] At the same time, paradoxically, as Allison Heisch and Louis Montrose have argued, the development of the centrally administered nation states created positions of exceptional political power that could be held by women, as the women who came to rule in France, Spain, and England demonstrated.[9] (The evidence indicates, however, that Elizabeth and Catherine de Medici were acutely aware that their position was anomalous. Catherine took steps, in the Caron designs of 1568, to represent her rule as an adjunct rather than a challenge to the rule of the son who would succeed her.[10]) The figure of Cleopatra VII, combining in one person a challenge to the public rule of the male and the domestic control of the husband, could not be anything but problematic for this period.

In choosing to confine myself to these two illustrated texts by Petrarch and Boccaccio, I have been concerned to identify an early and I believe crucial form in which Cleopatra's image became disseminated. Throughout the sixteenth century it was repeatedly renegotiated in painting, sculpture, engraving, and drama, but it is in the early texts by two men usually considered among the first to register a post-medieval consciousness that she was initially inscribed in a culture that we can recognize as our own.[11] But it is not just the pre-eminence of the authors that makes their account so important. Elizabeth Eisenstein, in *The Printing Press as an Agent of Change*, has argued that the invention of the press and its commercial development should be seen as the most significant Renaissance activity, marking a change in cultural practice so decisive that it can be described as defining the start of a new phase in human experience.[12] By means of print, ideas could achieve rapid and wide dissemination: what is more, they could be perpetuated. While the survival of texts depended on manual copyists, there was always a risk that an individual work might not be popular enough to be copied in sufficient numbers to ensure its survival. Both the texts in this essay survived, and in the form discussed here. They were able to reach a wider audience, reiterating their assessment of Cleopatra, and to lend their authority to the mistrust and subordination of women, thanks to the powerful new mechanism for the wholesale inscription of the word, the printing-press.

For the same reasons the woodcuts and engravings in these early illustrated books achieved a currency unknown to previous graphic images. The 1473 edition of *De Claris Mulieribus* was published by Johann Zainer of Ulm: known as the Ulm Boccaccio, it was the first illustrated book to have been printed in that city, where a Latin and a German edition were both published in the same year.[13] Although woodcuts had been included in typeset books for the first time in southern Germany around 1460, still in 1473, William Levin suggests, in spite of a growing technical sophistication, the woodcut's function was 'locked in its meaning and hardly attached to its aesthetic character; its purpose was to convey a simple idea or fit a concept'.[14] These ideological messengers were the images that formed the basis for illustrations to subsequent editions of the book, such as those in Augsburg (1479), Louvain (1487), Strasbourg (1488), and Saragossa (1494). The edition of Petrarch's *De Remediis utriusque Fortunae* in question was published by Heinrich Steiner of Augsburg in 1532, in translation under the title *Von der Artzney bayder Gluck, des Guten und Widerwertigen*. It was accompanied by a series of very fine wood engravings designed and executed specifically for this text by Hans Weiditz: it was the first complete and fully illustrated published translation of the text into German. The translation, which in fact had been completed in 1521, was quickly superseded, owing to the rapid transformation of the vernacular brought about by Luther's translation of the Bible and the vast increase in vernacular publication. The engravings, however, continued to be used and can still be found at the end of the century in the Frankfurt editions of 1572, 1584, 1604, and 1620.

It should be emphasized that these are both texts of the highest cultural privilege, empowered by the authority vested in their writers as scholars and moralists. Knowledge itself was being rewritten by these early humanists, as lost texts from antiquity were recovered, studied, synthesized, and made the instrument of a redefinition of current experience. *De Claris Mulieribus* was one of the group of great Latin texts, including *De Montibus, De Casibus Virorum Illustrium*, and *Genealogia Deorum Gentilium*, in which Boccaccio disseminated the knowledge of antiquity and gained for himself a cultural authority comparable with that of the classical writers he was recuperating for his own society.[15] This obtained, Branca judges, until the early 1700s; Bacchi della Lega records nearly a dozen editions of *De Claris Mulieribus* in France before 1600, seven in Italy, six in Germany, and two in Spain.[16] The Petrarch text wields a comparable cultural potency. Critics agree in describing the *De Remediis* as enormously influential until modern times.[17] Despite the popularity of his lyrics, this was Petrarch's most widely read work and it stayed popular till the eighteenth century when the last printed edition was issued. Fiske notes

numberless manuscript copies preserved in European libraries and remarks
the Latin text's appearance between about 1474 and 1758 in Germany,
Italy, France, Switzerland, Holland, and Hungary. It was also translated
into eight modern languages.

Inscribed in the classical texts from which Renaissance scholars were
deriving a knowledge of the divinities of the ancient world and its history,
geography, poetics, and philosophy was also a knowledge of Woman. It
is this knowledge that in recent years feminist scholarship has attempted
to deconstruct by identifying the place allotted to women in Greece and
Rome under the law, by custom, and in fantasy as revealed in myth and
literature.[18] Complex and contradictory as that knowledge appears, it is
self-evidently phallocentric. The legal systems of both Greece and Rome
institutionalized male advantage. The rights of citizens were not assigned
directly to women. The formal status of individual women in relation to
the community was not even always stable. It was sometimes adjusted
in order to regulate the size of the group qualified to confer the birthright
of citizenship on their children. It was difficult for women to amass
property or to pass it on to their daughters.

This is to say nothing of the influence of individual writers such as
Aristotle, with the misogyny his teaching institutionalized, or of the way
in which individual women had been inscribed. Epitaphs for Roman
wives, composed, it must be assumed, by husbands who erected the
memorials, pay tribute to their chastity, regularity in keeping the house,
and skill in such tasks as weaving.[19] What is celebrated, though it sometimes includes reference to an affection we can relate to companionate
marriage, is the acceptance of a prescribed set of obligations based on
gender difference. Memorial tablets apart, there was almost no way in
which the individual woman could be identified without bringing her
sexual probity into question; Gaia Afrania, a contemporary of Caesar,
who brought lawsuits herself, without the intermediary of any (male)
lawyer, became a byword, and her name was used to designate *any*
woman of low character.[20]

The form of Cleopatra's inscription in Roman culture was determined
by the threat she posed to these cultural patterns.[21] In the first place, the
law of Egypt did not subject women as the law of Greece and Rome did;
they enjoyed one freedom that made them a scandal to the men of Rome:
they were free to choose their own husbands.[22] Then, Cleopatra followed
the tradition of the queens of her house, known for their court intrigues
and political murders, in her active pursuit of political power within her
own country.[23] It was her further ambition to re-establish the empire of
her ancestor Ptolemy that brought her repeatedly into confrontation with
Rome. She became the lover of Julius Caesar and claimed to have had a
son by him, whom she called by a derivative of his name, Caesarion;
Livy's letters claim that when she was living in Rome as Caesar's mistress

she challenged that categorization by insisting on being called 'queen'. As he represents her, Cleopatra was resolute in appropriating and reinstating a term which they had placed beyond the law, rendered unsayable. But it was not only her determined appropriation of what Roman patriarchy wished to define as a male prerogative, political and dynastic power, that made her a threat. Her very origin in the East, already, as Said asserts, boldly demarcated as the 'other' by the time of Homer, played its part in overdetermining the manner of her inscription as a figure of opposition to the rule of Rome, as the Woman who in herself embodies the Sign of the Transgression of the Law, Virgil's 'monstrum fatale'.[24] It is as a threat to the Law of the Father rather than as an erotic symbol that Cleopatra impinged on Rome. The construction of her as a seductress, the delimitation of her power, and its redefinition in terms of female sexuality, however, began almost immediately.

In the first place, Cleopatra was the object of a deliberate and intensive propaganda campaign on the part of Octavian, intended to promote the reunification of the divided empire against a common enemy without.[25] She was incorporated in the culture specifically in order to identify and impersonate the other, to form an image against which Rome could constellate its own attributes and identify itself. This, Williamson suggests, is the reason for the surprising uniformity of allusion to Cleopatra in the poets of the period, Horace, Propertius, Virgil, Ovid, and Lucan. Cleopatra is regularly represented as the epitome of the foreign and barbaric, with careful emphasis on cultural differences, particularly as manifest in Egyptian religion. In the course of these accounts, Cleopatra's sexuality is arraigned: it is part of her otherness both as female and as non-Roman (Lucan writes of 'the night which brought the wanton daughter of the Ptolemies to the arms of a Roman general'), but it is also made to bear the guilt of otherness in its totality; and so Cleopatra becomes defined as the harlot queen.

What Boccaccio was transmitting, then, when he engaged in his pioneering task of presenting the lives of 104 famous women from antiquity, the collection of biographies, *De Claris Mulieribus*, was in itself problematic. The problems were compounded by new ambivalences: the preface to the work defines the women who are to be its topic by repeatedly setting them over against the women of the Judaeo-Christian tradition. It is going to describe the energies and achievements of 'pagan' women rather than the submission and restraint of 'the ladies of sacred history', who,

> following in the paths and the rules of their holy Teacher, often to attain true eternal glory, forced themselves to tolerate adversities almost beyond human comprehension. Pagan women, on the other hand, attained glory – and with what a burning strength of spirit – either

owing to a certain natural instinct; or, more probably, because they were driven by a spark of the fleeting splendour of this world; and sometimes beneath the blow of crushing fortune also faced most severe tests.[26]

Masculine vulnerability to the ambiguous attraction of the Other Woman with her self-determining force is evident, although any 'glory' she attains is distinguished from the real thing. This stands in the way of any easy categorization of the enterprise. Among the flood of discourse concerning the nature of women appearing in the fifteenth and sixteenth centuries, Constance Jordan groups *De Claris Mulieribus* with Sir Thomas Elyot's *Defence of Good Women* (1540) and Bruni's *De Studiis et Litteris* (1409) as 'humanist in character and apologetic in purpose'.[27] Joan Kelly-Gadol, however, sees it as one of the new texts of gender differentiation that provoked Christine de Pisan and her followers to initiate the long literary debate in which women opposed the terms of their cultural inscription, a debate which she traces up to the eighteenth century.[28] Certainly, the highest praise Boccaccio can offer a woman, in *De Claris Mulieribus*, is to allow that she has done as well as a man, that she has succeeded in attaining a 'manly' level of achievement, and, as I shall argue, the utmost censure of a man is to accuse him of failing to live up to male potential, of being 'effeminate'.

The life of Cleopatra is number 86 in Boccaccio's anthology, and about two thousand words long. He had already written of her in the *Fiammetta* (1354) and *De Casibus Virorum Illustrium* (1359); his attitude in *De Claris Mulieribus* is markedly more critical. This hardening may be attributed to the particular project of *De Claris*, the inscribing of (the Other) Woman by means of presenting a collection of the lives of individual women from the pagan past.[29] It brought him up against the other as the site of contradictory meanings, containing both what is repressed and what is desired: both the desire noted in his preface and the wish to control are constellated in his inscription. Cleopatra's beauty, her drive, and the amplitude of her resources are all registered, but only to be categorized as forms of transgression. The law which they transgress is the Law of the Father, and it is this, which empowers only men at the expense of women, that is invoked to define how Cleopatra has transgressed.

By the terms of Boccaccio's discourse, the desire to rule and sexual potency in Cleopatra are juxtaposed in such a way that both are discredited. At the opening we are told that

Cleopatra was an Egyptian woman who became an object of gossip for the whole world . . . She gained glory for almost nothing else than her beauty, while on the other hand she became known throughout the world for her greed, cruelty and lustfulness.[30]

Cleopatra is first stripped of her royalty and defined in her otherness before being presented as a public scandal. She is put before the reader as a figure of shame, even before Boccaccio goes on to construct the distinction between what would be appropriate in a warrior hero – the gaining of glory and universal renown, the desire for prizes, and a ruthless ambition – and what is legitimate in a female ruler. Cleopatra's sexuality is admitted, in the reference to the power of her beauty, but it is to be used only as the means of delegitimizing her – it wasn't the proper way of gaining glory, and the sexuality is itself rendered untrustworthy and discredited by repeated identification with a sexual intimacy which destroys:

> burning with the desire to rule, as some say, [she] poisoned the innocent fifteen-year-old boy who was both her brother and her husband, and ruled the kingdom alone . . . Thinking that she would obtain her kingdom if she could draw Caesar, the conqueror of the world, into lustfulness, and being very beautiful and captivating anyone she desired with her shining eyes and her eloquence, with little trouble she brought the lustful prince to her embraces.

Her sexuality is depicted as compromising Antony's potency as well as Caesar's. She consumes him metaphorically by the insatiability of her demands. There is a constant exchange in progress between Cleopatra as site and sign of sexual power and as site and sign of political ambition. Both attributes, equally at odds with the Law of the Father, reinforce, stand in for, and duplicate each other in identifying her as transgressor. A significant tool, in the deprecation of her potency, is Boccaccio's repeated definition of Cleopatra as oriental.

In identifying her as other, outside the law, he appropriates her attributes to define, by contrast, what the law permits.

> Thus Cleopatra, having already acquired her kingdom through two crimes, gave herself to her pleasures. Having become almost the prostitute of Oriental kings, and greedy for gold and jewels, she not only stripped her lovers of these things with her art, but it was also said that she emptied the temples and the sacred places of the Egyptians of their vases, statues, and other treasures.

Here female sexuality, unregulated by the constraints of marriage and exacting substantial economic reward, is fantasized, under the guise of condemning Cleopatra's ruthless oriental greed.

In the influential Ulm Boccaccio of 1473 what strikes the readers' eyes as they turn to the account of Cleopatra is the woodcut at its head and the decorated capital which draws their gaze into the first line of the text. Thus the graphic image is presented in close perceptual as well as spatial conjunction with the legend 'Cleopatra egiptia femina fuit totius orbis'

CLEOPATRA •ANTONIVS •

Plate 2.1 Woodcut from the Ulm Boccaccio, 1473, British Library.

(see Plate 2.1). 'Fabula', on the next line, completes the sentence: what the reader is being offered is a visualization of the text: 'Cleopatra was an Egyptian woman who became an object of gossip for the whole world.' The woodcut is presented as the emblem of a scandal. Two images, side by side, engrave the form of this scandal. On the left, the larger area represents the banquet described by Pliny where Cleopatra dissolved a pearl ear-ring and drank it off, in order to fulfil her boast to Antony that she could have a dinner costing more than 10,000,000 sester-ces.[31] And on the right Cleopatra and Antony are shown at the point of their death.

Boccaccio's text presents a clearly 'classical' story:

Antony thought that this could not be done; nevertheless, wishing to see and devour, he asked her to try it. Lucius Plautus was called to be the judge. The next day, when the food did not exceed the customary, and when Antony was already ridiculing her promises, Cleopatra ordered her servants to bring the second course. According to the instructions they had received beforehand, they brought in only a goblet of strong vinegar. Cleopatra immediately took a pearl of great value which she wore as an ornament on one of her ears, according to the custom of Oriental women, dissolved it in the vinegar, and then drank it.

It is, on one level, a literal narrative detail from Boccaccio's text that the woodcut illustrates, but it has a metaphorical force beyond its immediate reference. The 'Oriental' sign is interpreted and transmitted as difference. What the graphic artist has done is to construct a scene where a female on the left sits with a bowl to her lips, boldly looking over it at two male figures to the right of the picture. The figure closer to her, presumably Antony, holds up an admonishing finger, while the servant's horror is expressed by his dropped jaw and stance of affronted withdrawal. The impression of a confrontation across the division of sexual difference is emphasized by the writing in, under the picture, not only of Cleopatra's name, which might have been expected on its own, but of Antony's too. Hers is on the left, his on the right.

There is no attempt, of course, at any authenticity of historical detail: the effect is to constitute the male/female opposition in contemporary terms. This makes Antony's coronet, in comparison with Cleopatra's head-dress, a quite specific indication of superiority. And the horned head-dress that Cleopatra sports, a fashion item in the 1430s, had been identified by the Church as the sign of female licentiousness. A bishop had preached against them as early as 1371 and they were compared to the horns of the devil in the *Miroir aux Dames*. The tradition of manuscript illustration in which these woodcuts were formed made use of this coding: the deadly sin of Lust is frequently shown as a woman wearing one of these head-dresses.[32] Sexual desire in women and the enjoyment of wealth are not demarcated from each other in the image. There appears to be a deliberate attempt to indicate that this is a wealthy household – apart from the badge the servant wears in his hat and the fine table-cloth whose generous folds are displayed, the window space between Cleopatra and Antony is leaded. The visual image presents a fifteenth-century scene where a lady of rank is appalling the men of the household, from the husband, who should rule her as his coronet implies, to its steward, by her display of wanton self-indulgence.

The second incident chosen for illustration is Cleopatra's suicide. Again Cleopatra is on the left, Antony on the right. This is the passage in Boccaccio which prompts the picture:

> Angry at hearing that she was being reserved for the conqueror's triumph, and without hope of safety, Cleopatra, dressed in royal garments, followed her Antony. Lying down next to him, she opened the veins of her arms and put two asps in the openings in order to die.

Much of this detail, particularly its intimation of tenderness ('her Antony' – 'suum Antonium'), is ignored. As it stands, the image is quite ambiguous: the sword in Antony's breast could have been thrust in by Cleopatra. While he is utterly prostrate, upside-down, his eyes turned up (though still wearing his coronet), Cleopatra, in defiance of Boccaccio's assertion, is upright and active. Although her sleeves are rolled up to display the asps, it also makes her look as if she is ready to do a job of work. Although it does give an indication of Cleopatra's own suffering, in this second image the threat implied in the first is brought to realization. The woman, who had defied the good sense and control of the men about her with her immoderate appetites, is seen presiding over the death of her husband.[33]

If the woodcut panel in its entirety is less than accurate in its rendering of narrative detail, it is entirely in accord with the ideology of Boccaccio's text, with its emphasis on Cleopatra as a consuming or devouring figure. Like the text, it calls on readers to (mis)recognize the self-evident truths of gender relations: men must set a limit to the all-consuming appetites of their women or be destroyed by them.

> As the insatiable woman's craving for kingdoms grew day by day, to grasp everything at once she asked Antony for the Roman empire. Perhaps drunk or rising from such a noble supper, Antony, who was not in full possession of his mental faculties, without properly considering his own strength or the power of the Romans, promised to give it to her, as if it were his to give. Good Lord, how great was the audacity of the woman who requested this! And the madness of the man who promised it was no less! How generous was this man . . . as if he wanted to give it away at once like the ownership of a single house!

Issues of political, domestic, and sexual power are collapsed in a single image.

It was in these words and by means of these graphics that Cleopatra was first made available to a wide European audience. These subjects, Cleopatra's banquet and her death by the asps, here available for the first time in print, were to endure in European graphic art, repeatedly renegotiated.

These are the issues which continued to crystallize around the figure of Cleopatra and to be variously inflected and renegotiated, principally through the twin subjects of her banquet and her death by the asps. This is where it becomes feasible to start making some suggestions about the interpretation of the de Braij family group, introduced at the opening of this discussion. For, although Boccaccio and his graphics establish a firm identification between the figure of Cleopatra and a challenge to patriarchal power, they cannot enforce an immutable symbolism on the scenes depicted. As I have implied, the representation of Cleopatra's self-administered death could be made to bear ambiguous overtones: members of the

School of Fontainebleau and later Reni, Guercino, and Artemisia Gentileschi invested the unclothed single figure of Cleopatra and the snake with
the suggestion of a provocative or challenging auto-eroticism. But the
same image could be inflected negatively: instead of a figure of *jouissance*,
for Holbein and Beham in particular, Cleopatra with the snake is a figure
not of abandon but of muscular power suffering in physical constraint.
The banquet scene, too, then, is capable of specific inflection.

De Braij's family portrait can be read in the context of the visual
representation of fatherly authority noted in Jonathan Goldberg's study
of Stuart family images, where the arrangement and positioning of female
members in relation to male constitutes a visualization of the power of
the father.[34] The structure of de Braij's portrait differs radically from the
Boccaccio woodcut in the way in which it represents the relation of male
to female, although that relation is clearly at the centre of its project
(Plate 2.2). In the woodcut, Cleopatra draining her bowl is an object of
horror to the men with whom she is shown. In the portrait, although
the principal male and female figures are shown in close confrontation,
the look that Antony turns on Cleopatra, though not without ambiguity,
is not one of alarm.[35] For her part, she does not defy the laurelled figure
at her side but, as she reaches towards the fine pearl visible between her
fingers, raises her eyes to his, as if for approval. Nor is she alone in her
submissiveness: the way in which the family group is constructed again
reflects the authority of the father. To her right are two female figures,
a grown-up daughter and a daughter-in-law, echoing each other and their
mother by their meek profiles and smoothly coiffed heads. One of them
offers a tray on which two glasses – symbolizing their status as the weaker
vessels – are proffered, while on the left of the picture yet another
decorous young woman (like the others, notably well dressed) extends a
shallow bowl to the viewer, inviting us to witness both her family's
wealth and its internal dynamic. Her father is the one who has command
of discourse, as his almost preaching hands demonstrate: all the women's
mouths are firmly closed and their hands occupied in gestures of submission. Two silent male figures observe: one, possibly the painter, gazes
out at the viewer from between his mother and his sisters; the other, at
the extreme left of the picture, where he seems to command the gaze
even of the younger and less socialized and decorous members of the
family group down to the dog, holds a halberd which leans slightly
forward into the picture space. By implication, it is the phallic and martial
authority of this figure and all it represents that converts the raw material
of unformed childhood and slovenly undisciplined youth (the serving-boy
is hurried, not erect, a fallen vessel lies on his tipped tray) into the ordered
household. Wealth as well as order is the mark of patriarchal achievement:
from the pearl, which in this context is displayed as part of the *family*
treasure, to the Turkey carpet and embossed metal dish in the left-hand

Plate 2.2 De Braij family portrait, 1669, Currier Gallery of Art.

corner which take up about a sixth of the picture space, all reflect credit on the laurelled head of the father.

The pearl, though, as de Jongh's study 'Pearls of virtue and pearls of vice' has demonstrated, was more than a symbol of material wealth when depicted on a wife's ear in seventeenth-century Dutch painting.[36] It made specific assertions about her chastity and about the fulfilment of her duties as a wife. He quotes a passage from Francis de Sales's *Introduction à la vie dévote* of 1608, which was reprinted in its Dutch translation of 1616 thirteen times in the course of the seventeenth century. In a chapter entitled 'Advice for the married' de Sales wrote:

> Women of both ancient and present times customarily hang pearls in their ears because of the pleasure they derive (as Pliny observes) from feeling them swinging when they touch each other. But because I know that God's great friend, Isaac, sent earrings as the first token of his love to the pure Rebecca, so do I believe that this jewel signifies spiritually that the first part that a man must have from his wife and which the wife must faithfully preserve is the ear, so that no speech or sound may enter it other than the sweet sound of chaste words, which are oriental pearls of the Gospel.

It is in Pliny's chapter on pearls that he tells the story of Cleopatra's wager: in de Sales's devotional treatise the ancient author's representation of the pearl ear-ring as symbol of transgression of the Law of the Father is transformed, so that the ear-ring becomes the very index of her orthodoxy (as Freud was to agree).

That the image of Cleopatra's banquet, in Boccaccio such an emblem of the scandalous, could be so inflected 200 years later is to be explained in part by the new doctrines of marriage that had developed as a result of the Reformation. What was disruptive and threatening in women's sexuality was ideologically laundered: marriage was advanced as the normative condition and woman presented as a helpmate to her husband.[37] She was now to be his deputy, still subordinated, but bound to him by the ties of a companionate marriage, and accorded a new respect.[38] This inevitably involved a problematizing of the role and position of those women who were not, by definition, wives – such as the prostitute and the nun – and a renegotiation of the relationship of authority between husband and wife. The stresses and ambiguities involved in making these adjustments are particularly clear in the Weiditz illustrations to *De Remediis*, created in about 1520, half-way between the Boccaccio woodcuts and the de Braij family portrait.

The original text of *De Remediis* is fourteenth-century and Italian; it has been described as the most medieval in tone of Petrarch's works and the purveyor of a monkish misanthropy.[39] Weiditz's woodcuts, however, are the product of Reformation Augsburg; and they reflect a set of assumptions and anxieties not articulated in the written text. Word and image do concur, however, in using the transgressive fact of Cleopatra's political power as evidence to discredit women generally. Both Petrarch's text and Weiditz's woodcut are concerned with intimate private relations between the sexes: here it is the power Cleopatra wielded through her sexuality that is emphasized. In this sense she is capable of being constructed as the representative of all women, at the same time as she is a warning to them. She is both what they must not be and what they inevitably are.

Petrarch's text creates her as the site of these contradictory meanings only incidentally: his project in the sixty-ninth dialogue, 'Von angenehmer Lieb und Buhlschaften', in which she features, is to discredit Pleasant Love.[40] His attack is based not on ridiculing the follies of the lover, as one might expect, but on reminding the reader of the unworthiness and unreliability of Woman as a love-object. In the sense that this chapter reiterates familiar misogynistic material, it is nothing new. But the context offered by the work as a whole secured this material, a reading privileged in more than one aspect. *De Remediis* is made up of 254 dialogues, divided into two books: in the first, Reason (Ratio) argues with Joy (Gaudium or Spes) and, in the second, with Fear (Metus), in an attempt to promote a stoical acceptance of the vicissitudes of life. It is not a theoretical work but addresses itself to direct experience, including the problems of family life. That it was long and widely read I have indicated; the particular kind of attention such a handbook for the disturbances of daily life would have received is no less important. As a work to be turned to under pressure, a sedative against disabling excitement or distress, it would have enjoyed a special kind of reading. Returned to repeatedly, and its assertions incorporated uncritically, it offered a systematized set of defences against anxiety.

The method of this discourse is as important as the misogyny which it reinscribes, for by it misogyny is being articulated into a system of power relations. The method itself is a paradigm of the power relation where *jouissance* is displaced by *logos*: Petrarch's dialogues proceed on a pattern of naïve assertion on the part of Joy, countered by crushing rhetoric from Reason, which is established from the outset:

> *Joy.*   I enjoy pleasant love.
> *Reason.*   Thou shalt be overcome with pleasant snares.
> *Joy.*   I burn in pleasant love.
> *Reason.*   It is well said thou burnest: for love is a secret fire, a pleasant wound, a savoury poison, a sugared bitterness, a delectable sickness, a sweet punishment and a flattering death.

The association between love, deception, bait, injury, and death is maintained throughout.

This is no conventional rhetoric of idealized eroticism: the text carefully

locates this love in a real and possible world and works to identify the
impulse towards intimacy and trust, when it arises in the male, as leading
directly to a perilous loss of autonomy. Hierarchy is safer, or, as Petrarch
expresses it, the impulse to love, though universal, seems to him 'servile'
and 'base'. In order to maintain this rationalization of the fear of intimacy,
it is necessary to define the nature of Woman's inferiority: she is presented,
in sexual intimacy, as the very figure of deceit.

> *Joy.*   I love, and am loved again.
> *Reason.*   The first thou mayest know of thyself: the second thou mayest
> stand in doubt of, unless thou take thy sweetheart's secret
> talking in the night for a testimony thereof.
> *Joy.*   Without doubt I am beloved.
> *Reason.*   I perceive she hath persuaded thee, and it is no hard matter
> to persuade one that is willing, for all lovers are blind and
> quick of belief. But if thou think that there be any trust in a
> lover's oath, then bring forth the bill of thy lover's hand
> which was written in the brittle ice, whereunto the southern
> winds were witnesses. But O thou foolish man, never give
> credit to a dishonest woman: fear, heat, lightness, custom of
> lying, desire to deceive, and the gain of deceit, every one of
> these, and much more, all these maketh it suspicious whatso-
> ever cometh out of her mouth.

With this last exhortation, it becomes clear that the unpredictability of
the human condition, against which the dialogues are offered as a protection, can be blamed in this case on the inherent nature of woman herself.

It was Cleopatra's power to achieve a sexual conquest over the most
powerful man in the world, Julius Caesar, that challenged Petrarch's ideal
of the autonomous male and brought her into the argument. But she was
defined on this occasion in parallel with the prostitute who seduced
Hannibal: by implication stripped of her royal status and political power,
she is punished by being degraded to equality with the nameless harlot.

> Julius Caesar, being conqueror in France, Germany, Britannia, Spain,
> Italy, Thessalia, and Egypt, and again shortly after in Armenia, Pontus,
> Africa and last of all again in Spain, like to have the upper hand: in
> the midst of so many conquests he himself was conquered at Alexandria
> by princely love. Hannibal being conqueror at Ticinium, Trebeta, Trasi-
> menus Cannas and at length to be overcome in his own country, first
> was overcome at Salapia, a city of Apulia and that the matter might
> be more heinous, he humbled himself to the love of an harlot.

Love and humiliation for the warrior hero are inescapably linked. A man
wishing to construct himself as Caesar – that is, to model himself on the
ideal of the warrior statesman – must recognize in any woman with

whom he develops a tender sexual relationship the figure of the harlot/ Cleopatra. Issues of politics and of psychosexuality are persuasively entwined. The realistic fear of intimacy, based on the unconscious recognition of its reminder of original loss, is (mis)represented as exclusively the fear of domination.

It is these two examples, Caesar and Hannibal, that gave Weiditz his starting-point (Plate 2.3). But there are no labels, as there were in the Boccaccio pictures, to identify for the reader what he or she is looking at, no images taken from a narrative to pick out: the whole undertaking is more sophisticated and more riddling in the way in which it confronts the reader (see, for instance, the inventiveness which turns the division between images into a wall of masonry). The difference may be referred to the vastly differing circumstances of production: the woodcuts of the Ulm Boccaccio had been derived from Franco-Flemish manuscripts created between 1366 and 1473, but the Weiditz woodcuts were made in Augsburg, probably by 1521, and devised specially for the Augsburg publication of 1532. They take their place in the explosion of graphic inventiveness that accompanied the social and religious upheavals of the late fifteenth and early sixteenth centuries in Germany. They are rooted in the experience of Reformation Augsburg, from early on a Lutheran stronghold, particularly in its attempts to negotiate the relationship of classical to vernacular and to renegotiate the position of women, including the figures of the prostitute and the nun. There is no need to know anything about Cleopatra, or indeed much about the text with which the woodcut made its appearance, in order to read the icon.

It was 1532, the year in which *De Remediis* was finally published – it had been completed by 1521 and shelved for eleven years – that saw the closure of the city brothel in Augsburg.[41] Since the 1520s, as Lyndal Roper has shown, the evangelical preachers had been involved in the campaign against prostitution in the city: like adultery, clerical concubinage, and illegitimacy, it was a target of the reformers throughout northern Europe.[42] Sexual behaviour was being regulated and regularized within marriage.[43] Men and women were being herded into matrimony. Celibacy, or the hypocritical pretence of it, was being abolished: the clergy were to marry, nuns were expelled from their convents. The virgin and the harlot were equally disallowed. In Weiditz's woodcuts something of this paradoxical equation can be seen.

As in the first example, the visual field is divided, to give a larger image on the left and a smaller on the right. On the left, the dominant figure is a standing man, with a crown which is also like a helmet. He is bearded and wears a sword and is dressed in flowing garments girt up to free his feet. His right hand is extended, holding a sceptre, which is also grasped just above the base by a woman who is kneeling before him. She too is elaborately dressed, with jewellery and a low-cut gown. Her

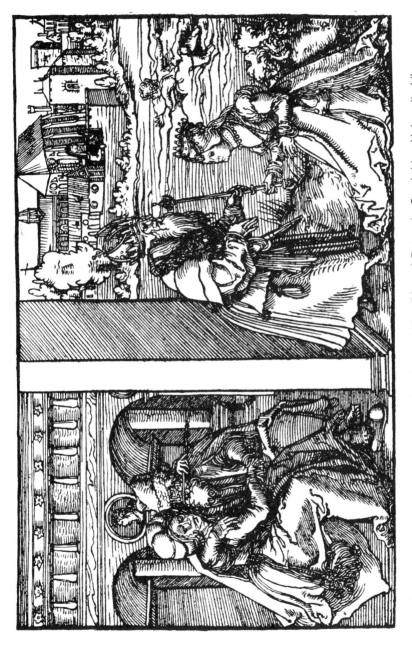

Plate 2.3 Hans Weiditz, illustration to the Augsburg 1532 edition of Petrarch, Cambridge University Library.

flowing skirts hide and impede her feet. This might be read as a decorous statement of sexual difference, were it not for the slightly ambiguous double grasp of the sceptre. What looks like equality and comparability is made problematic by this. What is seen behind these figures, however, develops the ambiguity of the foregrounded image a good deal further. A naked male figure swims, behind the queen's back, towards a shore where a woman stands watching him. This female figure is positioned directly above that of the queen, with whom a connection is thereby suggested. This second figure, taken on her own, would also look decorous enough: she is dressed as a nun and stands behind the wall which surrounds what looks like a church and is marked with a cross. Outside the wall is a tree and the suggestion of flourishing vegetation and the abundant waves through which the swimmer strikes towards her. The image suggests the hypocrisy of the enclosed female figure, apparently waving to her lover, and when we remember the fact that in Augsburg the brothel was known as 'the virgins' court' an implied comparison with a prostitute's behaviour is reinforced. At the same time the image permits a certain pathos: the woman is hemmed in, in a constructed world, while the male is naked, moving vigorously through the natural element. What is reflected here is something like the attitude of Bernhard Rem, who wrote, urging his daughter to leave her Augsburg convent in 1523, 'when a sister is "walled in" from the world, her carnal desires are not "walled out" '.[44] Ozment argues that contemporary critics saw monastic life as inhuman, anti-sexual, and anti-social. Marriage would redress this cultural deprivation.

Both female figures are constrained by their clothes – only the nun's face and hands are visible, and the queen, though her chest is displayed, sinks amid the folds of her skirts. Although the foregrounded image seems to display a queen graciously deferring to a king, the totality of the image is more problematic: free male activity is contrasted with female constraint and perhaps explained or justified by the linking of sexual activity and hypocrisy in women. And there is a suggestion of both the scandalous and the pitiable in the waving nun. That the hint for the background image may be found in Petrarch's passing reference to 'Leander lost in the surges of the sea' does not, I think, begin to account for the meanings Weiditz liberates by his design. To explain that Hero was a priestess of Aphrodite is in no way to account for the teasing ambivalence of the secondary female figure, or for the way in which it appropriates centrality for itself, disrupting the placid foreground. But the image is not yet complete: to the right of this panel is a narrower one, in which male and female are again juxtaposed. In this composition, set indoors, in contrast, the figures are not separated but brought into close conjunction. They are bourgeois rather than regal, everyday rather than special, and in this also suggest a deliberate contrast of meaning with the group on the left. Man and woman are sitting embraced, the hands of each positioned in a manner that is mildly suggestive. The strongest clue to interpretation lies in the straw which the woman can be seen to hold. According to Stewart, who includes this woodcut in her study of images of *Unequal Lovers*, this implies 'distraction through flattery'.[45] The laurelled or helmeted head on the wall behind them is in austere contrast to their rather impugned intimacy. This woman, unlike the handsome if stern-faced queen on the left, looks lined and worn. Scheidig, in his edition, identifies this scene with Hannibal's succumbing to a harlot cited above.[46] I cannot, however, see any grounds in the image for construing it in this way. Read in conjunction with the first image, it seems rather to suggest that the viewer has been transported into the enclosed space from which the nun, not waving but drowning, gestured to the swimmer. Male and female are united in this space but they are also confined. There is no river, no growing thing – only the manipulating straw. The man in this image has still a good deal in common with the pope-emperor on the left – big, impressive headgear, a beard, shoes prominently displayed – though he is shown in a caricature of humiliation. The woman may be getting her own way, in the trivialized terms implied by the straw metaphor, but she is suffering. Above their heads, and perhaps by implication creating and endorsing these conditions, is the classical head, detached and severed from its body.

That the complex and contradictory meanings of these images reflect anxieties about the new attempt to channel, enforce, and delimit sexual activity within marriage, and doubts about the new ideology of marriage, even while they reproduce an older mistrust of women endorsed by the new learning, seems inescapable. At the same time they must be compared with the figure of the richly attired prostitute which Roper notes in contemporary engravings: Weiditz's images share a reliance on the unacceptability of the sight of the powerful woman flaunting her sexuality and the riches it has brought her.

By the time of the de Braij portrait in 1669 there were conditions in which it was possible for a woman to gain legitimate access to wealth because conjugal marriage had been institutionalized and its doctrines elaborated. Enclosed in the conjugal family, Cleopatra's appetites are licensed and transposed into duty. Dryden's treatment of her at the same period, in *All for Love* (1677), is defined by the same translation into domesticity which closes off all ambiguity and threat. If it were not for the power of Shakespeare's intensely conflicted representation of Cleopatra (1607), which precludes a unitary interpretation, it would seem that patriarchal discourse had succeeded in shutting her up.

Interestingly, although the image of Cleopatra at her banquet is not found much after the mid-eighteenth century, there is evidence that the image of her as a housewife defined and confined in terms of domesticity continued to be influential a hundred years later. In Chapter 19 of Charlotte Bronte's *Villette*, 'The Cleopatra', the tortured protagonist, Lucy Snowe, confronts an image of Cleopatra which she describes at considerable length and with the greatest bitterness.[47] She gazes into it as into a distorting mirror and hates what she sees: a figure whose abundance she can only characterize as gross. She describes her, insistently, in terms of household management and domestic confinement – the symbolic accessories are 'a perfect litter of flowers and rubbish'. The novel uses the image of Cleopatra as a means of identifying the way the institution of Christian marriage has constrained women and of the alienation experienced in consequence. At the same time she is an image of forbidden sexuality: Lucy Snowe is banned from regarding her, though she must tolerate the voyeuristic comments of the men she overhears admiring the picture. She takes some comfort from the fact that the man she idealizes, Dr Bretton, has no time for the Cleopatra; but what he prefers is his mother.

Chapter 3

Newton and Cleopatra

In the Palazzo Labia in Venice, in a room now used for conferences by the Italian radio and television company RAI that owns the building, stands a monument to the name of Cleopatra. Every surface, except the floor and a long wall of windows, has been decorated in an elaborate scheme. The ceiling is painted to represent a sky, statues are painted on to the walls. A salmon-pink *trompe-l'oeil* doubles and replicates architectural detail designed in genuine marble, cold to the touch. The chief images, however, are two frescoes of Antony and Cleopatra by Giambattista Tiepolo. Two complete walls are taken up with them. On the right, as you enter, is the *Banquet* and, on the left, a scene known as the *Incontro* or meeting. These frescoes also extend and complicate the actual space of the room and its verifiable surfaces by suggesting that the walls they are painted on are pierced and offer views into spaces beyond the room itself. The spectator looks through them into a kitchen or a piazza, a quayside or the sea.

This baroque concentration of painted fictions is not only a monument to Cleopatra. It stands as a silent memorial to Newton's experimental method, or, more accurately, to the wider cultural impact of that method. Such a claim rests on the understanding that the key term at issue both in the Labia frescoes and in Newton's work is the spectacle, something presented to be looked at. Newton's innovation, in constructing the experimental method which is now understood as his most significant contribution to the development of scientific thought, was the attempt to associate spectacle and the demonstration of truth. It brought the gaze under a new discipline.[1]

The impact of that move to redefine the gaze and its object prompted Tiepolo to a radical reworking of the image of Cleopatra's banquet. His fresco (Plate 3.1) is clearly indebted to an earlier painting of the theme by Trevisani (Plate 3.2). But, if the fresco quotes Trevisani, it is only to transform his work and put its assumptions to the test. In the fresco it is not the question of controlling Cleopatra but the fascination of looking at her that organizes the image. An immense cultural shift separates the two. Between the completion of Trevisani's *Banquet* early in the century and the painting of Tiepolo's fresco in 1746, Newton's work on optics had become known and generally accepted throughout Europe.

The figure of Cleopatra offered Tiepolo an image by means of which to register and work through some of the problems that Newtonian accounts of the spectacle posed for him as a painter. There was nothing arbitrary about his choice: the figure had already been publicly implicated in a discussion of Newton, looking, and women. The text in which this had occurred is an account of Newtonian optics by Francesco Algarotti, first published in Italy in 1737, *Newtonianismo per le dame* (Newtonianism for ladies).[2] As the title suggests, the work extends beyond a mere treatise on optics to imply a way of life, a cultural system permeated by the thought of the master. Algarotti was the first to coin the totalizing expression 'Newtonianism' and his work presents it as a force to transfigure social reality, not just to explain what is seen. As a result, Algarotti's text raises issues well beyond the scope of Newton's original *Opticks*. Some of these, like the question of the moral value of instrumentally enhanced vision, are part of a public debate already in process. Others, like his wish to square the work of the painter with the work of the demonstrator, arise from his own enthusiasm for art. His text is preoccupied, too, with the question of how women look both as subject and object of vision. It is with Algarotti's version of Newton, rather than with Newton's *Opticks* itself, that Tiepolo is in dialogue.

The first step is to clarify what this distinction means. I will start with an account of Newton's attempts to establish the authority of what he called his *experimentum crucis*. This was the primary spectacle advanced as the guarantee of his optical theory. It came to be taken as an emblem of the new science of the Enlightenment. It will be followed by a reading of Algarotti's text. The polemic of Algarotti's work functions rather differently from Newton's own. He is attempting to persuade Italy and in particular Venice to acknowledge the authority of Newton. It is this specific address that engages Tiepolo. But *Newtonianismo per le dame* is a text to trouble a Venetian painter. Algarotti makes regular use of a cross-reference between experimental demonstration and the work of painting which denies any significant difference between the two activities. In consequence the frame of meaning within which art is produced is tacitly brought under question. Put simply, if the point of the spectacle is to demonstrate truth, what legitimacy or scope is left for the painter's skill in creating pleasure? And what about his training in the use of perspective to create illusion? The middle section of my argument will trace how these issues became fused in Tiepolo's repeated attempts to represent Cleopatra and suggest how the decorated room in the Palazzo Labia may be read as Tiepolo's show-down with Newton.

Lastly, I shall consider what kind of figure has been produced in the

Plate 3.1 Tiepolo, *Cleopatra's Banquet*, Palazzo Labia.

Plate 3.2 Trevisani, *Cleopatra's Banquet*, Palazzo Spada.

Labia frescoes in the name of Cleopatra. The woman Tiepolo paints in the *Banquet* is represented as both queen and whore. She also occupies the authoritative place of the demonstrator at a public experiment. It is the attempt made by experimental philosophy to achieve transparency and to fix meaning that produces this enigmatic image.

It was Newton's experimental method and the truth-claims he made for it that historians of science now identify as his most crucial contribution to the development of Western thought. Although it caused his work to be extremely controversial in his lifetime, delaying the publication of his *Opticks* until 1704, by the time of his death in 1727 or soon after his theories were generally widely accepted. So was his method and not only for private work in the laboratory. Public shows and lecture demonstrations where his most famous experiments were restaged increased after his death: great care, too, was taken to provide exactly appropriate commentaries, drawn from the work of Desaguliers, the Royal Society demonstrator who had put on Newton's experiments for the Society, and from Newton's own texts. The scrupulous alignment of word and image in their exact reciprocity was maintained, the meaning of the spectacle preserved intact. It is in such shows – the theatre where self-identical presence itself was staged – that the Enlightenment assumption of the perfection of fit between concept and representation can be seen installed as social practice.[3]

Although Newton is now associated with the general principle of demonstration, in the eighteenth century he was identified throughout Europe with a single famous experiment. This was the one he himself called the *experimentum crucis*, the crucial experiment. It involved passing a beam of light through glass prisms. An engraving of this experiment was used to head the French edition of the *Opticks*, the *Traité d'Optique*, published in Paris in 1722. It was probably the most handsome edition of the *Opticks* ever produced, with folding plates and decorated initial letters. When work on it was nearing completion, Newton was told that on its first sheet a blank space had been left above the half-title, where a vignette would be engraved. He was asked to 'think of an idea' appropriate to his book and responded by sending a sketch of the prism experiment. This was redrawn for publication. Interestingly, the sketch and the later engraving included the words 'nec variat lux fracta colorem', 'refracted light does not change its colour'. The emblem was dependent on linguistic formulation for transparency. The publication of this book was decisive in securing widespread acceptance of Newton's experiments and theory of colour in France. So famous did the experiment become that it was used as a symbol to represent Newton himself. In a painting of the 1740s by Pittoni, commissioned in Venice as part of a series celebrating British achievements, Newton is modelled not in his own person but by this '*experimentum crucis*' where light is passed through prisms.[4]

The experiment with the prisms achieved emblematic status and thus appeared to be imbued with a specific and recognizable meaning, though the two examples of its use just cited, in the French edition of the *Opticks* and in the Pittoni oil, show that meaning was in fact open to variation. It became so well known because Newton himself had earlier chosen to make it the test-case of his work in optics. A variety of options were open to seventeenth-century experimental philosophers when trying to make authority for their work. The virtues of relying on a long series of trials or on a single decisive experiment, direct witness or reading detailed reports were debated among the experimental community. Newton chose to base his claim to authority on the evidence of a single decisive experiment reported in circumstantial detail and replicated for public assent. This was the prism experiment.

But, as Simon Schaffer has shown, right up till the 1720s, the decade of Newton's death, questions concerning both the practical detail of the experiment and the exact interpretation that was to be put on whatever was supposed to transpire during it remained obscure or confused.

Although the *experimentum crucis* was a focus of controversy over many years, Newton was vague or contradictory on the topic of experimental protocols, instrumentation, and even the meanings that were attached to the experiment. It was a slow and erratic process agreeing on what the visible evidence should be, how it would be produced, and how it should be interpreted.

The matter of instrumentation was specially fraught. The prism, on which so much of Newton's theory of light and colours depended, had no previous significant history in experimental use before the middle of the seventeenth century. Newton had obtained his first prisms in all likelihood at the Midsummer Fair in Cambridge. They were relatively cheap: in 1668 he paid three shillings for three. They probably came from Venice, the leading source of glassware. Later, when Newton had refined his experimental requirements, English prisms were specified. This move did not reduce the element of international rivalry between experimenters.

There was no standardized form of prism available and Newton came to define as an adequate prism one which produced the effects predicted before the experiment took place. Arriving at an agreed form and interpretation for the experiment itself was a matter of reciprocal internal adjustment of the components at issue. In Schaffer's summary,

> the status of the *experimentum crucis* was hard to fix. There was no agreed criterion for a competent prism experiment or for a good prism. Only when the status of the experiment was fixed did this criterion become available. Replicability and meaning both hinged on the establishment of this emblem. Some of Newton's audience read the experiment as a claim about colour immutability. Newton sometimes provided them with grounds for this reading. By the 1720s, in fact, he seemed to have come to agree with this reading. That is, the experiment which Newton now counted as his decisive one had a new and fixed meaning: 'refracted light does not change its colour'.

Even when this stability of reference had been achieved, a reminder of the ambiguity of vision was cemented into the experimental process. The emblem of this newly won identity between meaning and spectacle was the 'good' prism: the redeemed toy, previously used for entertainment and associated with a playful kind of deceit. Kenelm Digby writing in 1644 reported that they were known as 'Fool's Paradises'. On such unstable bases rested the precarious equivalence between signifier and signified claimed by the new science.[5]

Francesco Algarotti wrote *Newtonianismo per le dame* to celebrate the triumph of demonstration. He had been a student at the University of Bologna where the staunchest Italian Newtonians, Eustachio Manfredi and Francesco Bianchini, were based, and in 1728, as a young student, had been involved in attempts to replicate Newton's experiments. He kept up the intellectual contacts he made at this time for the rest of his life. But he was writing in the context of hostilities and accusations of intrigue between experimental philosophers of different nationalities.

Enthusiasm for Newton was not universal in Italy. His appropriation of the prism and advocacy of English glassware could be felt as a specific challenge to Venice, the premier European source of quality glass. Between 1719 and 1741 the Venetian natural philosopher, Giovanni Rizzetti, was active in challenging both Newton's reports and his doctrine.[6] Writing *Newtonianismo* was not a politically neutral act and its tone is often disconcertingly polemical. The work could not be published in Venice and reviews were not wholly favourable. Nevertheless, on the European scale, it was unequivocally successful, being translated into German, French, and English within five years.

It was a very different kind of book from Newton's own. Instead of being addressed to the community of experimental philosophers it was written 'for the ladies'. It would not necessarily be appropriate to read this as a sign that its explanations were aimed at readers with less intelligence or a more restricted education. The University of Bologna, where Algarotti had been instructed in Newtonian theory, had two women professors. (It was the only university in the world that did.[7]) It was a woman of 22, Elizabeth Carter, who undertook the translation of *Newtonianismo* into English. In the early eighteenth century a number of aristocratic women were prominent as both patrons and students of philosophy. Among the women taken seriously as students of philosophy by Leibniz, Newton's great scientific contemporary, were the British Lady Anne Finch, Viscountess Conway; Sophie, the Electress of Hanover; her daughter Sophia Charlotte, queen of Prussia after 1701; and the latter's ward, Princess Caroline, later queen of Great Britain. It was in answer to her questions that the entire Leibniz–Clarke correspondence of 1716 was directed.[8]

A principal expounder of Leibniz's system was Madame Emelie du Châtelet: to her Voltaire dedicated his version of Newton, published a year later than Algarotti's. And with her Algarotti himself conferred about his own *Newtonianismo*, though he disappointed her by failing to acknowledge her help in his dedication.[9] Perhaps in the figure of this woman, where intellectual distinction and, for Algarotti, an unavowed relation of dependence and social inferiority coincide, can be glimpsed something of the complex associations that might be in play around the figure of the learned lady in *Newtonianismo*.

Instead of Madame du Châtelet, Algarotti dedicated his book to Bernard de Fontenelle. In 1686 de Fontenelle had published *Entretiens sur la pluralité des mondes*, a series of six dialogues between an instructor and a lady of quality, in which the moral and philosophical implications of knowledge about the natural world are explored. It met with great success and has continued to be read up to the present day. The six-dialogue form became a classic of scientific exposition: imitations of it were produced even before Algarotti adopted it as a model and they continued long afterwards.[10] By choosing it and by dedicating his book to Fontenelle, Algarotti inserted himself into a dynastic sequence of authority.

The dialogue form had a powerfully determining effect. Algarotti's *Newtonianismo* reinstates Newton's thought in the dense and hetero-geneous social world from which the discourse of the *Opticks* had attempted to secede. This critical shift is to be traced to the personalized form of address. In *Newtonianismo* instruction on the theory of light and colours is offered couched in the form of a series of dialogues between the author and a lady of quality, the 'marchese'. Algarotti engages with the form so whole-heartedly, taking on the full implications of the mode of address, that optical theory is transformed by inserting it into the field of social relations and of gender relations in particular.

In *Newtonianismo* the austerity of Newton's *Opticks* gives way to quite a different tone. The axioms, precepts, laws, and propositions that structure Newton's argument, with the formal account of experimental method and conclusions, are displaced. Lines and mathematical figures are expressly excluded. What is substituted for this abstraction is pleasure: appeals to the experience of looking at painting are used in the place of diagrams. Pleasure, the question of how men look at women, and the problem of interpretation of visual evidence deriving from his original are inextricably bound up with each other in Algarotti's text.

This makes it an extremely complex piece of writing. The focus is unstable: should the text speak of love or of light and colours? The dialogue form produces a social interaction which reads as drama. The crises and resolutions of this drama are all played out in terms of the relation between the marchese and her instructor. These are unequivocally defined in terms not of the library but of the salon. Flirtation and gallantry are offered by the instructor, with a liberality which threatens to bring his whole project into disrepute. When the lady asks to see some experiment which cannot possibly be explained by any other system but the Newtonian, the instructor answers, 'This . . . is the very thing necessary to prove not only the different Refrangibility but every other Principle in Philosophy; and this Sir *Isaac Newton* has done (without knowing, perhaps, that it would one Day give Pleasure to a fine Lady).'[11] The reincorporation of the woman of rank as a social presence disturbs the terms of discussion to the point of overturning them. Newton's intellec-tual achievement is rewritten as personal compliment. If the instructor speaks of colours he is led into the same impasse, by way of a flattering reference to 'that lively Bloom on your Complexion'. It is the lady herself who objects:

I should not have thought, answered she, that the colouring of my Cheeks would ever have entered into the *Cartesian* system. It enters, answered I, into other Systems more generally understood, and of somewhat more importance than those of Philosophy. But even these must receive great Honour from the Explication of so beautiful a Phaenomenon.[12]

In spite of compliments like this, which foreground the marchese's body, it is not in fact an erotic submission which is sought but an intellectual victory. The marchese is to yield her intelligence rather than her beauty to the instructor's arguments. But her very presence within the text threatens to disperse the discursive field which grounds the discussion of philosophy.

It is the pleasure of looking at the body of the marchese that unsettles the Newtonian project. Newton's account of looking had no place for pleasure. Algarotti reinstalls pleasure in dramatizing relations between the sexes. The argument comes round repeatedly to a consideration of the marchese's own beauty and the charm of women in general. In his introduction Algarotti had characterized women as 'that Sex which had rather *perceive* than *understand*': they did not use their minds to explore what their eyes took in.[13] The instructor's strategy confirms a belief that, for a woman, being looked *at* must always constitute the primary experience of seeing.

The importance for women of being looked at is persistently dramatized by the movement of the dialogues, in which both the argument and the gaze are repeatedly drawn back to the person of the marchese herself. Whether it is a question of her volunteering that lying in the bath she had observed the way her body then seemed 'deformed and crooked' – an opportunity to explain the refraction of light in water – or of her instructor's teasing her about the time women spend making up, the female body is never out of sight for long. Although ostensibly a discourse on the theory of optics, Algarotti's text, both in its structure and in its argument, recognizes the female body as the privileged object of vision and, more importantly, of visual pleasure.

Algarotti's text has a divided commitment, which it labours to reconcile. Determined to argue the case for demonstration as the staging of visible truth, it is also involved in the validation of visual pleasure, which it calls Beauty. Towards the close of the final dialogue it declares that the 'pleasing Attractions of Beauty . . . are preferable to any Speculation whatsoever'. It is a potentially disabling conflict because the role of deception in pleasure was philosophically well established. An acknowledgement of the deceptive nature of appearances is used to negotiate this difficulty. According to Newtonian theory, vision can only give a coded intimation of the laws of the universe. And so, for Algarotti, explaining

Newton's theories to the marchese involves disillusioning her of the com-
mon-sense view. She must learn that the laws of Nature that underlie
appearances are much more complex than she might have imagined. She
must accept that, in that sense, the evidence of appearances is *not* to be
trusted.

This process of disillusion is dramatized throughout the first dialogue:
it culminates in the marchese's explicit concession that 'if what you say
be true, Things appear to us very different from what they really are'.[14]
This points towards the recognition that embracing Newtonianism means
admitting that unaided vision cannot interpret what it sees correctly. It
later becomes possible, in the fourth dialogue, to suggest that the initial
pleasurable illusion does not have to be surrendered but can be held in
parallel with a more instructed understanding of what is seen. 'Let me
entreat you, said the Marchioness, to make me a compleat *Newtonian*. I
plainly see that by my Conversion I shall acquire the Knowledge of Truth
without losing that Pleasure which I found in being deceived.'[15]

These attempts to confront and resolve the rival claims of truth and
pleasure cannot dispose of the problem of what happens when the gaze
is turned on the female body. Where is its truth to be found? *Newtonianismo per le dame* produces the marchese's body as the site where scientific
or truth-seeking, looking and the look of pleasure, meet. It is a moment
of crisis. Under the microscope, the beauty previously perceived in the
marchese's skin not only vanishes but is revealed as mere illusion. The
eye was deceived, or more accurately was shown to be incapable of
registering the true nature of what lay before it. And pleasure evaporates.
The text confronts and negotiates this crisis by side-stepping the issue
and transposing it into a matter of ethics or aesthetics.

> It would be very bad for us, if our Touch was exquisite enough to feel
> all that the Microscope discovers to our Sight. We should certainly be
> extremely unhappy, answer'd I, if our Sensations were so perfect, that
> in handling the smoothest Surface our Touch should fail us at every
> Pore, and every little Eminence should make us shudder. It is to the
> Silence of our Reason and the want of more refined Senses, that we
> owe our Perceptions of Pleasure. And he gave a very just Definition
> of our Happiness, who affirm'd that the most tranquil Possession of
> Pleasure consists in our being agreeably deceiv'd.[16]

Deception is redefined as a necessary component of a pleasure that is
firmly located in the body of the woman.

It is at this unarguably critical moment in Algarotti's text that the figure
of Cleopatra is brought into play. In one sense, she is merely part of the
classicizing frame used to give authority to the argument. But it is by
means of that authority that the woman reader and by extension the
woman in the text are characterized in their relation to male sexuality.

For example, the fact that the book is ostensibly written for women is underlined by the fact that it is prefaced by an epigraph from Virgil's tenth eclogue, 'quae legat ipsa Lycoris': 'Lycoris [i.e. the recipient's mistress] can read this too.' Lycoris was a Roman courtesan, the mistress of Gallus, first Roman governor of Egypt, to whom the poem is addressed. The reference eroticizes the female reader in the moment of calling her into being, granting her literary and cultural interests at the price of defining her in terms of male desire. The part that the name of Cleopatra is called on to play in Algarotti's argument confirms this contract, which demands that the woman's sexuality must be kept firmly in view.

When the marchese, filled with anxiety by the power of the microscope to take away her beauty, is consoled by her instructor, he reassures her in the following terms: 'Not all the Microscopes nor all the Philosophy in the World, answered I, could ever hinder your appearing agreeable to the naked Eye, and even a *Cleopatra* might be contented with this.'[17] The sight of a beautiful woman is identified as the acid test, as it were, of a Newtonian/mechanically assisted looking that seeks to penetrate behind appearances. Her body, or the ways of looking that preserve her as a site of visual pleasure, offers a resistance to the hegemony of Newtonian optics. Algarotti constructs out of this resistance something resembling an equation. On one side of it lies the extreme testing of the body, subjected to scrutiny by all the microscopes in the world and yet remaining agreeable to the naked eye. On the other stands the name of Cleopatra, used to measure the triumph of the look of pleasure. The balance of the equation, like the equivalence claimed between signifier and signified in Newtonian methodology, is fugitive and unstable. The question of what is the truth about woman, here temporarily sutured, threatens to split open again under pressure.

The struggle in *Newtonianismo* to establish an acceptable equilibrium between looking, pleasure, and understanding was also carried out in terms of an underlying argument about painting. At 25, when he published *Newtonianismo*, Algarotti was already in command of a highly developed visual taste. He was to become one of the leading art patrons in eighteenth-century Venice from the 1740s, acting under the commission of Augustus of Saxony on behalf of the Royal Gallery at Dresden and on his own account.[18] His enthusiasm for art qualified Algarotti's response to Newton's method. His account is marked by a tacit anxiety that the new demonstration might be impossible to reconcile with the older spectacle of art. Algarotti's repeated attempts to hold painting and demonstration in unproblematic alignment betray that Newtonian accounts of the spectacle were an implicit challenge to painting and its traditions.

It is a clash that has not received much critical attention in histories of the impact of Newton's theory, though it has been observed that throughout the eighteenth century painters struggled to appropriate Newtonian optical theory for themselves, encountering repeated failure in the process. Martin Kemp in *The Science of Art* denies that any conflict of interests was to be perceived. He claims that the conservative insistence on academic fundamentals such as perspective proved 'surprisingly compatible with ideas from the new sciences in the particular form in which they were absorbed into the mainstream of Italian thought'.[19] This is not the case. Here in *Newtonianismo* some recognition of fundamental issues at stake in this encounter between artists and experimental science can be found.

In the first instance it is the energetic denial of any difference between Newtonian or experimental looking and the look that is addressed to a painting that is striking. This reveals itself in a repeated attempt to map the one on to the other. *Newtonianismo* is a book about optics which is illustrated not with diagrams but by verbal appeals to the evidence of painting. This occurs in order to retrieve the place of pleasure in the gaze: experimental looking has no room for it.

Writing of the colours obtained when white light is split, one of the two central arguments of Newton's *Opticks* and the one with which his name was then and is now most closely associated, Algarotti specifically sets out to link them with the achievements of the painter's art. 'Neither *Corregio*, *Titian* nor his Rival *Rosalba* did ever unite and shade their Mezzo Tinto's with so much Exactness to form the Oval of a Face.'[20] Newton's original experiment produced the colours in the form of an ellipse: in Algarotti's comparison, that shape is the product not of an experiment but of the painter's skill. The movement which maps experimental evidence on to visual artefacts is repeated many times.

Looking at a fresco is used to test the theory that strings of small bodies arise from a coloured source to strike the eye and make that colour visible:

> Let us fix upon one Point in the Air to which your Eye and mine may be equally directed while we are both looking at the same Time upon different Parts and different Colours of this Wall. Do you, for instance, place yourself at this Pilaster and look upon the red on the vesture of Achilles. I will stand at the Window, and look upon the blue of the Sea. . .[21]

In a particularly striking development of this gesture, *Newtonianismo* attempts to assert a complete identification between the work of the demonstrator and of the painter. Variations on an experiment are compared to variations on a painter's theme: any difference between the truth-status of the activities is implicitly suppressed.

> This Experiment varied in as many Ways as the fruitful Imagination of a *Paul Veronese* would vary the Subject of a Picture, always succeeded

so well, as to have greatly confirmed this System, if its Author had suffered it to need any Confirmation.[22]

The move appears to deny or erase the difference between the kind of purity and trustworthiness claimed for one kind of vision – the one sustained and accounted for by Newtonian theory – and painting's long commitment to making the eye see what is not there.

It may be more helpful, however, to see the attempt to assert the truthfulness of painting in terms of Norman Bryson's account of an earlier crisis in figuration. When the discipline of perspective came into general use in Italian painting, Bryson claims, the effect was that paintings could thenceforward be understood as windows on to sacred spaces and transcendental truths. Perspective was at once the means by which the visual space was organized and by which the sacred truths revealed in it were guaranteed. Later, where the Reformation took hold, this access to the truth in visible form was blocked by the assertion that transcendental truth did not belong to the realm of the visible but must be decoded from it by means of scripture. From that point on figuration was chastened and subordinated to figures of speech.[23] Perspective, a visual technique, could no longer function to guarantee transcendental truths: words became necessary. Transparency was lost and the image depended for its legibility on a textual source. In eighteenth-century Italy, although this consequence of the Reformation had been avoided earlier, a similar stand-off between the image on its own and the image authorized and authenticated by a text was under way. Algarotti's constant appeals to painting in the very act of promoting Newtonian looking present that struggle.

It is a struggle of special moment to the painters of Venice. If Algarotti's text was ostensibly addressed to women, it also hailed its readers as Venetians. Algarotti was a Venetian by birth, though as an adult he had travelled and made contacts all over Europe. The painters whose work he quotes most often, Titian and Veronese, belong to the Venetian tradition of the sixteenth century: in fact painting in *Newtonianismo* is all but synonymous with the Venetian tradition. And both the marchese and her instructor are presented as natives of Venice, for the text speaks of 'our fine city founded by the gods upon the ocean', a reference to one of the complex of founding myths by which the state of Venice asserted its right to political authority. The subtext of *Newtonianismo* poses the problem for Venetian painters of continuing to work within the powerful and highly specific visual tradition of their inheritance under the pressure of a new way of calling the look to account.

In the Venetian tradition of Titian, Veronese, and Tintoretto, illusionist skills, particularly the use of perspective, were the very foundation of the painter's art. Looking at Venetian pictures involved spectators in learning to see what was *not there*: and to read from the perspective code a multiplicity of depths and forms out of a single plane surface. The painter depended on the trained but independent reading skill of the viewer to produce the space of the picture. But, if illusionist art, which of course was practised not only in Venice but across Europe, demands collusive looking, it also grants relative autonomy to the eye: it is subject primarily to visual codes and it creates its own pleasure. Words, though they may constitute the painting's title and indicate its subject, are not required to govern and legislate for every aspect of the image that the eye must read. Newtonianism threatened to revoke this independence, to yoke the act of vision with the perception of univocal truth, and to make it subject to linguistic formulation.

According to Newton, what the eye saw, in certain formalized circumstances, could properly be identified with truth. That is to say, his experimental method was grounded in the possibility of demonstrating truth, of obliging it to appear in the form of a spectacle to be taken in by the eye. Not by an unaided eye, however. Only the instructed viewer, who understood the spectacle in its relation to a particular set of concepts and mathematical formulations, could perceive in it the demonstration of a law of nature. Truth, in the Newtonian experiment, was mathematically and linguistically formulated and that precise formulation used to regulate the act of visual perception. The Newtonian eye must operate in subjection to codes that were beyond the remit of the visual. The experimental method Newton pioneered in the *Opticks*, and more importantly the truth-claims he made for it, signalled a denial of that ambiguity and independence of vision on which illusionist practice was based. At the time of Newton's death, when Algarotti was fifteen and Tiepolo was in his thirties, the Newtonian method had won recognition throughout Europe, though its authority was never uncontested: a whole new ideology of the eye as guarantee of a univocal truth had been broached. It stood in broad contradiction to the older acceptance of the ambiguity of vision and to the function of that ambiguity in producing visual pleasure through the eye's work of interpretation.

In the opening chapter of *Painting in Cinquecento Venice*, David Rosand identifies two distinct principles of construction that inform work in Venice in the sixteenth century, when the paintings that were to be most influential on later artists were produced.[24] One is the general Renaissance commitment to perspective, from which followed clarity and commensurability, that is, legibility in the treatment of space. The other is the specific local value set on a particular use of colour to create pictorial structure. This, he argues, has a tendency towards the allusive and the implicit. Both, however, insist on subjective participation. In a Newtonian demonstration, meaning is invariable, subject to prior linguistic formulation and coded within the spectacle: it is the property of the object. The eye is merely the passive register of a truth designated by words. In the paintings of the illusionist tradition, on the other hand, meaning is the property of the eye and like the eye is by no means fixed. Reiterated pleasurable acts of interpretation are required. Even the legibilities of perspective are called into play to alert the spectator to the undecidability of vision: at its most obvious, the picture plane is both a real surface marked with lines and colours and a window through which we look on to a fictive world; the picture-frame is the index of an illusion and at the same time a material object in a real world. In this tradition, viewers are called on to recognize and collaborate in their own deception. The tradition's practices and its sophisticated understanding of visual pleasure do not sit easily with any notion of vision as direct access to a truth regulated by linguistic formulation.

This, I am arguing, indicates the predicament of Tiepolo, born in Venice in 1696 and employed there with increasing distinction, being first set down in the Fraglia, the list of Venetian painters, in 1717. There was a sense in which he was the ideal reader of Algarotti's work and there is no reason to suppose it was unknown to him. Everyone else was reading it. *Newtonianismo* in its own way made formal recognition of the new pressure on the act of looking and it gave a name, Cleopatra, to the difficulty of interpreting what you saw when you looked at a woman. When Tiepolo repeatedly reworked the Cleopatra theme in the years after 1743 it was the status of truth and illusion in his art that was being renegotiated.

In 1743 Algarotti and Tiepolo came into direct contact when the former had returned to Venice with a commission to collect pictures for Augustus III, King of Poland and Elector of Saxony. A friendship appears to have developed and a letter of Tiepolo's laments his incarceration at the Villa Cordellina where he was finishing some frescoes, when he would so much have preferred to spend the day with Algarotti talking about painting. Algarotti's letters and account-books for the period are in fact among the prime sources of information concerning Tiepolo's work at that time. It is Algarotti who provides the first mention of Tiepolo's involvement with the theme of Cleopatra, in the January following Algarotti's arrival in Venice in May 1743. The period of his stay in Venice 1743–4, was roughly coterminous with Tiepolo's early work on the Cleopatra theme, before the final exposition in the Palazzo Labia.

It will be useful at this point to give a brief account of the surviving images of Cleopatra made by Tiepolo before his work on the Labia frescoes. The picture Algarotti saw, and ordered for Augustus III, was a *Banquet*, and it is now in Melbourne (Plate 3.3). It had in fact been preceded by a smaller version known to have been in existence in 1743, when it was engraved, with the pearl suppressed, under the title of *Nabal's Feast*. This earlier version, which broadly corresponds with the Melbourne *Banquet*, is now in the Musée Cognacq-Jay, Paris (Plate 3.4). Three times

Tiepolo worked on a pair of Cleopatra scenes: there are three more versions of the *Banquet*, all of them with pendants showing a meeting between Antony and Cleopatra. There is an oil sketch of the *Banquet* in the National Gallery, London (Plate 3.5); in a private collection, New York, there is a *Meeting of Antony and Cleopatra* that Levey identifies as its pendant (Plate 3.6). The composition of both these is horizontal. Another pair, where the *Banquet* is now in Stockholm (Plate 3.7) and the *Meeting* in the National Gallery of Scotland (Plate 3.8), are vertical (like the frescoes). On stylistic grounds Levey suggests that these all belong to the period 1743–4. There are in addition various preparatory works that are associated with the frescoes: a pen-and-wash drawing for the *Meeting* in the Metropolitan Museum, New York, drawings and pen-and-ink studies in the Victoria and Albert Museum and in the National Museum, Stockholm, and a quantity of chalk drawings on blue paper in the Meyer–Ilschen Collection, Stuttgart. The frescoes were not under way until 1746–7 and were completed by 1752.[25] If the need to prepare for them might account for Tiepolo's initial interest in the Cleopatra theme, it does not explain the unprecedented quantity of highly finished material he produced or the extent of the reworking this accomplished painter, renowned for his speed and facility, found appropriate.

There were no contemporary precedents for treating the theme of Cleopatra's banquet in Venice itself, though it was one that had recurred in Western painting: the banquet and the death were by far the most common topoi in treating Cleopatra. Pigler records over forty banquets and more than a hundred and twenty death scenes between the sixteenth and eighteenth centuries.[26] In the preceding century eroticized accounts of Cleopatra's suicide had been produced in Venice for the collections in German courts. There was one sixteenth-century fresco *Banquet of Cleopatra* in the Veneto, where the whole ground-floor *sala* of a villa had been frescoed with scenes from ancient history by Fasolo and Zelotti. There were a number of seventeenth-century Italian versions of the banquet, the best known of which were probably a version by Giacinto Gimignani that was engraved and an emblem from Maccio's collection, circulated in book form.[27] For Tiepolo in the 1740s, however, the immediate models were a *Banquet of Cleopatra* by Francisco Trevisani, now in the Palazzo Spada at Rome (Plate 3.2), and the resources of the Venetian tradition.

Great feasts, usually with a religious pretext, like Veronese's *Feast in the House of Levi*, his *Marriage Feast at Cana*, or the *Last Supper* itself, were a common theme in Venetian painting of the sixteenth century. In spite of this sacred origin, the feast did not necessarily have a particularly devotional aspect: a *Last Supper* by Veronese was so thoroughly secular that it had to be renamed as *The Feast in the House of Levi*. In the Venetian tradition the feast offered an occasion for the management of ambitious architectural and perspective schemes and for showing large numbers of

Plate 3.3 Tiepolo, *Cleopatra's Banquet*, National Gallery of Victoria, Melbourne.

Plate 3.4 Tiepolo, *Cleopatra's Banquet*, Musée Cognacq-Jay, Paris.

Plate 3.5 Tiepolo, *Cleopatra's Banquet*, National Gallery, London.

Plate 3.6 Tiepolo, *The Meeting of Antony and Cleopatra*, New York, private collection.

Plate 3.7 Tiepolo, *Cleopatra's Banquet*, Stockholm University Art Collection.

Plate 3.8 Tiepolo, *The Meeting of Antony and Cleopatra*. National Gallery of Scotland, Edinburgh.

diverse participants variously engaged – servants, pages, dwarfs, guests, including women and splendidly dressed 'orientals', monkeys, dogs, and even horses. These are the elements that go to form Tiepolo's *Banquet of Cleopatra*.

Tiepolo's art was closely identified both by the painter himself and by others with the tradition of sixteenth-century painting, particularly with the work of Veronese. It was as the most Veronese-like of his contemporaries that Algarotti wrote of him. Tiepolo himself declared this alignment most clearly in his fresco for the Villa Cordellina, *The Family of Darius before Alexander*. Veronese's canvas of the same name was one of the most famous paintings in eighteenth-century Venice. Tiepolo's fresco version quotes it very extensively, to the point of suggesting a public gesture of identification. It was while he was working at the Villa Cordellina that the painter wrote of how he would have liked to spend the day with Algarotti, talking about painting.

Trevisani's *Banquet* (Plate 3.2), the immediate iconographic precursor of Tiepolo's, also had its base in the Venetian tradition. Although Francesco Trevisani is known as a Roman painter, who worked in the city from the age of 22 in 1678 until his death in 1746, he had come there from Venice, where he had been trained from the age of 10 or 15. Dated provisionally between 1705 and 1710, Trevisani's painting was made for the Cardinal Fabrizio Spada-Veralli, to accompany three other pictures of famous women from antiquity, Guercino's *Death of Dido*, Campana's copy of Reni's *Rape of Helen*, and Daniel Seiter's *Lucretia*.[28] To the feast motifs of the Venetian tradition it marries the uncompromising morality of Maccio's emblem, where Cleopatra's action is presented as a type of the folly that comes with wealth.

Antony, in a dramatic gesture of arrest, reaches out to intervene before Cleopatra can let fall the pearl she holds over her goblet. At the same time the presence of a range of other observers and participants, including some bearing choice provisions, complicates the scene and its meanings. These figures include a second male seated at the table with Antony and Cleopatra, a number of servants crowded up behind the tableau, and in the foreground a dwarf, pulling at a spotted puppy. This dwarf has his back turned to Cleopatra and looks instead at Antony, in a grouping that suggests his effort to control the dog is being compared to Antony's attempt to control Cleopatra. The lead he pulls on is paralleled by the broken line of the human arms, where Cleopatra's arm bends away from Antony's, above his head. The foregrounded presence of the dwarf and his dog links Trevisani's *Banquet* with Tiepolo's designs but in Tiepolo's versions the references to control have been erased, Antony is less prominent, and Cleopatra herself is the focus of attention. A common emphasis on witness separates these two versions from the Fasolo and Zelotti fresco mentioned above. In the earlier version there are only four observers apart from the two main actors in what is essentially a private scene; in the eighteenth-century versions Cleopatra's act has become a spectacle for a gaze that is public, if not, in Trevisani, unequivocally focused on herself. It is Tiepolo who makes an absolute cynosure out of Cleopatra.

In Tiepolo's version of *Cleopatra's Banquet* both Trevisani's design, with its dog and dwarf, and the public feasts of Venetian tradition, in their spectacular architectural framing and multiplicity of presence, are quoted and recalled. Both, however, are given a new value, in the intense concentration of specularity that Tiepolo creates. This is in the first place a matter of framing the looks of the spectators portrayed within the banquet scene itself so that they focus on Cleopatra, but it is also a question of directing the non-illusionist spectator, outside the painting, to perform a set of repeated recognitions of the problematic nature of vision and of the status of illusion in the painter's art.

I shall deal with the centring of Cleopatra first, by considering the evidence of Tiepolo's various treatments of the scene. First, the diminution of Antony. In the earliest, Paris version (Plate 3.4) Antony is a surprisingly reticent presence, unlike the authoritative helmeted figure whose reach extended more than half-way across Trevisani's canvas (Plate 3.2). It was this reticence which made it possible to issue the engraving of this picture under the title of *Nabal's Feast.*[29] Antony, in his helmet, drops easily out of the dynamic of the composition. The striking male presence at the table with Cleopatra is a patriarchal bearded figure, not a Roman one, who sits facing the viewer, though slightly turned away, towards Cleopatra. Trevisani also shows a second male seated at the table, presumably the Plautus mentioned by Pliny, but in his canvas the effect of this figure is muted. Attention is on the gestures, the outstretched and bent arms of Antony and Cleopatra. In Tiepolo that balance has been reversed, partly as a consequence of putting Antony firmly on the near side of the table. With his back to the viewer, only his profile visible, while his heavy plumed helmet leaves only the lower part of his face exposed, Antony no longer competes with Cleopatra for attention. And, if Plautus has taken up a prominent place in the composition, it is to emphasize his spectatorship.

The Melbourne canvas (Plate 3.3), which is extremely close to this version in most details, nevertheless takes an important further step in emphasizing the role of the spectator both inside and outside the picture and with it the status of Cleopatra as the paramount spectacle. It is done by an adjustment of the architectural forms displayed in the background. In the Paris version (Plate 3.4), a balcony with some figures can be seen through the arch on the right and continues briefly in the space of the main arch. This has been extended and brought forward in the Melbourne canvas (Plate 3.3) to make a strong horizontal line across the picture, challenging the verticals of the pillars: with this bold assertion the company of onlookers who stand on the balcony are brought into structural significance. It has two effects: first the introduction of disengaged spectators at a remove assimilates the action to the Venetian tradition of scenes of miracle and witness and of notable human action, like Veronese's *Family of Darius before Alexander*, which it closely follows in its use of the balcony. At the same time, a firm dissociation between foreground and background, supported also by the use of colour, is established. The perspective control of the picture space becomes more assertive – and poses itself as problematic: Martin Kemp has remarked on the exaggerated perspective of the floor tiles in this second treatment. In comparison with its predecessor the number of horizontal intervals has been doubled and the viewer is no longer dealing with square tiles of clearly determined plan. If the tiles are square, Antony's chair and drapery would span an improbable distance.[30]

In both the London (Plate 3.5) and Stockholm (Plate 3.7) canvasses the parade of perspectival illusionism and the creation of a spectator presence within the picture continue to be worked over. The London composition pushes the table and the protagonists back into the middle ground, where they are positioned at the head of a broad flight of steps that leads down to the spectator but stops short of the edge of the canvas. On and around these stairs stand spectators, among them a dwarf and a lap-dog he is coaxing, while others stand to the side of the table and even behind it and a solitary turbaned figure gestures from a balconied roof-top. In a plane behind this stands the strong horizontal of the arched wall established in the previous picture, but in this case it is unpeopled. There is no Plautus figure here and Cleopatra maintains the assertive pose assigned to her in the Melbourne canvas (Plate 3.3), with arm outstretched. In spite of this, her position, set back in the picture space, muffles her impact.

A fourth canvas, now in Stockholm (Plate 3.7), resolves these issues in a manner close to the solutions of the final Labia fresco, though it has a number of marks of unease. Like the fresco, it is a vertical oblong. Perspective illusion is on parade: it creates a sequence of receding planes, from the foreground steps, through the banquet table, the four massive pillars of a loggia, and the broken pediment of a distant wall, finally to an impossible object which the eye reads as 'obelisk'. The perspective, which implies that the 'obelisk' stands at quite a considerable distance, also indicates that to take up the space it does in the image it must be much taller than any known obelisk. More critically, it must be differently proportioned, very much broader at the base in proportion to the tip, and so must resemble a tall thin pyramid. The viewer's habitual skill in reading perspective is thrown into disarray. Spectatorship within the image is divided between a row of observers on the balcony above the loggia and less than half a dozen others disposed close about the table.

The balcony viewers, like the obelisk, disrupt confidence in perspectival accomplishment as a shared language between painter and viewer, for they are impossibly small and remote in relation to the central scene. As the contradiction between viewing as reliable witness and viewing as illusion is screwed tight, absurdity threatens.

Here Plautus, the prime witness, is restored and the final placement of the three figures confirms his importance in that role. Antony now sits behind the table for the first time; this allows Plautus to be moved round, to sit with his back to the viewer, in the position formerly taken up by Antony. Its most important effect is to make Plautus, positioned across the table from the protagonists, constitute with the dwarf on the steps, who stands closer to the viewers outside the picture-space and mimes them, the exemplar of a disengaged scrutiny. Like Antony he looks at Cleopatra, but from an angle that those on the other side of the table – that is, everyone but the black servant on the right – cannot share. He shares with the dwarf a different view of Cleopatra and one that is more complete. In him the intent regards of the other spectators of the feast converge: Cleopatra has been produced as the object of scrutiny *par excellence*.

The emphasis of this grouping is reproduced in the Labia fresco (Plate 3.1), the image at the centre of this argument. In the fresco, however, it receives yet further intensification, as the painter includes images of himself and Mengozzi, his collaborator, as spectators to the left of the picture. The arrangement of the figures had already thrown the representation of Cleopatra itself under pressure: in the fresco the painter enacts his own imbrication in the problem of looking at Cleopatra. What can be seen in her? Her pose, with the pearl held out while she reaches for the transparent vessel with which Tiepolo replaced the original silver tankard of the Paris canvas (Plate 3.4) at an early stage in his exploration of this theme, suggests the demonstrator at a public lecture of the kind that became popular after Newton's death, the exponent of a visible experimental truth. Her place, at the centre of an intent and heterogeneous crowd, and the spartan table-dressing support this identification. Yet the act she is engaged in is patently fabulous, a gesture of the boldest extravagance, and, to be strictly realistic, pearls do not instantaneously dissolve in vinegar. The 'demonstration' she is in the act of giving does not compute. There is no law that it makes visible. Like Escher's perspective traps, the pearl 'experiment' locks the viewer into cognitive impasse.

If I have suggested that the Stockholm canvas (Plate 3.7) forces the gaze of truth and the gaze of illusion into a tense conjunction, the particular circumstances of the Labia frescoes offered a yet more highly keyed questioning of the relation between the two. In the Palazzo Labia, the images of Cleopatra that Tiepolo had been working on for so long changed their form from easel paintings to frescoes and with that change moved from being independent self-bounded images to playing a part in a very much larger enterprise, the creation of a full-scale illusionist decorated room. They became subordinated to a scheme of decoration in which the surfaces of wall and ceiling were emphasized and transformed by the addition of *trompe-l'oeil* architectural forms, pillars, pilasters, balconies, and cornices. The wall planes were also illusionistically dissolved, by the use of frescoes. This was a tradition of decoration that can be traced from before the painting of Masaccio's *Trinity: trompe-l'oeil* is set to work in collaboration with perspective schemes that are by no means self-evident or simple. It demands the virtuoso display of illusionist skill.[31]

Applying this to room decoration did not simply mean a strict adherence to the formalities of perspective but the ability to adapt the rules in order to match the capacities of the viewing eye more closely. For example, it was Veronese's practice, with which Tiepolo was familiar, to produce 'an artistically flexible space of a predominantly non-geometrical kind'.[32] Ways of modifying the strictness of perspective and of softening it by manipulation of the focal point, for the sake of comfort in reading the space, were taught. By 1625, when Pietro Accolti called the book he published in Florence *Lo inganno de gl'occhi*, the deception of the eyes, it was possible to make a direct equation between perspectival skills and deception. It was agreed that creating the architecturally illusionistic ceiling was the most difficult undertaking of all in the field of perspective. Illusionistic room decoration involving the sophisticated deployment of perspectival deceptions was further elaborated by the seventeenth-century *quadraturisti* of Bologna. In its readiness to modify theory for the sake of the viewer and in its conscious intent to deceive, the perspective decoration of rooms could be called an art without principle. As such, it was not easily to be assimilated to a viewing practice that claimed to regulate itself according to notions of truth and accuracy.

Decorating the Labia ballroom was an ambitious project to put perspective decoration to the test. It followed on the refurbishing of the palace, built late in the previous century, when a large public room, usually referred to as the ballroom, was carved out of the interior. None of the documents relating to the commission have survived and it is only by circumstantial details that a considerable time-lag between the creation of the room and its decoration can be inferred.[33] The room was prepared by Tiepolo's long-term colleague, the *quadratura* specialist, Carlo Mengozzi, whose work characteristically did not hesitate to use perspective for effect rather than strict logic. Mengozzi recreated the internal space by adding illusionistic architectural features to the walls and ceiling. The salmon-coloured marble of the actual door frames was imitated in fake columns and socles; the two walls destined to be frescoed were pierced with apertures; false balconies were painted beneath real windows; the ceiling was opened with a central oculus to allow an apparent view into the sky beyond. At every turn the enclosed nature of the space – it was bounded on every side but one – was dissimulated.

Mengozzi was a highly sophisticated exponent of a classic art in which the illusionism of perspective was doubled by the illusion of surface in the peculiar character of *trompe-l'oeil*. Both work through deceiving the eye but in ways that are fundamentally opposed. *Trompe-l'oeil*, it has been argued by Jean Baudrillard, does nothing less than undermine the world of perspective viewing. It does this by offering an imitation or simulacrum which undoes the real and throws doubt on the reality of the third dimension. By it the viewing practices which since the Renaissance have organized vision, the perspectival construction of space, are at once exposed as mechanisms for staging reality. *Trompe-l'oeil* insists on its own artificiality: what it offers in display is its own technique. It invites the viewer to take pleasure in that technique as a means of faking the presence of real objects. At the same time *trompe-l'oeil*, in abandoning the vanishing point, abolishes the gaze and with it the individual viewing subject's mastery of the object of vision. It produces a world where such mastery has been debunked. Where it is used in decorative schemes, Baudrillard argues, 'trompe l'oeil at once ridicules architecture, is wedded to it, betrays it, emphasises its role, and puts it out of circulation by making unbridled use of its techniques'.[34] In the Labia *sala di ballo*, the salmon-tinted mock-marbles, the painted sculptures, and the shields of the wall and ceiling decoration mix the disciplines and play false with them all. *Trompe-l'oeil* makes play of weight, solidity, and resistance: the human figure features in it only to mock the mass of veridical architecture, as Veronese puts characters leaning over balconies or half-opening a false door or as Tiepolo here seats mythical figures on a cornice.

The vast and elaborate frame in which the Cleopatra images, with their dedication to problems of vision and interpretation, were to be set thus redoubled the questioning of representation and its base in perspective illusion. Several new images of this anxiety appear for the first time in the Labia ballroom. Two concern the act of reading and specialized forms of notation. The spaces made available for Tiepolo's Cleopatra images were tripartite, in this final location, so that new material to fill the side-panels was devised. To the left of the banquet scene proper is shown a figure checking a list, as in Veronese's *Feast in the House of Levi*. Above the banquet table and well to its rear, as the relative size of the figures indicates, is set a balcony with musicians. It is both a perspective marker, staking out a specific height and depth for perception, and a reference to what is at stake at a moment of textual relay. The choir-master is shown reading, his interpretative activity underlined by the fact that he is wearing glasses; like the natural philosopher he requires the assistance of the lens. From his reading of musical notation sound will be produced, as space is from the viewer's reading of perspective.

Plate 3.9 Tiepolo, *Page and Monkey*, Palazzo Labia.

But the clearest statement that the mimetic function of the painter is under strain or question, the image that associates the attempt to paint Cleopatra with a possible failure of both vision and reading, stands high on the wall outside the purview of the two main images. Here a black page leans over a painted balcony, close to a real window, as Veronese's figures had leaned to mock the architect. Below him and to one side, a pet monkey clings to the fretwork of the balcony, or may already be in the act of falling. It is not just the monkeys from Venetian feast paintings or even the alert monkey given so prominent a position in *The Family of Darius* that it recalls, though it does speak of a tradition. The monkey, as Janson has documented, serves as an ancient figure of the painter's debased and futile imitation of the world.[35] In Tiepolo's uncomfortable image, the illusionist skills of his profession and the way of looking on which they rely for their recognition threaten to lose their anchorage and founder.

The final part of this argument moves on to consider how the pivotal figure in all these images, Cleopatra, was itself made to bear the mark of its identification with the problems of looking for pleasure and looking to make sense.

Algarotti's Cleopatra, I have argued, is produced as the limit case of woman's visibility and as a site in which the look of pleasure and the look of knowledge are in dispute. It is this contest which may account for the fact, not much commented on, that Cleopatra at her banquet is shown in the final Labia banquet fresco as wearing a dress which completely exposes her breasts. Nudity of this kind, where a formal dress discloses the breasts, is clearly quite distinct from the nakedness regularly found in representations of Cleopatra's death and was exceptional in treatments of the banquet. This display troubles interpretation on more than one count. It cannot be dismissed to a footnote, for its implications are locally and historically quite clear. In the Venetian tradition, for example in the work of Paris Bordone, only courtesans were shown with exposed breasts. (Pearls, too, could be a sign of the high-class prostitute.[36]) It had continued to be a sign of transgression: two women who ventured into the Piazza San Marco in 1757 with their breasts exposed had to be rescued from the fury of the crowd.[37] Tiepolo's image reads as both erotic and scandalous.

It is not difficult to see how a primary commitment to constituting the image of Cleopatra as the site of the most pleasurable looking at a woman might produce this bare-breasted queen. The visibility of the breasts indicates the satisfaction of the look of pleasure. It also permits the satisfaction of the look of knowledge that penetrates below the surface to the true nature of things. The breast is the visible sign of sexual difference, of the identity of woman: to show it exposed is to indicate that the eye has mastered the knowledge of woman. No explanation, however, disposes of the scandalous implications of that image. Cleopatra is presented as a whore. This categorization seems inextricably bound up with defining the figure as the cynosure of male attention, the object men attempt to comprehend by a looking that is felt to impart a knowledge which is both intimate and specifically sexual. It also debases its object. She is promiscuously available to their scrutiny, penetrated by their common gaze. This reading is held in tension with the alternative, noted earlier (see p. 68), that Cleopatra, the pearl held out in her hand, is taking the leading part in demonstrating an experiment. The tendency is inexorably to cast both the figure as woman and the act of demonstration into disrepute.

No such innuendo disturbs the image of Cleopatra transmitted in the *Incontro*. But it has its own problems. Here the emphasis falls on the failure of meaning, the inability to name and the figure's refusal or inability to deliver that clarity of vision that *Newtonianismo* seemed to promise. This emerges with increasing force through the versions of the scene which culminate in the Labia fresco.

The *Incontro*, as the ambiguous name by which it has come to be known suggests, is a non-theme. That is to say, it has no tradition and no origin. Cleopatra's death, which has both, would have been an obvious pendant for the banquet. There are no models for a generalized 'encounter' between Antony and Cleopatra that I know of, and later accounts, like Alma Tadema's picture showing Cleopatra reclining on her barge where Mark Antony comes to welcome her, can be placed with reference to a classical narrative, as the banquet scene can.[38] But in the *Incontro* Cleopatra is unambiguously placed in relation to no object, like the pearl or the barge, that would ground her representation in an originary narrative.

The image of liminality, of being on some kind of threshold between land and sea, like Venice itself, is an organizing principle of the *Incontro* group. There are only two versions of the *Incontro* that predate the final fresco and they are quite distinct in setting, though both show Antony kissing Cleopatra's hand. The earlier (Plate 3.6), pendant to the London *Banquet*, is placed in the open air, close to the sea. This littoral or marginal context is the easiest thing to read from the image; to the left of the protagonists there is a wagon with a suggestion of slaves and booty, while masts, spars, and pennants indicate the presence of a ship. This is obscured, however, by a large ruined monument in masonry in front of which Cleopatra is standing. In the slope of its sides this monument suggests a tapering masonry form which defies identification: neither an obelisk nor a pyramid, like the *Incontro* itself it cannot be given a proper name. The obelisk noted in later developments of the banquet scene had not yet been introduced in the companion piece to this work, the London *Banquet* (Plate 3.5). It seems most likely that the image of the distorted, and therefore troubling, obelisk in the later banquet scenes was transferred from this first version of the *Incontro*.

Uncertainty, a confusion bound up with a liminal context, continues to be a theme in subsequent reworkings, although in the second version (Plate 3.8) the setting has been transformed. Now the indication of liminality is no longer made by a suggestion that the meeting is taking place in the wilds by the shore: instead, at the centre right of the picture is set an explicit image of the threshold, the gangplank, instrument of transition. Attention is made to linger on the object by a carefully realistic treatment, which includes showing how it has been repaired. At the far end of it are the vessels and the sea, at the near end is terra firma. Antony bends over Cleopatra's hand. It is not possible to define confidently the relation in which the pair stand to the nearby vessels; possible originary narratives and the visual evidence do not support each other. It was Cleopatra who was famous, since Plutarch, for travelling by barge, so perhaps she has just arrived; on the other hand, among the figures apparently landing at the top of the gangplank is one wearing a helmet: perhaps Antony has disembarked. Or are the gestures we are shown those of farewell? The interpretative difficulty is embedded in the terms of the image and the viewer is obliged to attempt it.

In the final version from the Palazzo Labia (Plate 3.10) a shift of emphasis has occurred which brings the image into an unexpected alignment with the Trevisani *Banquet* (Plate 3.2). The parallel established in that picture between Antony's attempt to control Cleopatra and a dwarf's tugging at the leash of a lap-dog is recycled. On the left of the foreground (Plate 3.10), Antony, no longer bending over her hand, leads Cleopatra forward. To the right, a black page holds back a greyhound. The extended arms, as in the earlier picture, stress the connection between the two pairs, master and mistress, servant and dog. In Tiepolo's version, however, the image of the dog is tricked out with some surprising accessories that require first interpretation in their own right and then to be understood in reference to the figure of Cleopatra.

In this image the liminality already suggested by the gangplank is brought into dramatization. It is the second time that the figure of a black male servant is used to identify a crucial image: the third instance, though probably the originating one, is in the *Banquet*, where the glass in which the pearl is to be dissolved is proffered to Cleopatra by a black page. The *Incontro* page with his charge offers an image of the threshold transgressed: the greyhound is a hunting dog, inside instead of outside. Between the dog's feet lie a dropped dish and rucked-up fabric. It stands amid the disorder its presence creates. The entire *Incontro* is an image which foregrounds limits and boundaries and at the same time produces a sense of confusion. Something more than a generalized moral observation is at stake here: it has a precise reference to the conditions of signification. As Saussure has taught us, it is not on the existence of fixed terms but on the maintenance of difference between terms that the possibility of meaning depends. The perception does not appear in Tiepolo's work as a theorized proposition, naturally, but in the form of a symbol, like a dream. The image of the greyhound allows the disorder caused by the obliteration of demarcating boundaries to be proposed in a specific case. By means of it the *Incontro*, an image founded on inscrutability, gestures towards a state of confusion where no sense at all can be made and the possibility of signification is wiped out.

And where is the figure of Cleopatra in all this? Like the greyhound, she disturbs the categories, refuses to stay in place. Instead of proving a useful marker of boundaries and a term in the exchange of ideas between men, her body offers a certain resistance to a fixed reading just as in the fresco it leans away from the pressure of Antony's intentions.

I have proposed that what is at stake for Tiepolo in the Cleopatra enterprise is the possibility of readable representation itself. *Newtonianismo* attempted to offer the figure of the woman's body as a site where visual pleasure, illusion, and knowledge could be reconciled: Tiepolo's Cleopatra

Plate 3.10 Tiepolo, *Incontro*, Palazzo Labia.

frescoes put that proposition to the test. The fixed and stabilized meaning promised by Newtonian demonstration failed to materialize. Instead, the intensification of the gaze produced only the threat of loss of meaning, failure of identity. If it is a timeless psychic predisposition which places a woman's body at the focus of the look, it is also true that there is evidence of a historical resistance to this role. The scientific ladies of the eighteenth century dedicated themselves in the greatest numbers to those branches of enquiry that involved instrumentally enhanced vision, the microscope and the telescope. They did the looking.[39]

Chapter 4

Spaced out: Cleopatra and the citizen-king

The named environment, familiar to all, furnishes material for common memories and symbols which bind the group together and allow them to communicate with one another. The landscape serves as a vast mnemonic system for the retention of group history and ideals. Porteus denies that the Arunta tribes of Australia have any special memory ability, although they can repeat extremely long traditional tales. Every detail of the countryside is a cue for some myth, and each scene prompts the recollection of their common culture. Maurice Halbwachs makes the same point in reference to modern Paris, when he remarks that the stable physical scene, the common memory of Parisians, is a potent force in binding them together and allowing them to communicate with each other.[1]

With these words Kevin Lynch, in an argument recently taken up by Fredric Jameson, points towards the way landscape can be used both to constitute and signify group identity.[2] Accepting and developing this notion, however, involves exposing the fact that in the case of modern Paris, the example he actually quotes, the relation between a city and its history is a good deal more evasive than Halbwachs's sanguine assertion might suggest. It might be more realistic to see in the stable physical scene of Paris a sealing off or cauterization imposed under Louis-Philippe, to censor the record of the past and effectively to inhibit future rethinking of the nation's history.

It is by means of the remodelling of the Place de la Concorde, which took place early in the reign of Louis-Philippe, that the memory of the guillotine was expunged from the public space of the street. It was to be a continuing absence, for it was remarked that the recent bicentenary celebration of the Revolution, 'La Liberté ou la mort', did not feature the guillotine.[3] There was good reason to want to forget it. If the Revolution had established the French as unique in Europe for their attempt to replace an absolute monarchy with a system designed to promote the sharing of power between equals, the guillotine had made France the scandal of Europe.

The blood shed by the guillotine – so copious and so offensive that it had to be moved to a site with specially constructed drainage – could never be favourably represented. With its reminder of the arbitrary betrayals of the Terror, it was a monument not to the nation but to disunity and fratricidal destruction. But the site was not left blank. What was set up in place of the guillotine was an Egyptian obelisk. That enigmatic symbol, so clearly made into a signifier of *something else not present*, offered itself to the collective imaginary as the sign of the guillotine. Civic restructuring, however, could not rob the guillotine and the traumas of the Revolution of their continued force in the psychic life of the community or do away with the need to come to terms with them. It simply offered another form under which the repressed could return, a form which was accepted and developed by both Théophile Gautier and Eugène Delacroix. Both made use of the implicit identification made in the Place de la Concorde between ancient Egypt and the revolutionary history of their own city, when they explored the figure of Cleopatra. For Cleopatra, the queen who killed herself rather than endure to be taken in triumph through the city, had a particular resonance in the Paris which had seen the public humiliation and execution of its own queen, Marie-Antoinette, within a profoundly ambiguous period of the nation's founding history.

That execution had psychological as well as political consequences. Although Marie-Antoinette's death and the sufferings that led up to it have received full documentation, the trauma occasioned in the society that killed her has not been much explored. Recent critics have been alert to the patricidal aspects of putting Louis XVI to death. Cultural practices apparently generated by the regicide of 1793 have tentatively been identified and investigated by Neil Hertz and Marie-Hélène Huet.[4] Little attention has been paid, however, to the cultural aftermath of killing the mother: it is not always recognized that the maternity of Marie-Antoinette was an important element in the way she was represented.

The queen had borne four children, as the portrait painted by Elisabeth Vigée-Lebrun in 1787 indicates. It shows only three living children but the Dauphin points to the empty cradle in a reminder of his sister Sophie who had recently died (Plate 4.1). After the long delay between her marriage in 1770 and the birth of Madame Royale in 1778, her eventual fertility was a cause for celebration. At the announcement of her first pregnancy, a ballet whose theme was maternity was staged at court.[5] The rejoicing at the birth of the Dauphin in 1781, though it tended to elide the role of the mother in enabling the all-important transmission from Father to Son, was extended and intense: the tradesmen of the capital marched out to Versailles to the sound of music – an ironic pre-echo of

Plate 4.1 Vigée-Lebrun, *Marie-Antoinette and her Children*, Musée de Versailles.

Plate 4.2 Bouillon, *The Trial of Marie-Antoinette*, Musée Carnavalet.

the procession of October 1791 that would drag the royal family ignomini-
ously back to Paris – while there were bands dancing and free wine
throughout France.

At her fall, Marie-Antoinette's maternity was emphasized. An important feature of her trial was the allegation that her son, the 8-year-old
Dauphin, who had succeeded to the title on the death of his elder brother,
was induced to make against her. She was accused of child abuse: it was
claimed that she had taught her son to play sexualized games. Her
response was to emphasize her identity as a mother and to insist on her
connection with other mothers: 'If I do not answer, it is because Nature
prevents any mother from responding to such an accusation. I appeal to
all mothers present here.' This famous declaration was the subject of an
engraving, one of a series put on public sale by Royalist sympathizers
(Plate 4.2).[6] The public humiliation and death meted out to Marie-Antoinette were directed specifically at a maternal figure and, more exactly, a
maternal body. Her judges timed her trial to coincide with the onset of
her period.

When Delacroix exhibited his salon picture, *Cléopâtre et le paysan*
(*Cleopatra and the Peasant*), in 1838 and Gautier produced his short story,
'Une nuit de Cléopâtre', in the same year they were engaging with

material with a disturbing local resonance, rather than reaching into a romantic distance. The figure of Marie-Antoinette could be mapped on to the figure of Cleopatra, as I have indicated, and it also carried an additional psychic charge in its reminder of a communal matricide. Through the image of Cleopatra the execution of Marie-Antoinette returned to haunt the newly re-created urban spaces of the daily newspaper. Thanks to the fantasies that condensed in that image, revolutionary symbolism surfaced too, in the painter's meditation over Shakespeare's text as well as in the columns of the newspaper. But the struggles of the present moment also played their part in producing Cleopatra: most of all, the hope that under Louis-Philippe the abandoned revolutionary programme would now be reinstated. In a network of meanings involving the geography of Paris, the shift to the market economy, and the struggle for the franchise, Cleopatra became a node where the struggles of the past and of the present intersected.

Disentangling these threads to offer new readings of the Cleopatras produced by Delacroix and Gautier will be the work of this chapter. Its aim will be to register the overlapping images constituted by communal fantasy and symbol as they are brought into play around the figure of Cleopatra. Any interpretations offered will be shifting and unstable, not amenable to full resolution, any more than the dreams of an individual. But the analysis will establish that interpreting these Cleopatras in terms merely of privatized sexuality is inadequate, arguing that they are marked by the traces of a desire that is public, national, and political.

It is not surprising that these images present reading difficulties of the kind I indicate: they were produced at a moment when the status and the location of the political were intensely confused. Newspapers were being depoliticized, in answer to commercial pressures as well as to meet the demands of censorship. At the same time a sustained programme was turning the central space of Paris and its monuments into a new text from which an official account of national history could be read. Before exploring the concatenations of fantasy around the figure of Cleopatra, I will begin with the remodelling of the Parisian streets and go on to discuss the changes in the sale of newspaper space, which both played an important part in qualifying Parisians' understanding of their own society and its relation to the past.

The importance of city layout has often been recognized but, paradoxically, it is Haussmann's remaking of Paris between 1852 and 1870, rather than the earlier changes brought about under Louis-Philippe, that is most often identified as the crucial intervention in design of the built environment of Paris, the one that most firmly determined how life should be lived in the urban environment and was most evidently formative in the citizens' sense of identity. In this instance there has been no difficulty in recognizing the political nature of the decisions involved. Every guidebook points out that the *grands boulevards* which opened up the city, enabling the movement of people and goods, also spoiled it for guerrilla warfare. The priorities established under Haussmann – water, drains, lighting, transport – continued to be influential decades after he had been dismissed by a city no longer willing to foot the bills for the ambitious construction works his plans required. The enduring authority his layout had over people's minds is even more remarkable. The *Histoire de la France urbaine* puts the case in the language of scientific purity:

> The bold lines of this town planning are so indispensable to succeeding generations that their ability to reconceive the centre of Paris is sterilized. (Les lignes directrices de cet urbanisme s'imposent à la génération suivante, jusqu'à stériliser . . . les imaginations.)[7]

It killed off potential alternative cultures. The interventions made under the July Monarchy aimed to achieve no less.

In one sense, they were completely successful, for the history that was written on to the streets in the 1830s has become the authorized version, blandly endorsed by such statements as Maurice Agulhon's that 'It is under Louis-Philippe that the affective map of Paris was constructed.' ('C'est de Louis-Philippe que date l'essentiel de [la] carte sentimentale [de Paris].'[8]) The definition of a space contested by revolutionary, Napoleonic, and monarchist symbols as a 'carte sentimentale' (affective map) denies the urgency of the contest. But it is also true that it was soon recognized that the recollection of common culture prompted by the revised cityscape had something odd about it.

It was only a decade after the remodelling of the Place de la Concorde that Michelet, writing the very first study of the Revolutionary period, remarked on the absence of built memorial to the Revolution in the city of Paris.

> The Champ de Mars is the only monument left by the Revolution; the Empire has its column and has furthermore taken the Arc de Triomphe over almost entirely for itself; the monarchy has its Louvre and its Invalides; the feudal Church of 1200 is still enthroned in majesty in Notre-Dame; even the Romans have the thermal baths of Caesar. And the Revolution's monument is . . . emptiness.[9]

This emptiness constitutes a speaking absence at the centre, in the Place de la Concorde.[10] It was in this space, its name changed from Place Louis XV to Place de la Révolution and transformed by the supreme revolutionary act into a theatre of justice, that the guillotine was placed on 21 January 1793 for the execution of Louis XVI. (Here, between 1793 and 1795, when the protests of local residents about the smell of blood caused it to be moved, more than a thousand other persons of lesser symbolic significance, including Queen Marie-Antoinette, were brought in open vehicles through the crowd to their death.)

Erasing the memory of the guillotine was only one feature of a pro- gramme of civic restructuring, by means of which the July Monarchy was reforging the sense of the national past. It was an urgent political necessity. The July Monarchy based its mandate on its claim to have restored the connection with the new national identity broached at the Revolution and developed under the Empire. The period of the Bourbon Restoration was represented as a brief anomaly. Historical continuity in the cult of the nation had to be demonstrated in the public spaces of the city, where the battle to institute a definitive history had been in progress since the moment of the Revolution. The city space had been claimed and reclaimed by those who wanted to inscribe in its streets and monu- ments their own master narrative of the nation's history. The transient public spectacles of the revolutionary pageants were not enough. The names and meanings of the city's landmarks were struggled over, in the battle to secure a hold on and fix the future play of public imagination.[11]

Seeking public forms that would endorse his own authority, Louis- Philippe joined in this contest of signs with a view to creating a synthesis between royalist, Napoleonic, and revolutionary strands in the national past. Particularly skilful management of public space was demonstrated in the decision to set up his own July column. Clearly, in one sense, replicating the authority of the column in the Place Vendôme by which Napoleon had commemorated his victory at Austerlitz, it also permitted a firm association to be made between the July Monarchy and the least ambiguous traditions of the Revolution. Set up as a memorial to the Three Glorious Days of July 1830 which had brought Louis-Philippe to power, the column stood on the site of the Bastille, allowing a tactful association between the original and largely symbolic revolutionary act of 1789 by which the Bastille's seven inmates were liberated and the street fighting of 1830 by which the Bourbons were deposed. Unlike the guillotine, it offered a tolerable monument to revolution and became the focus of annual celebrations.[12]

Distancing himself as he must from traditional monarchy, Louis- Philippe could reassert the link with Napoleon but care had to be taken to protect himself from suffering by the comparison. If Napoleon had restored French pride, shaken by the confusion and compromise in which revolutionary hopes had collapsed, and was therefore a figure indispens- able to a programme of national reconstruction, he could still pose a threat to present unity through the power of his personal cult. It was with the greatest tact that Napoleon was reinstated in the city's narrative. An important step was to secure the return of his body from St Helena, where he had died in 1821. Negotiations, begun in 1833, were successfully completed in 1840, when it was returned for burial in Paris. Popular feeling inclined towards a tomb at the Vendôme column, already the centre of a number of memorial practices, but choosing this site would have given too much emphasis to the personal cult. What the government chose instead was to create a tomb within the Invalides, the vast barracks for military pensioners founded by Louis XIV. In this way Napoleon's individual achievement was to some extent assimilated to a national and historical framework.

At the same time the occasion of Napoleon's state funeral was used to confirm the obliteration of the guillotine and the scandals of the past. The procession was arranged to celebrate the reworked text of Paris and dramatize the new history of France, as created under the July Monarchy. One of Louis-Philippe's recuperative moves had involved completing the work on the Arc de Triomphe, initiated by Napoleon as a tribute to the French military but abandoned under the Restoration. Four years after it was finished, on 15 December 1840 when Napoleon's body was returned to France, the cortège was made to pass in solemn procession beneath the Arc de Triomphe, along the Champs Elysées, and across the Place de la Concorde on its way to the Invalides.

Not only had the name of the place of execution been changed, but the meaning of the whole area had been transformed by additions undertaken by Jakob Hittorf in 1836. Each had their political force. Around the octagonal space, the eight plinths of Gabriel's original design were now filled by (female) statues representing the cities of France: Brest, Rouen, Strasbourg, Lille, Bordeaux, Nantes, Marseille, and Lyon. The importance of the non-metropolitan centres was recognized and their weight in the new order publicly demonstrated: only 3 per cent of the total population of France lived in Paris in 1830 and the national divisions occasioned by post-revolutionary politics were to be avoided.[13] Of the guillotine, of course, there was no sign: its site was washed by the waters of one of the two new fountains.[14]

If the area had been redecorated to disavow its past and assert a new political order, its central monument, in its ambiguity, to some extent undid that work. The obelisk from Luxor, which reached France in 1833, had been intended as a gift to Charles X from Mohammed Ali, viceroy of Egypt. In so far as it was a recognizably Egyptian structure, it flattered national pride with its reminder of Napoleon's conquest of Egypt and again asserted, in the very spot where rupture was being created, a continuity with a proud national past.[15] By its emphatic positioning in that historic space and even by its arbitrary foreignness (on which Gautier mused in *Emaux et Camées*), the sign of the obelisk could not escape association with the displaced and obliterated signifier of the guillotine.[16] Obelisks already carried funerary associations, a connection so strong that a famous satirical drawing dating from the Revolutionary period itself shows an obelisk in parallel with multiple guillotines, of which it is the monument. On it is written 'cy gît toute la France' (Plate 4.3). Ironically, the monument which at once repressed and evoked the memory of a dead queen simultaneously pointed to the realm of her most fascinating predecessor.

In spite of these bold redefinitions of the built environment, the image of continuity and of unified national identity masked troubling and potentially cataclysmic contradictions. Napoleon's reign, though it had restored national pride, had in fact cancelled some of the freedoms most precious to the Revolution. Slavery had been abolished unanimously by the Convention on 4 February 1794, almost without discussion; Napoleon as first consul restored it and with it the slave trade, which continued till 1830 in spite of the fact that it was banned at the Congress of Vienna. In 1816 one of the first acts of the restored Bourbon monarchy was to put an end to divorce, which had been permitted under the liberalized marriage laws of September 1792. In 1826 inheritance rights cancelled under the Revolution were restored, to substantial public protest. In its constitutional charter of 9 August 1830, the newly established July Monarchy had undertaken to make good some crucial promises of the Revolution: among these were electoral reform, to give male citizens of 25 and over the vote, the disestablishment of the church, and a commitment that press censorship would never be reinstated. This neo-revolutionary commitment, as is well known, was not sustained. The period became distinguished for rigid governmental control over the press and it was the failure to enfranchise working men that finally brought Louis-Philippe and his ministers down. They had still not abolished slavery, in spite of proposals dating from 1838, a commission under Tocqueville which asked for universal simultaneous enfranchisement of slaves to be considered in the 1841 session, and the demonstrations of workers in Paris and Lyon. All these issues, the franchise, abolition, and relations between the sexes, can be found disputed and mapped on to each other in the representations of Cleopatra proposed for discussion here.

The first of these, Théophile Gautier's story, 'Une nuit de Cléopâtre', was written to come out in six parts in *La Presse*, a daily newspaper, in the winter of 1838.[17] Its format as newspaper fiction makes two things clear: it was addressed to a wide audience and it was produced in the matrix of commercial pressures that were transforming contemporary journalism. At the same time as the text of the city was being rewritten, a new form of public space was being manufactured in the columns of the daily newspaper, a space theoretically dedicated to freedom but in fact kept under firm political control.[18] Accompanying this, paradoxically, the bid to secure an extended readership was producing a new and previously unsought appearance of disinterest and objectivity in reportage. In 1830, as under the Restoration, newspapers had tended to identify themselves with specific political factions, but in 1836 Emile de Girardin

Plate 4.3 Anon, *Robespierre Guillotining the Executioner*, Musée Carnavalet.

made a number of innovations in establishing *La Presse* that decisively changed the character of newspapers' circulation base and created for the first time the possibility of a wide-spectrum or mass readership. It was not only a commercial venture in the self-evident sense. Its great innovation was in effectively devaluing reportage in comparison with sales pitch. This was done by lowering the price to individual subscribers, thus achieving a wider distribution, which subsidized the price cut by attracting an increase in the revenue from advertisers. Advertising became more important in the paper's fight for success, journalism less.[19]

It was also novel in being without party affiliation and thus laying claim to a kind of objectivity not previously projected as possible. The newspaper began to constitute a widely shared experience and to offer the possibility of constituting a greater homogeneity of attitude, of playing, indeed, something like the part of the cityscape in offering forms of group identity and value. An important feature was the part played by newspaper layout. The page of newsprint held random items of information in factitious and unexplained relation, packed together within its margins. This produced a graphic suggestion of the possibility of homogeneity and reconciliation, of the denial of difference and conflict:

> [what is of greatest moment in] the newspaper's disposition of space, [the] topology of its interpenetrating discourses . . . is the manner in which their juxtaposition schooled readers to the neutralisation of any active perception of contradiction.[20]

At the same time the newspaper, by its own commercial practices, fostered some confusion between what was news and what was advertisement. An important, though not widely publicized, trade practice beginning in the period after 1836 was the sale of space for covert advertising under the guise of journalism. Covering four sheets of newsprint, papers ostensibly devoted the first three to the reporting of news, while paid advertisements were admitted to the fourth. In fact, space on the third, second, and even front pages could be bought, at appropriately increased rates, so that the distinction between public information and private advantage was irretrievably confused. No public space was protected from being turned into a commodity.[21] The citizen, depoliticized, was evolving into the consumer. Théophile Gautier, in addition to writing fiction for *La Presse* was also employed as manager of its *feuilleton* and so was responsible for the miscellaneous non-news articles of the paper. He was working with and within these developments.

Important changes in retailing were taking place too. The roles of buyer and seller were being modified. Only in the 1830s was the *prix fixe* being introduced in stores. The buyer submitted to a prearranged price and did not negotiate terms. Before that, customers declared their intention to purchase by entering the shop and when inside bargained with the

proprietor to arrive at an acceptable price. With the advent of the department stores, entering a shop no longer implied the intention to make a
purchase: it became possible for the first time to go 'just looking'.[22] It
was up to the shopkeeper, in these conditions, to seduce the customer
into desiring goods they had not made a previous decision to buy.
Terdiman argues that a new situation had been created, where it was a
problem to know who was in charge of retail transactions (in the shops)
or even where a retail transaction was at stake (in the newspaper). This
confusion may help to explain Gautier's choice of the Cleopatra narrative,
as I shall indicate.

If I begin by characterizing Gautier's tale as one of consumption and
trade, it is not to underestimate the difficulties in approaching what
presents itself as an almost unreadable text. It is replete with a contemporary and revolutionary imagery which unequivocally establishes a political
register, but at the same time it concerns itself almost exclusively with
individual desire. The disparity between the registers of privatized eroticism and the politics of class and nation challenges the composition of a
satisfactory reading. It seems likely that the most convenient way to
resolve the contradictions of the text was to read Cleopatra and her
behaviour in the light of the developing bourgeois ethic of woman as
wife, domestic inhabitant, and consumer: Cleopatra both as monstrous
anti-woman in her sexual independence and as Emma Bovary – she
wanted to die, she wanted to live in Paris. Such a simplified reading,
however, may be rejected in favour of retaining the text's contradictions
and highlighting the public and the political in it.

The story, divided into six chapters, each about two thousand words
in length, recounts how Cleopatra came to take a young commoner to
her bed for a single night, on the understanding that he would die the
next day. The tale offers less a narrative than a symbolic amplification of
this theme: not much action, lots of description. The first chapter sets
the scene in Egypt and introduces the figure of Cleopatra, languid but
well served in the interior of her barge. It closes with the climactic
exclamation 'O Charmian! she said, how bored I am' ('O Charmion! dit-
elle, je m'ennuie'). In the second she complains of her isolation and
longing for change: as it closes the reader is shown a young man of
striking physical prowess following the queen. Chapter 3 is largely
devoted to informing the reader about Meiamoun and his infatuation with
Cleopatra: he sends an arrow through her window, carrying the message
'I love you' ('Je vous aime!'). By the end of Chapter 4, although Cleopatra
could not succeed in identifying her admirer, he was able to gain admission to her presence by the notable expedient of diving through the
underground conduits leading the Nile water to Cleopatra's baths. Only
in Chapter 5 do they confront each other, amidst the luxury of the baths,
and Cleopatra agrees to reward his desire before having him killed on

the following day. The final chapter, in which the orgiastic banquet, the 'nuit de Cléopâtre' of the title, is described, closes with Cleopatra presiding over Meiamoun's draught of poison.

Gautier's story does not draw on the familiar Cleopatra material of asps and dissolved pearls and Antony is almost entirely absent from it. What it offers is an account of consumption and trade couched in terms which present a radical confusion. How the roles of buyer and seller are to be assigned and what is the commodity under transaction are all unclear. This confusion is reminiscent of and is perhaps patterned by the dissembling of economics in retailing and in the layout of *La Presse* and other newspapers. The source of the story is Sextus Aurelius Victor's assertion: 'She became so debauched that she frequently offered herself as a prostitute; but she was so beautiful that many men bought a night with her at the price of their own death' ('Haec tantae libidinis fuit, ut saepe prostiterit, tantae pulchritudinis ut multi noctem illius morte emeruit').[23]

This turns away from the historical, from connections with a world politics located in the first century BC; it is a fantasy of female power (so beautiful) equated with female shame (so debauched): both rooted in the body. Its contradictions, Oedipal in tone, enclose specifically male fantasies of the female body: the fantasy of female appetite, the vision of a female sexuality sufficiently empowered to command its own satisfaction; the conjunction of the untouchable and unattainable queen as bought female flesh; the restoration of the queen as all-powerful even to the point of killing her lovers.[24] What locks them firmly into a time and place is their production in the site of the compromised space of the newspaper. Freedom of the press had mattered enough to be featured in the constitutional charter at the start of the reign: now the space was being lost to politics and becoming the arena of an ambiguous commerce. Freedom, or, in the terms of radical iconography, Liberty, was prostituted. And so, curiously, the story about Cleopatra may overlap with the story of Liberty.

There is some confusion in Aurelius Victor, however, about who is being prostituted and to whom. Notice how the men are not figured quite as bought male flesh, though that is what in effect Cleopatra is doing, buying sexual gratification. She pays with her body, not with money. The hint of male subordination can be retrieved and transformed by the fact that her lovers pay with their lives – a price so high that it becomes a heroic rather than an economic term. (In fact, the ordinary economic terms of prostitution, on which the scandal value of the tale is sprung, are notably absent.) The woman's power is absolute; what the men pay is absolute.

If the power relations of the narrative outlined by Aurelius Victor strongly resist investigation, this is true also of Gautier's account, where he traces the circumstances in which Meiamoun, a young man of the people who has fallen in love with Cleopatra, manages to get a night with her. At the point where Cleopatra speaks the terms of the deal, which are themselves ambiguous – 'je te l'achète' (I'll buy it off/for you) – the reader cannot be clear what she is buying. Meiamoun's life? Sexual pleasure? If he is selling his life, he is paid a night with Cleopatra. If pleasure is what he's selling, then pleasure is what he is being paid with. But it is in either case Cleopatra who is the buyer: positioned not as the prostitute but as the client. Ambiguity steps over into contradiction.

This reading difficulty is not accidental. It is produced by the contradiction of the clashing registers established in the text. They work together, the historical, the political, and the privatized, to prevent or forestall the composition of a coherent reading and it is only by careful attention to the divergent implications of each that progress in understanding can be made. We have seen something of how the text bears the traces of the power relations within which it was produced. Yet it names itself as an episode in the life of an individualized Cleopatra living in a remote past. At the same time it gives it to be understood, by sustained and repeated gestures within itself, that it is as reluctant memorial of Marie-Antoinette, the French queen who died by the guillotine in 1793, that the writing functions.

It is in the representation of the body of Cleopatra, delayed for several pages from the tale's opening, that the primary and authoritative identification is made. Fetishistic, disturbing, what the text offers to the gaze, set amidst the trappings of an orientalized boudoir, is the image of a severed or disembodied female head, the neck resting on a curved wooden support like the bowl of the guillotine:

> in the background stood a small bed on griffin feet, with a bedhead decorated like a sofa or a love-seat of our own time, a set of stairs with four steps to climb up to it with, and, a rather singular refinement according to our idea of comfort, a sort of semicircle made of cedar wood, standing on a base, intended to encompass the outline of the nape of the neck and to support the sleeper's head.
>
> On this strange pillow was lying a very charming head.
>
> (au fond s'élevait un petit lit à pieds de griffon, avec un dossier garni comme un canapé ou une causeuse moderne, un escabeau à quatre marches pour y monter, et, recherche assez singulière dans nos idées confortables, une espèce d'hémicycle en bois de cèdre, monté sur un pied, destiné à embrasser le contour de la nuque et à soutenir la tête de la personne couchée.
>
> Sur cet étrange oreiller reposait une tête bien charmante.)[25]

But, immediately the gesture is made, it is denied. The body and the head are not separated, have never been abused, are almost omnipotent:

On this strange pillow was lying a very charming head, one look from which caused half the world to be lost, an adored and divine head, the most complete woman, the most queenly, a wonderful specimen to whom poets have been able to add nothing and whom dreamers find at the end of their fantasies still: I need hardly say it was Cleopatra.

(Sur cet étrange oreiller reposait une tête bien charmante, dont un regard fit perdre la moitié du monde, une tête adorée et divine, la femme la plus complète qui ait jamais existé la plus femme et la plus reine, un type admirable, auquel les poètes n'ont pu rien ajouter, et que les songeurs trouvent toujours au bout de leurs rêves: il n'est pas besoin de nommer Cléopâtre.)[26]

Only a determined regime of normalization and naturalization can extract a harmonious and congenial reading from this text. It is full of disturbance: the isolation of the head presented on the pillow, like the Baptist's head on a charger, is at odds with the insistent lyricism. The implied absence of the body makes the assertion that the woman is complete discomfiting: while the idea that *poets* have failed to make up what is absent is at least as possible a reading as the more consoling and conventional one, that no poet could improve on her beauty. The mounting rhetoric of this eulogy may intelligently be read in terms of hysterical denial. Personalized erotic fantasy will hardly account for the intensity of this writing or for the political curiosity, in the reign of consciously democratized monarchy, of coupling the terms 'the most complete woman', 'the one most a queen', and 'un type admirable'.

The ambiguity of reference brought to crisis in this first presentation of Cleopatra is by implication present from the start of the tale. Paradoxically it is achieved by a heavy emphasis on the remoteness of the period and the exoticism of the surroundings in which the events are situated. Already, in 1831, Jules Janin had brought out a novel, *Barnave*, in which Alexandrian Egypt had metonymically represented France during the Revolutionary period.[27] The more encrusted with Egyptian detail the account – and many sources were available to Gautier from the ethnographic to costume history – the more questionable the singularity of its reference grew.[28]

This contradiction is foregrounded by a passage from Gautier's fourth chapter when Cleopatra sends for her chief oarsman, Phrehipehbour. She intends to send boats in pursuit of her unknown lover, who, having made his passion known, is swimming away in the darkness.

Phrehipehbour appeared: he was of the Nahasi race, with big hands, muscular arms, wearing a red cap, rather like a phrygian bonnet, and dressed in narrow breeches, diagonally striped in white and blue. His chest, which was completely bare, gleamed in the lamplight, black and polished like a ball of jet. He received the queen's orders and withdrew forthwith to carry them out.

(Phrehipehbour parut: c'était un homme de la race Nahasi, aux mains larges, aux bras musculeux, coiffé d'un bonnet de couleur rouge, assez semblable au casque phrygien, et vêtu d'un caleçon étroit, rayé diagonalement de blanc et de bleu. Son buste, entièrement nu, relulisait à la clarté de la lampe, noir et poli comme un globe de jais. Il prit les ordres de la reine et se retira sur-le-champ pour les exécuter.)[29]

Impossible conjunction between the gratuitous red revolutionary bonnet, unequivocally represented here and so radical a symbol that it was banned as a violent and seditious emblem in the early 1870s, and the absolute power over its wearer attributed to the queen. Even the red, white, and blue of the total outfit recalls the invention, two days after the fall of the Bastille, of the tricolour. Some of the first flags of the Garde Nationale were striped in white and blue: striped trousers are frequently worn in contemporary caricatures of Revolutionaries (Plate 4.4).[30] However she is overtly named, the queen who is invoked here, face to face with the man wearing the symbols of the Revolution, is Marie-Antoinette. Yet it is also true that the queen from whom such men took their instructions was known as Liberty.[31]

Plate 4.4 Le Sueur, *The Prison Tribunal*, Musée Carnavalet.

The confrontation between power and labour – at its most absolute in the slave trade – is repeatedly problematized in this text in terms of a physical, if not always an erotic, encounter between the sexes. The emphasis on naked flesh, on skin texture and colour, while undoubtedly indebted to ethnographic practice, provides the means of mapping the political on to the private body. This is what produces the reiterated assertion of the queen's delight in destroying (male) bodies: only our long training in making individual sexual taste the primary focus of critical attention can obscure the political meaning of these images. They are repeated: when Phrehipehbour fails in his quest, it is suggested that 'You would have to be a very gentle queen and a very merciful one, not to have this wretched Phrehipehbour crucified' ('il faut être, en vérité, une reine très douce et très clémente, pour ne pas mettre en croix ce misérable Phrehipehbour').[32] 'It's obvious, Charmian said very quietly, that the queen has had no lover and has put no one to death this last month' ('On voit bien, dit tout bas Charmion, que la reine n'a pas eu d'amant et n'a fait tuer personne depuis un mois').[33] 'Trying out poisons on slaves, making men fight with tigers or gladiators do battle with each other, drinking dissolved pearls, eating up a province, all that is tame and banal!' ('Essayer des poisons sur des esclaves, faire battre des hommes avec des tigres ou des gladiateurs entre eux, boire des perles fondues, manger une province, tout cela est fade et commun!').[34]

At the same time the terms for a redefinition of sexual difference are also being offered. In this it is consumption, in confinement, whether of pearls, provinces, or the product of others' labour, that is the part assigned to the female figure: the male conducts his life out of doors and is identified with work. (It is a distinction confirmed by the text's overt construction of a gendered readership: 'nos lectrices' (our lady readers) will want to know what Cleopatra is wearing.) Here a domestic reading to the exclusion of the political, a private rather than a public rendering of the text, begins to yield the crystallizing forms of bourgeois domesticity.

The representation of Meiamoun as a figure of Labour is quite specific and historically grounded. Lynn Hunt has documented the development of a radical revolutionary icon that was male.[35] In the Revolutionary period the figure of Hercules was set up in opposition to and competition with female allegorizations of the radical republic. It was introduced, or at any rate elaborated, specifically in order to counter the growing political mobilization of women. This first made its appearance on 10 August 1793 during an elaborate festival planned by David, where a colossal figure of Hercules, representing the French people, used its club to shatter the hydra of federalism. At the end of October the Convention outlawed all women's clubs, to avoid 'the kinds of disruption and disorder that hysteria can produce'; in November they chose Hercules rather than a female figure of Liberty to represent the people of France on the seal of state (Plate 4.5).

The image focused contests of class as well as gender. The transformation of Hercules, with his club and his lion skin, into a symbol of the people, projects them as essentially physical rather than intellectual, a natural force bringing light and truth to the world through strength, courage, and, above all, labour. Hercules spoke, mutely, of the value of the work to which the common people's lives were bound, in contrast with the idleness of the rich; at the same time he demonstrated the limitations of their range. Ingres revived the figure in a sketch made to celebrate the revolution of 1830: he drew a naked man with a club, entitled *The People Triumphant in 1830* (Plate 4.6).

The representation of Meiamoun, in Gautier's story, though no less contradictory than other features to which attention has already been drawn, does derive quite patently from the imagery of Hercules. Before he is even named, the exceptional physical strength that makes him single-handed able to outpace a vessel with fifty rowers is identified; 'although he had been rowing for a long time, he was showing no trace of tiredness, and on his forehead there was not a single pearl of sweat' ('bien qu'il ramât depuis longtemps, il ne trahissait aucune fatigue, et il n'avait pas sur le front une seul perle de sueur').[36] Before getting out of his boat he drapes a lion skin round his shoulders. At the opening of the next instalment the reference is made explicit in the ascription to him of 'une force herculéenne'. But the model is interestingly reinflected: Meiamoun combines in his person both female and male attributes to the point of androgyny.

> although he had almost the delicate grace of a girl and although Dionysus, the effeminate god, did not have a chest more rounded or more smooth, he kept nerves of steel and a herculean strength hidden under this soft surface; it was the exceptional privilege of a few beings in antiquity to combine a woman's beauty with a man's strength.
>
> (quoiqu'il eût presque la grâce délicate d'une jeune fille, et que Dionysius, le dieu efféminé, n'eût pas une poitrine plus ronde et plus polie, il cachait sous cette molle apparence des nerfs d'acier et une force herculéenne; singulier privilège de certaines natures antiques de réunir la beauté de la femme à la force de l'homme.)[37]

And even if he is shown elsewhere as immeasurably below Cleopatra, his brow wears, in contestation of this inferior social status, a serene majesty. This is a self-conscious fantasy of the obliteration of the symbolic divisions of class and gender, the demarcations that construct the world of the social. It attempts to restore the child's early pre-Oedipal world, as its appeal to 'antiquity', the remote past, indicates. In that world of an experience which does not yet register sexual difference, the mother

Plate 4.5 Dupré, Hercules design for the seal of state, Musée Carnavalet, Paris.

Plate 4.6 Ingres, sketch for *The People Triumphant in 1830*, Musée Ingres, Montauban.

is all-important. Gautier's text briefly gestures towards a fantasy reconstruction of the phallic mother, whose woman's body – the breast, roun-
ded and smooth – is not yet known to be socially designated as inferior
to the man's. Gautier endows it here with an idealized power, which
brings it into alignment specifically with the strength of working men.
(This conjunction will be repeated in Delacroix's *Cleopatra* and I will
discuss its implications when I deal with the picture.) It is in the field of
force around the image of Cleopatra, particularly its associations with the
dead mother, Marie-Antoinette, that this fantasy is produced: it is a work
of unacknowledged mourning.

Delacroix's *Cleopatra*, shown in the Salon of 1839, like Gautier's newspaper serial could seem to endorse a simply private and eroticized reading.
In the painting, Cleopatra is seated, her chin on her right hand, gazing
out of the picture space and ahead of her to the right (Plate 4.7). On that
same side of her stands a male figure, who has drawn back a fold of the
leopard skin he is wearing to disclose a snake, lying on top of a basket
of leaves. Cleopatra may be looking at the snake; she is impassive and
absorbed. Her face, with its large eyes, long straight nose, and a mouth
that is heavily curved but not slack, stands slightly above the centre of
the picture: her arm and the hand supporting the chin mark that centre.
She is aloof: some spectators might enjoy seeing her as alone with her
destiny.

But the vitality of the male figure, eager to engage her attention, makes
it unconvincing to treat Cleopatra as if she were overwhelmingly more
important. Who is this man? The clown that Shakespeare brings on stage
in this scene makes his presence felt by a change of verbal register that
counterpoints the heroics of Cleopatra's situation; Delacroix's peasant is
himself a heroically physical being.

The leopard skin worn by this male figure, with its muscled shoulders,
makes reference to the same complex of Hercules/Dionysus found in the
Gautier text; if the brawny shoulders and animal pelt suggested Hercules,
the leopard skin was specifically associated with Dionysus. At the same
time the boundaries of a strong gender distinction between male and
female are marked out. In the visual image Dionysus is not used as a
marker of ambiguous sexuality but of an emphatic masculinity. Heavily
bearded, a leopard skin over one shoulder, and his thick hair bound with
leopard-skin thongs, untamed energy and spontaneous vigour are the
qualities the figure derives from the Dionysiac association. This overlaps
with and modifies the meanings to be discovered if the figure is read
simply as drawing on the Hercules trope, making it more clearly threatening and potentially disruptive.[38]

In some respects the pair of figures are constructed to echo each other.
Both have the left shoulder and upper arm bare, the man's hair, if not
as long as the woman's, is abundant, their hands are positioned in parallel

Plate 4.7 Delacroix, *Cleopatra and the Peasant*, Ackland Art Museum.

– at the point where their garments almost touch they seem to mirror each other. But the differences within this close comparison are marked: the man's nakedness reveals muscle, the woman's indicates the rise of a breast. A jewelled head-dress keeps the hair off the woman's forehead, while the end of the mottled band tied about the man's head looks disconcertingly like the head of a snake. A highlight concentrates attention on the back of the man's left hand. Down to the start of the fingers it is covered by the paw of the leopard skin in which he is draped: his finger nails and the top joints of the fingers have the force of animal vitality, without losing their human definition.

It is the woman's right hand that is counter-poised with this sign of vital capacity: turned back on itself, pinned down by the weight of the chin resting on it, the fingers are at once clenched and impotent, like a club-foot. On the other hand, resting idle in the folds of her wrap, is a ring: like the bracelets which she wears on both arms it signals wealth and yet can be read also as encirclement or constraint. (The ring the man wears is in his ear and boldly signals a gypsy or oriental escape from the restrictions of European dress codes.) The man's left hand, posed at the same level is broad, extended across its lateral surface, the thumb spread, to grasp the basket he supports with the flexed muscles of the forearm.

If this could be called the image of a missed conjunction, it is because it is by no means clear that the male figure has succeeded in engaging the woman on the terms that he wanted. Intent, swarthy, he offers for her attention, from beneath his leopard skin, a frankly phallic configuration of a snake, one nestling, moreover, amid fig-leaves. The woman's gaze, though it travels in the snake's direction, is markedly unmoved and almost unseeing. It reflects self-absorption rather than vision. Her pallor, contrasted with the man's ruddy flesh tones, and the fact that she is shown physically supported by an opulent piece of furniture mark her off from the life of external activity.

Although this picture makes clear reference to the account given in Plutarch and amplified by Shakespeare of how Cleopatra was brought the snakes by which she died, the image owes more to the public iconography of post-Revolutionary France under the July Monarchy than it does to the staging, actual or imagined, of Shakespeare's play. There is no evidence that *Antony and Cleopatra* was among the plays staged by the English theatre company on its visit to Paris in 1827, the most obvious immediate source.[39] Ducis, who translated and adapted a number of Shakespeare's tragedies for the Revolutionary stage, did not include *Antony and Cleopatra*; the only record of a play about Cleopatra performed in Paris between 1800 and 1847 refers to the five-act tragedy by Soumet.[40]

In fact the picture itself confounds the attempt to place what is going on in terms of period or scene. Datable details, like the chair, Cleopatra's clothing, and her jewellery, offer contradictory evidence. No authentic

Egyptian furniture had been recovered at the period: knowledge of furniture design was drawn from wall-paintings and it does not appear that Delacroix was basing his account on those. The design of the chair is essentially contemporary, based on the classical *klismos* chair, current from the 1780s and derived from those shown on Greek vases. The arm-rests, with their stripes and palm or lotus motif, are Egyptianizing, like the designs of Thomas Hope, rather than Egyptian. The columnar supports could owe their design to the architectural capitals illustrated by Denon but their representation by Delacroix is so impressionistic that it could not be claimed that the viewer was being reminded of the finely incised line of any one of the range of styles shown by Denon's engravings.[41]

Cleopatra's dress and her ornaments are equally ambiguous. There is no attempt at specificity in her costume: something like a shift has slipped off her shoulders, darker fabric wraps the lower part of her body. Its vagueness is emphasized when the picture is compared with the portrait of Lady Londonderry dressed as Cleopatra for Prince Borghese's ball in Florence in 1825 (Plate 4.8). (Representing herself as Cleopatra at a costume ball may well have been less fraught with ambiguity for a wealthy and beautiful young married woman than the act of representing Cleopatra on canvas was for a man living in post-Revolutionary Paris.) The Londonderry outfit could be recreated now, garment by garment, and its classicizing style dates itself firmly. In the Delacroix picture Cleopatra, by her dress, is delivered from any historical specificity.

Her jewels are another question, however. They are firmly contemporary in design and there are a lot of them. Sleeve clasps like hers can be found in Lawrence's portrait of Lady Londonderry, and in Winterthur's portrait of Madame Ingres there is a bracelet with a clasp like the one on Cleopatra's left arm. The design of the necklace is common in the period, when the jewelled medallions were linked by gold chains 'en esclavage' (slave-style) rather than by pearls. In spite of the quantity of ornament, the overall effect is neither brilliantly extravagant nor particularly regal. There are puzzles: why is there only one small ring worn in what is rather a showy tenue? Is it a wedding-ring? Frontlets, like small tiaras, were regularly worn as part of evening-dress in the period: there is no such crown on Cleopatra. The three buckle-like objects that hold back her hair have no parallels in contemporary dress.

Her hair is down, suggesting a dishabille at odds with the evidence of the jewellery. The eyes (echoed by the shape of the head ornaments) and the brow are emphasized but royalty is played down. The ear-rings are timeless top-and-drop design, not the pearls associated with Cleopatra. And a detail that might have been expected, the snake bracelet fashionable in the period and particularly appropriate to Cleopatra, is missing.[42] Uncertainty over the sitter's identity builds as the picture is scrutinized. She may be named as Cleopatra outside the picture: inside it her meaning

Plate 4.8 Lady Londonderry as Cleopatra, private collection.

floats more freely, drifting away from the royal and historical towards invoking both seated figures of Liberty and the figure of contemporary women.

It was simply no longer possible to think Cleopatra according to the tradition. Changes in the social contract could be seen enforcing changes in signifying practice: in a Palais Bourbon frieze Delacroix had recently drawn on motifs regularly used by the painters of the school of Fontainebleau to designate Cleopatra, the snake on the arm and the elaborately coiffed hair bound with pearls. Yet he had insisted, by the label *Industria*, on the production of a new meaning for these signifiers.

For Delacroix, no less than Gautier, was producer and product of the reorganized politics of public space. Seven years previously he had shown *Liberty Leading the People* at the Salon and seen it bought and sent into storage by a regime not eager to see such a radical emblem on display. Now he was a successful painter, commissioned by the state to celebrate the order of modern France. In the period immediately before the completion of *Cleopatra* he had been employed in decorating the Salon du Roi in the Palais-Bourbon and would go on to paint the famous cycle of the Bourbon Library.[43] These commissions involved making over the walls and ceilings of what had been an aristocratic property, the Condé palace, to its new role of housing the legislature of a democratized monarchy.

The legislature that these decorations were designed to celebrate was one, in spite of its claims to revolutionary antecedents, which excluded two major groups of citizens from political power. The franchise was not extended to women or to working men. It is not coincidental that in Delacroix's *Cleopatra and the Peasant* these are the matched, ambiguously involved groups that receive representation.

In spite of the control of the press established under the July Monarchy, the traces of the protest provoked by the exclusion of women and work-ing men from the franchise are to be read in contemporary accounts. Ambiguously, *La Presse* reports that workmen who had been persuaded to petition for the vote had seen their mistake and withdrawn.[44] For some women, however, it was possible to make their own case in the press. A group of proletarian women under Suzanne Voilquin brought out *La Tribune des femmes* from 1832 till it was banned in 1834; between 1836 and 1838 the bourgeois *Gazette des femmes* campaigned for women to be allowed to petition government directly, one aim of which was to petition for the franchise. During the Revolutionary period women had become politically active – though it was in quite diverse ways, their interests very much divided along the lines of class, with little common ground between the market-women and the bourgeois activists. It was, however, as a group, as women, that they were in April 1793 excluded by the Convention from the rights of citizenship, along with the demented and minors.[45]

The attempt to claim full civil rights by women and working men was resisted by Charles Nodier, mentor of the first romanticists, in *L'Europe littéraire* no. 2, in an argument whose mystifying tendencies offer an invaluable insight into the cultural sleights of hand at work in the texts of both Gautier and Delacroix. In his piece, 'La femme libre' ('The free woman'), the right to vote is transposed into an issue of sexual potency and the relationship between the sexes transposed into the politics of class, even of slavery. The actual past is repudiated; women are instructed to recognize that they dwell outside the scope of historical investigation and can only discover the truth of their condition through fiction rather than by consulting the evidence of 'a stupid coarse reality' ('une sotte et grossi-ère réalité'); 'Let women not deceive themselves, the story of their kind is to be found in the pages of novels' ('Que les femmes ne s'y trompent pas, leur histoire à elles, c'est le roman'). They should recognize that, thanks to their 'charming organization',

> there is not a single woman who does not exercise around her more influence than a peer of France . . . Christianity and chivalry, which found them slaves, made sovereigns of them.

(il n'y a point de femme qui n'exerce autour d'elle plus d'influence qu'un pair de France . . . Le christianisme et la chevalerie, qui les trouvèrent esclaves, les ont faites souveraines.)[46]

But the sort of queens Nodier had in mind were bourgeoises, sited primarily as wives: Balzac's assertion, in *La Physiologie du mariage*, of 1829, that 'the married woman is a slave whom one must be able to set on a throne' had recently brought a new cynicism as well as a new domesticated turn to the concept of the woman as sovereign.[47] It was underpinned by the fact that Napoleon's civil code had in 1804 confirmed the total submission of women to marital authority and in 1816 divorce had been abolished. (Slavery itself, of course, banned under the Revolution, was also restored under Napoleon. The term 'l'esclavage' (slavery) was in use in the *Tribune des femmes* to refer both to the condition of the disenfranchised workers and specifically to the multiple social disadvantages of women.)

Possibly most remarkable is Nodier's equation between the exercise of public power, in the maintenance of law and control of finance, and the possession of full male sexuality. In his account, there is an intimate relationship between the franchise, the exercise of sexuality, and the maintenance of sexual difference.

> I fancy indeed that a woman who passed laws, who debated the budget, was responsible for public funds, and sat in judgement over courts, would be at the most a man.
>
> (J'imagine en effet qu'une femme qui voterait les lois, qui discuterait le budget, qui administrerait les deniers publics, et qui jugerait les procès, serait tout au plus un homme.)[48]

And, if a politically active woman must in fact turn out to be a man, the reason no man of a lower class, a *prolétaire*, can vote, is that he literally has no sex: 'All workers in France are at the same stage as old women; they have no sex' ('Les prolétaires en sont tous en France au même point que les vieilles femmes; ils n'ont point de sexe').[49]

Suzanne Voilquin, writing in *La Tribune des femmes*, saw a simple answer: radical as she was, even her language, however, could not escape contamination. Her imagery implies, if it does not ultimately appeal to, an idealization of marriage. The joined hands and 'holy equality' of the final phrase are difficult to discriminate from an image of matrimony.

> enfranchise the workers: is it maintained anywhere that they should not have a sex and recognized rights one day? And why are we not allowed to believe that the moment is at hand when women and the people, joining hands, should together cross this last barrier separating them from holy equality?
>
> (affranchissez les prolétaires: est-il dit quelque part qu'ils ne doivent pas

un jour avoir un sexe et des droits reconnus? Et pourquoi ne nous serait-il pas permis de croire que le moment est proche où les femmes et le peuple, se donnant la main, doivent ensemble franchir cette derni-ère barrière qui les sépare de la sainte égalité?)[50]

In all the texts examined in this chapter, fiction, painting, and journalism, the public register is jostled and contaminated by the private. The terms for conducting relations between the sexes are inextricably involved with the terminology of power and class politics. In the 1830s this permitted repressed desires obliterated from the public space and official memory to emerge in the private sphere and be read in its register. Later interpreters have ignored the organizing role played by emblems of national history and politics in both Gautier's and Delacroix's Cleopatras. The common memories and symbols that were invoked by the new obelisk at the centre of Paris are reinstated here. They meant that beautiful moody Egyptian queens, confined with men of a lower social class, who are eager to demonstrate their sexuality at all costs, are not just one more fantasy of erotic appetite. They speak of the memory of Liberty and the object of their desire is the franchise.

Chapter 5

A body for Cleopatra

Cecil B. de Mille produced his Hollywood version of Cleopatra in 1934, the year after the Vatican head was identified by Ludwig Curtius in Rome.[1] One account of Cleopatra was circulated among a mass audience, the other was available only to the specialist readers of a learned journal. Nevertheless, they are recognizably linked by a common strategy. It is a fantasy of the disrupted female body that governs both narratives. This fragmentation takes a specific and ritualized shape. It also involves substitution. Like the head of the medusa, the head of Cleopatra is made to stand in for the form of the female genital. What is at stake in representing Cleopatra in the 1930s is genital difference. The recognition of difference between the bodies of men and women provided the initial structure from which social organization was produced. It was by reference to this difference that political authority within communities was assigned. Internalized, the recognition of this difference as paramount served to structure the organization of the psyche. The male member, what was appropriate to it and what did not become those who lacked it, had been the unspoken arbiter of human association until Freud and, after him, Lacan began to direct attention to the case. It is at that point, by implication, that the possibility of discussing an alternative organization arose. There was, after all, another form of genital to consider.

The cue for this new perception was the shift of power away from the phallus that took place in the early decades of this century. As the franchise was extended to women in societies located in all parts of the globe, their historical exclusion from the rights and responsibilities of citizenship was coming to an end. The unfamiliar logic which divides and reinscribes the female body to turn it into a cipher of its own genital in both the film and the learned journal is produced by this political change.

It is in the governing form of Curtius's argument that the fantasy of the fragmented body is most boldly manifest. The logic of this fantasy, rather than any ratiocination, dictates his method of procedure, as I shall show. The same logic shapes the film representation. However, when the fantasy is geared to the resources of cinema, it is elaborated and explored.

This takes the form of two set pieces. These are the highlight of the second and third reels, a carnival of desire on 'Cleopatra's love-boat' and an inferno of destruction at the battle of Actium. The masochistic pleasures these extend to spectators of either sex will be analysed towards the close of this discussion.

The relation between this fantasy and the specific historical circumstances of its production is acknowledged by both journal article and film. Curtius's text draws on the racial theories of Nazism and Fascist ideology of womanhood in making his identification of Cleopatra's head in the Vatican Museum. De Mille's film addresses the phenomenon of the American woman of the period by means of a judicious casting policy that sets the scene as firmly in contemporary New York as in the imagined past of Alexandria. Both Curtius and de Mille develop their fantasy of the dismembered female body in terms of their understanding of contemporary women's lives. Film alone, however, commands the means of engaging with contemporary women. De Mille is able to address them directly, through his film, and to act on them through the pleasure offered by the cinematic experience. His film appears to make a flattering recognition of women's economic and sexual independence, offering in its representation of Cleopatra a figure with whom satisfying identification can be made. But in the register of fantasy Cleopatra is defined by the film in terms of the mother in the unconscious, as I shall demonstrate. Women spectators were encouraged in their identification with the figure of Claudette Colbert, the star who played the part: how this was intended to be acted out in their own lives will be explained by way of conclusion.

De Mille and Curtius were not the only interpreters, between the wars, to turn to the problem of Cleopatra. This chapter will argue that the widespread renewal of interest in Cleopatra is part of an attempt to come to terms with the changing political status of women across the world. The governing role assigned to the image of the fragmented body in both the film and the journal article can also be related to that attempt. The specific form of this fragmentation, as I shall argue, aligns these images produced in the 1930s with the ancient image of the medusa. Recent work on the medusa by Neil Hertz, Catherine Gallagher, and Tobin Siebers has stressed its political and social function.[2] Hertz has shown how it was produced at a number of moments of revolutionary change in the social order in nineteenth-century France. De Mille's film and Curtius's article will be placed in relation to the differing responses made by the societies in Europe and in the United States to the disturbance brought about by the emancipation of women.

First, however, the importance and scale of the political change under way across the globe. In the account that follows, particular attention will be paid to conditions in Germany, Italy, Britain, and the United States. It is hard to overestimate the disruptive implications, freshly experienced in the decades before the Second World War, of giving women the vote. Social, cultural, and psychic organization were at stake. All used the recognition of genital difference between the sexes as an organizing principle and all were vulnerable to erosions of difference.

It is not an accident that the move to put the sexes on a more equal footing should have been accompanied by an unprecedented attempt to rethink the human body and its sexuality.[3]

The profound readjustments involved were spread over many decades and are still in process at the close of the twentieth century. It would not be till the end of the Second World War that women would be allowed to vote in France (1944), Japan (1945), Italy (1945), and China (1947), while it was later still in Egypt (1956) and Iran (1963).[4] Nevertheless, active campaigns to improve the conditions of women's lives and narrow the gap between the rights enjoyed by men and women had been pursued in all these countries since the previous century.

Throughout the later decades of the nineteenth century women had been organizing themselves to ask that the opportunities of education and employment for women should be more comparable with those available to men. It was the first move in changing the terms on which responsibility was assigned between the sexes. It did not immediately register as a demand that women should be recognized as equal members of their societies and consequently be assigned an equal share in ordering and interpreting them.[5] In most cases that conclusion was reached very much later, if at all. Nevertheless, one of the means to make it easier for women to get decently paid work and a say in things outside the home was defined. The ideology of separate spheres which had been developed in the nineteenth century to accompany the restriction of women's powers to private life was under challenge.

Civil rights were central to what was at stake. Under the law of most countries women did not have the same rights as men.[6] They were not recognized as full citizens. In claiming the vote women set out to win the right to act as responsible members of a democracy. Having the vote and having access to an administrative role in society were closely connected. In Britain it was made unlawful to bar women from public office or civil or judicial posts in 1919, the year after women over 30 got the vote. In many countries the franchise was only gradually extended to women: initially they were allowed to vote only in municipal or other local elections.[7] Winning the right to vote on equal terms with men, when it came, meant that an important symbolic obstacle had been overcome: the disparity which confirmed women as creatures excluded from the process of decision-making and public responsibility was removed.

In 1934, when de Mille's *Cleopatra* was made, this disparity was no longer uniformly maintained. Some women had had the right to vote in national elections since before the First World War: since 1893 in New

Zealand, 1902 in Australia, 1906 in Finland, and 1913 in Norway. But the great wave of enfranchisement fell between the two world wars. In this period women from twenty-eight more countries acquired the right to vote on equal terms with men. These included Soviet Russia and the Netherlands (1917); Canada (1918); Germany, Austria, Poland, and Czechoslovakia (1919); the United States and Hungary (1920); Burma and Ireland (1922); Mongolia (1924); Britain (1928 – between 1918 and 1928 only women over 30 had a right to vote); Ecuador (1929); South Africa (1930); Spain (1931); Brazil, Uruguay, and Thailand (1932). Turkey, Sri Lanka, and Cuba enfranchised women in 1934.[8] The whole North American continent, Soviet Russia, Oceania, and the Baltic, together with a number of European and South American states, had moved to abolish the most important symbol of difference between the sexes in use in civic life.

The paid work done by women in all levels of society was increasingly hard to ignore and this too served to close the gulf between the sexes. When the suffrage campaigns in Britain and America took to the streets, one of their strategies had been to elicit recognition for the paid labour performed by women in the work-force. Lisa Tickner has written the history of this concerted attempt by women to move into the public space and take responsibility in their own persons for showing what they were and what they wanted. This involved a direct challenge both to notions of proper behaviour and to the models by which women were popularly represented. In *The Spectacle of Women* she describes how women organized together in a sequence of public demonstrations and processions between 1907 and 1913 to create new signs and put them into circulation in the streets of the capital city.[9] It was an attempt to displace the old system of signing sexual difference by which they had previously been defined.

To do this they had to commit themselves to transgressing powerful codes which dictated the terms of behaviour for women, enjoining reticence and unobtrusiveness in the public zone for those of the middle and upper classes. They assembled from all over Britain and marched together, so that their numbers could not be disputed. They dressed in symbolic colours to reinforce the visible meaning of their procession. Banners in brilliant designs and striking colours, memorable works in themselves, displayed new emblems of their cause. Nearly a thousand of these were carried in the march of 13 June 1908.[10] In the pageant of Women's Trades and Professions, the following year, they specifically took up the challenge of representing themselves as workers. A thousand women from ninety different occupations walked in groups, carrying emblems of their occupation which had been specially designed for the occasion. This time they were dressed for work. The nurses were in uniform, the pit-brow women wore shawls over their head, charwomen carried buckets, graduates were in academic dress.[11] Women elected to be seen and defined in terms of their paid labour, by which they took a full adult's part in society.

The suffrage campaign in the United States learned from its British counterpart to emphasize women's participation in the labour force.[12] Alice Paul, leader of the American movement after 1915, had spent the years 1907–12 in Britain, when she was sufficiently prominent in the British campaign to be arrested six times and also forcibly fed as a hunger-striker. When she returned to America in 1912, she was put in charge of organizing a massive demonstration, planned to take place on the day before Woodrow Wilson's inauguration as president. The ten thousand women her organization put on the streets, with their banners and bands and costumes made by the suppliers to the Manhattan Opera Company, made the suffrage register as an issue in America as never before. After that parades, including contingents of professional women, followed in other cities.

German women had not embarked on the same public contesting of established stereotypes of womanly nature and behaviour in the years before they were allowed the vote. They voted for the first time in 1919, when, following their country's defeat in the First World War, a Socialist government committed itself to a programme of reforms. Votes for women was only one element in a liberal package. It did not come in answer to organized agitation by a significant body of women acting on their own behalf. This meant that women's exercise of the franchise was not accompanied by or prepared for by any troubling of established patterns of representing 'womanhood' and so that notion remained unchallenged. It also followed that the dislocating force of the change was not fully expressed and remained substantially unexplored. Terms for showing women as sharing in the labour-market and relating that to their exercise of political rights were not developed.

Claudia Koonz argues that German women seem to have been at a loss for a group identity once they were no longer united in their exclusion from public life.[13] Before 1914 their demand for the vote had often, though not always, been made on the ground that women had a natural right to it as equal members of the human race with men. During the twenties, increasing numbers of activists based their claims for women on a notion of their special 'womanly' contribution as guardians of the home and family. The 'difference', apparently erased when women were given the vote, was reinstated through an intense valorization of 'womanliness' and an emphasis on biological destiny. At the same period Hitler was outlining his vision of the place of women in a Nazi state: citizenship would be the reward of their monogamous heterosexual commitment and would come to them on marriage. That is, it would be tied to their conformity to a particular signing of sexual difference. More than one vote, Goebbels proposed in 1926, should be permitted to women who had borne many children.[14] When the Nazis came to power after 1933, women were systematically excluded from higher education and public life.[15] As the work of signing sexual difference was taken up elsewhere, the value of the vote, in the hands of women, dwindled. They retained the vote but it no longer promised to confer the rights of a citizen, which were defined otherwise and elsewhere and belonged to men alone.

The same move to focus on the body and to represent women not as citizens themselves but as wives and mothers of citizens was made under Mussolini, even though Italian women did not have the vote until after the Second World War. Maria-Antoinetta Macciocchi has analysed this campaign.[16] Mussolini made a theatre of the streets to reach right into the social formation with his images of womanhood. Women were assigned a group identity and a role in the public ritual of Fascism. But this role confirmed that for women membership of the social formation did not come directly but was extended through their relationship to men. In 1935 women who had surrendered their wedding-rings to the war effort in answer to an appeal were recompensed, in public ceremonies all over Italy, by iron replacements. These did better than restore the lost badge of wifehood: they were described as the pledge of a new marriage to Mussolini himself. It was women who had lost men, bereaved women, who were organized into squads of mourners, clothed in a uniform black, to appear on public occasions. Women were admitted to the public scene as the sign of absent men. As Mussolini demonstrated, the mechanisms of theatre, spectacle, and identification could be used to reinforce a socially constructed difference between the sexes as readily as they could to undermine it. Predictably, this reinforcement extended to the labour-market. Under Fascism women's wages dropped by 50 per cent.

The figure of Cleopatra had a specific force in this moment. In it political power and female sexuality were securely combined and above all publicly visible. It gave direct representation to the new political order, where the phallus was no longer the exclusive sign of political power. It had been contended both in nineteenth-century Paris and in Edwardian London that women who got or even wanted the vote would lose their sexual identity.[17] Neither sexual drive nor authority was in doubt in the figure of Cleopatra.[18] The figure attracted frequent reworkings, both in Europe and America, an interest that gained momentum in the twenties and went on to peak in the following decade. By the 1930s there was an international traffic in the image of Cleopatra, reciprocal and mutually reinforcing: at least five books about her, two written in French and three in German, were translated into English and the de Mille film was sent out from Hollywood to a world-wide audience. Two of these translations were specially republished in the States for the release of this film.[19] Though most of the works produced were intended for a popular market, influential redefinitions of the figure of Cleopatra also took place in academic publication at the period. One of the most famous judgements of modern times on Cleopatra was published in the *Cambridge Ancient History* in 1934, when W.W. Tarn concluded his account with the dictum: 'For Rome, who had never condescended to fear any nation or people, did in her time fear two human beings; one was Hannibal, and the other was a woman.'[20] It is a concession which permits Cleopatra stature at the cost of her individuality: she is defined, not by her name, but by her genital difference. It also associates that difference with fear: Tarn produces his own miniature medusa. This is the fantasy that shaped the accounts of Cleopatra produced by Curtius and by de Mille. It structured the most graphic of all the contemporary redefinitions by scholars, that is the claim by Ludwig Curtius to have identified a marble head of Cleopatra herself.

The terms in which this claim is made, his methodology, and his narrative strategy call attention to themselves. Supported as it is by impeccable researches and published in a prestigious journal, Curtius's argument is articulated by a tacit violence. It is this violence that I shall explore first before going on to discuss the meaning and function of the medusa image which it suggests. Curtius's article deals in photographs of stone figures. Inert and apparently distanced from the experience of live bodies, they are nevertheless used to produce a gratuitous imagery of dismemberment. The strategies at work and the economy they serve can be recognized as those that also produce the classical figure of the medusa.

Ludwig Curtius was a German art historian who had lived in Rome for many years when he made his 'discovery' of Cleopatra's head (Plate 1.1). It was published in the proceedings of the German Archaeological Institute of Rome in 1933, since when it has been repeatedly quoted as a source for the iconography of Cleopatra. Curtius was writing in the context of a Fascism whose determination to limit the public role of women has already been sketched. The account of the Cleopatra head takes up only half of his argument, pp. 182–92. The latter part, pp. 192–243, is devoted to a separate iconographic problem, concerning the representation of a man, M. Vipsanius Agrippa. The journal readership Curtius was addressing would recognize in the name of M. Vipsanius Agrippa the man who had commanded the Roman fleet at Actium; thanks to his skill, as the reference books have it, Cleopatra was disastrously and finally defeated. Curtius frames his iconographic argument within a reminder of Cleopatra's subordination and conquest. It is the first indication of a rhetorical strategy that is highly politicized.

Curtius was claiming to deal in matters of objective information. His material was drawn from the evidence of coin portraits; his methodology consisted of painstaking comparison of detail between the marble head he had designated as a portrait of Cleopatra and the images on a range of coins recorded in catalogues and reference works of the numismatists. Such an account of scholarly practice, however, does no justice to the

bold and arbitrary organization of his argument. Neither does it acknowledge the role allotted to overt fantasy or to the more covert endorsement
of Nazi ideologies of race and gender.

Curtius articulates his argument in a sequence of separation and substitution. Starting with the statue of a female figure then on view in the
Vatican's *Sala informa di Croce*, he proceeds to divide the head from the
body. They did not belong together, he argues, partly on the grounds
that they were made from different kinds of marble but presumably, in
view of the way his argument develops, also on the ground that nothing
in the appearance of a simple *Peplosfigur*, or woman in a peplos, would
support the identification with a ruler. To put it another way, an ordinary
woman's body would not be marked by the sign of authority in the way
that the head was by wearing the diadem. So Curtius makes his argument
about Cleopatra on the basis of a head that he has personally divided
from the body he found it joined to.

The significance of this only becomes apparent when, towards the close
of his account, he begins to speculate about what the authentic or original
body that the head went with in the first place would have been like. It
is at this point that a process that can be recognized as the second phase
of figuring the medusa began. By it the head is transformed into the sign
of the genital. This is how it was achieved: Curtius had already used three
photographs, of the head and two coins, to support his identification; now
he added three more, to suggest possible alternative body forms to go
with the marble head. These forms were all still fragmentary, multiplying
the images of the female body in a special kind of dismemberment: that
is, where the head and the genital, divided from each other, have been
defined as distinct and the genital function has then been used to obliterate
the functions of the head. This particular fragmentation produces an
image from which the capacity for thought, perception, cognition, and
judgement, the powers that might equip a citizen to take part in the work
of democracy, have been wiped in order to represent the woman as a
birth canal. Individual identity as represented in the face is suppressed by
the same token. By implication all cunts are the same.

The first of the new body forms advanced in the article was a terracotta
fragment of a woman, to the waist, with a winged child on her shoulder
(Plate 5.1). The other two show back and front views of a single object,
a draped female figure, this one headless, but also with a child on its
shoulder (Plate 5.2). This is labelled as a statuette of Aphrodite. The
association of this material with the marble head he was discussing was
wholly speculative, as his text makes plain. It is not, however, merely a
scholarly whim but a specific logic of fantasy that gives rise to this series
of visualizations. The eccentric sequence of division and substitution that
betrays the play of this fantasy is not the only trace it leaves. Elements
of it are elaborated and explored by Curtius himself, when he reminds

Plate 5.1 Fragment of a terracotta statuette, reproduced from 'Ikonographische Beiträge', Curtius, 1933.

Plate 5.2 Statuette of Aphrodite, reproduced from 'Ikonographische Beiträge', Curtius, 1933.

his readers that Julius Caesar had a gold statue of Cleopatra placed in the temple of Venus Genetrix. That is why he has illustrated his article with a classical representation of Venus/Aphrodite with Cupid/Eros. Isn't it likely, he asks in conclusion, that Cleopatra would have been represented as Aphrodite with Caesarion as Eros, and that the Vatican 'portrait' – identified by himself in the course of the article – is a copy of that original?

He has removed the body of an ordinary woman and succeeded in substituting for it a body uniquely characterized as the form of female sexuality. The classical fantasy of Venus Genetrix condenses the erotic and the generative function of the female genital: *The Oxford Companion to Classical Literature*, published in 1937, explains that under the title of Genetrix the Roman goddess of love was recognized as the mother of the Roman people and in particular as the protectress of the Julian house.[21] In Curtius the reproductive is emphasized over the erotic, however. The terracotta half-figure shows the woman's head, her breasts, and the child brought into juxtaposition: maternity alone is represented. In the case of the larger fragment, the headless statuette of Aphrodite, though the name indicates the possibility of sexual pleasure, the lower body is doubly draped. This carefully defined female sexuality, however, is only licensed to appear in his essay because he has invented a speculative relation between it and his original matter, the marble head. It is this head, now invested with the specific sexuality Curtius has invoked, that remains the subject of his essay and the reference point of his argument. It is as an article about 'the Vatican head' that the piece will enter the literature of the subject.

I have argued that the narrative strategy of this work, the separation of head from torso, followed by the inscription of genitality on to the head, marks it as a medusa figure. This implies that the text is orchestrated by the operation of the same drives that call into being the classical medusa. It is time now to consider what those drives might be and the cultural force of the image, particularly in the 1930s. The medusa is an image with a long history, used as an amulet or talisman in classical antiquity and recurring in Western art. It shows the head of a woman, the mouth usually open, the hair often represented in the form of snakes. Stories from antiquity that are told to account for this image centre on the execution of a monster who had at the same time something in common with ordinary women. Medusa alone of her sisters, the Gorgons, was mortal and could therefore be killed. She was very dangerous but she was also vulnerable. Her head, with its snaky locks, was too terrible to look at directly, however, so the story goes, and would turn the beholder to stone. It could only be safely viewed reflected in another object. She was put to death by Perseus, who made sure as he did so only to look at her reflection in the polished surface of his shield. In some later accounts he used the mirror image itself to kill her. In all versions, she was then decapitated and her head used by Perseus to petrify his own enemies.[22] The power of the look has no more authoritative myth.

It was in continental Europe, between the two world wars, that it was first suggested that the medusa's head was an image of the female genital. Freud is usually credited with the idea, though his own paper on the topic, 'Medusa's head', written while he was still living in Vienna in 1922, was not published until after his death.[23] Another analyst, the Hungarian Sándor Ferenczi based in Budapest, was the first publicly to compare the head with the female genital, in a paper published in 1923.[24]

This identification has been widely accepted. However, it was formed in the same cultural turbulence that produced the de Mille film and the Curtius article: Austrian women had got the vote in 1919, Hungarian women in 1920. The psychoanalytic account of genital difference is no less politicized than the film and the article: Freud was not able to allow the vagina to be registered as simple difference and leave open the question of why it should inspire such fear. In his account, difference becomes the sign of inferiority. Notoriously, he explained the fear inspired by the sight of the vagina as the fear of the image of castration. When he refers in print for the first time to Ferenczi's theory, in his own 1923 paper, 'The infantile genital organisation', it is to equate the 'horror' of the symbol with its lack of a penis; by the time of his second and final written reference, in 'New introductory lectures', the medusa's head is 'traced back to the . . . *motif* of fright at castration'.[25]

Charles Bernheimer has recently argued that Freud's invention of the castration theory is itself a defence against the simple anxiety of sexual difference.[26] In a detailed rereading of Freud's argument associating the image of the vagina with the threat of castration, Bernheimer exposes its failures of logic and its internal contradictions. Castration, Bernheimer argues, is a construct, created to justify the male perception of anatomical difference as 'uncanny and intolerable' in Freud's words. Bernheimer sees Freud's theory as an elaborate unconscious attempt to distract attention from the banal truth of anatomical difference. 'To consider women as castrated men is the most effective defence of the fetishist, whose fundamental fear is that women are intolerably, uncannily other.'[27] As a construct, castration has the further value that it creates a hierarchy out of difference. It legitimizes the social and cultural subordination of women by defining their difference as lack.

There are two points that I would like to take up and emphasize at this juncture: Bernheimer's stress on the banality of difference and Freud's perception of the female body as 'uncanny'. They are sharply polarized accounts of the same phenomenon. From Freud's perspective the bodies of ordinary women are freakish, in so far as they fail to resemble his own. As he had written in a letter to his fiancée, Martha Bernays, 'I always find it uncanny when I can't understand someone in terms of myself.'[28] If the ancient account of the medusa implied that the figure might be aligned with the run of mortal women, Freud's account makes no bones about claiming that ordinary women's bodies are monstrous. At that moment a new means was at hand to reach these women directly and confront them with their bodies – in the form of cinema. The *Cleopatra* film of 1934 attempted to locate women spectators within a fantasy of the female body defined specifically as maternal and charged with danger.

Representation of the female genital as an object of horror has a recognized function in public life. Recent studies of the occurrence of the medusa symbol have argued that it has been directly geared to the maintenance of social organization. Neil Hertz, Catherine Gallagher, and Tobin Siebers, writing from his very different perspective, have emphasized its political force and its association with violence in the community. Neil Hertz has shown that the symbol was produced in response to the violence of revolutionary change, by means of examples from the iconography of the French Revolution and of later decades in French history. In these cases it did not necessarily appear as a straight account of the classical figure but acted rather as a constituting and shaping force. The form of the medusa could govern the representation of the severed head of Louis XVI or an anecdote from the barricades of 1848. That is, reference through form or by implication to the female genital dominated these representations.

As Hertz sees it, fantasies of the vagina were to be understood in relation to political disequilibrium: they are found in political contexts in nineteenth-century France in conditions when it was feared that patriarchal social organization itself, with its relations of power and property, was under threat. In the early twentieth century such a threat became a worldwide issue, as the assignation of power between men and women entered into transformation. It was not a threat within a single national group but a challenge to the common dispensation of human affairs. I want to suggest that the representation of Cleopatra in Curtius and de Mille displays the same fascination with the vagina found in the nineteenth-century examples quoted by Hertz and that the film and the article are inherently political texts.

Catherine Gallagher explains the fascination with the vagina noted by Hertz in terms of social understanding rather than the physiologically grounded anxieties of individual males. She sees the fascination as a recognition of the vagina's inalienable role in the transmission of the social. Because the female genital gives birth, the reproduction of the social is ultimately dependent on it. Access to the name of the father, on which the transmission of power and property depends, is itself dependent on the reliability of the woman.[29] If the woman refused control and became completely independent, refusing the terms of the social, its trans-mission could no longer be maintained.

To say that the representation of the Cleopatras in Curtius's article and de Mille's film is governed by the image of the medusa is not to claim any obvious identity between them. What they have in common and are defined by is a series of moves which involve separating the head from the body and then using the head to represent the genital. In both article and film the woman's body is restructured in representation to emphasize the symbolization of the vagina. That Curtius brings this about while remaining within conventional disciplines has already been established.

It remains to show how his argument positions itself in relation to the question of contemporary women, before going on to locate the vagina in the Hollywood version.

The article in which Curtius produces Cleopatra bears vivid traces of a specific historical moment. The writing makes a number of assumptions about women and about race in order to argue the case for his identifi-cation of the marble head. These are not incidental but are made to carry some weight. It is clear, for instance, that a Nazi ideology of womanhood underpins the analysis of visual evidence that Curtius is offering. In the course of a long discussion of hair-styles shown on coins he writes with admiration of the style of wearing the hair in plaits round the head, as something that 'schöne Frauen' (beautiful women) used 'bei uns' (among us, in our country too) before the fashion for short hair won through ('ehe die Mode kurzgeschnittener Haare siegte').[30] This confirms that his reflections on the image of Cleopatra are inextricably entwined with his sense of the place and value of women in his own society. A fabricated version of the national past was used to ground Nazi propaganda concern-ing the distinct roles appropriate to men and women. This involved suggesting that women should favour the rustic simplicity implied by braids. Posters and photographs featured the style and prominent Nazi women wore it. Gertrud Scholz-Klink, chief of the Women's Bureau under Hitler, is shown wearing her hair in braids round her head on the cover of *Mutter und Volk*, the magazine for Nazi women.[31]

Nazi propagandists like Hans F.K. Günther were willing to make use of the eighteenth-century science of physiognomy to trace 'the mental characteristics of different races'.[32] Curtius was prepared to adopt the same science to 'read' the personality of Cleopatra, 'this great paramour', from the evidence of 'her' marble portrait. The attempt centres on discovering the traces of an independent sexuality, which is incidentally debased by hints about the incestuous practices of the Ptolemies, in the stone face. The strain of reading the features in accordance with this project is evident in its awkward attempts to yoke evidence and interpretation in a convincing manner.

What is perhaps most surprising is the severity of this countenance, the almost brooding reserve of this character. The wide open eye with its severe, entirely classicistic stylization gazes very knowingly yet indefinitely at the viewer . . . The slightly protruding lower part of the face with its evidently strong jaw which lies behind those glowing cheeks shows signs of a quite tenacious stubbornness. However, probably as a result of courtly education, all emotions are held in check and the sensuality of one later reviled as a whore is at most to be seen in the fleshy cheek and the full, pouting lower lip. The forehead is broad and high, rising steeply and positioned far forward in the face so that the eyes are deep-set and the nose protrudes at a fairly sharp angle; these too are the forms of a great, stubborn and artful intelligence.

(Vielleicht ist die Herbheit dieses Antlitzes die grösste Überaschung, die beinahe düstere Verschlossenheit dieses Charakters. Das weitgeöffnete Auge mit seiner strengen, durchaus klassizistischen Stilisierung blickt sehr wissend unbestimmt auf den Beschauer . . . Das etwas vorgeschobene Untergesicht mit gewiss sehr starken Kinnladen hinter den blühenden Wangen hat seinen besonderen zähen Eigensinn. Aber offenbar durch höfische Erziehung sind alle Affekte verhalten, und die Sinnlichkeit der später so oft als Dirne Geschmähten ist höchstens der fleischigen Wange und der vollen vorgeschobenen Unterlippe abzulesen. Die Stirne ist breit und hoch, steigt steil aufwärts und sitzt in dem Gesicht weit vorne, so dass das Auge tief liegt und die Nase in ziemlich scharfem Winkel ansetzt auch dies Formen grosser, eigensinniger und verschlagener Intelligenz.)[33]

He could even make out a possible 'touch of something negroid' in her inheritance 'that might explain the gloom of her countenance' ('In dem Gesicht scheint mir ein leise negroider Einschlag von irgendeiner lagidischen Nebenfrau her mitzuschwingen, der veilleicht die Düsterkeit der Physiognomie mitbestimmt').[34] The text Curtius wrote, like the images he put together, constitutes a fantasy restructuring of the woman's body: the head becomes the witness of genitality here too. But the textual fantasy is produced in its detail by the specific constraints of Fascist and Nazi ideologies.

That journal article was composed for a predominantly male readership of specialist academics: Cecil B. de Mille's film version of Cleopatra, though it too is structured by the fragmentation of the female body, addressed itself with particular urgency to ordinary women. The mechanisms of identification that cinematic technology engages were knowingly exploited in the film's enterprise of bringing the historic figure into flattering alignment with the women of its own day. Exploring this will involve taking stock of the material conditions in which Cleopatra was made and circulated as a Hollywood film in the 1930s: it also involves reflecting in detail on the imagery produced in the film. How were women spectators encouraged to align themselves with Cleopatra and how did that identification carry over into their lives outside the cinema? These are the considerations that will govern the discussion of *Cleopatra* that takes up the remainder of this essay.

De Mille already had sixty movies behind him when he came to make *Cleopatra*. Though he is now popularly considered as a more or less cynical producer of spectaculars with big box-office appeal, he was a significant innovator in the development of the cinematic techniques employed in classical Hollywood style. He had an exceptional grasp of the medium and a will to extend and intensify its hold over an audience. One way was through the use of low-key lighting to shape and give meaning to the shot while confirming the narrative effect. 'Lasky light-ing', as it came to be called, had been pioneered by de Mille at the Lasky studio in 1915, before being generally adopted in preference to the diffuse lighting that had been commonly used before. Contemporaries recognized that it brought 'a new dramatic force' into cinema. De Mille also developed his own production method in the 1920s, using multiple-camera shooting. Reports of how this worked vary but it appears that he set up one camera at a long shot, a second one right next to it with a longer focal-depth lens for a close-up, and several other cameras at angles for more close-ups and two-shots. The various shots would be edited together for the final version. Though the emphasis on varying depths of shot, a matter of central importance in the filming of *Cleopatra* as will be seen, was initially prompted by economic pressures, it indicates the technical assurance that gave de Mille such power over his audience. It should also be noted that Claudette Colbert was herself highly skilled in film technique, particularly questions of lighting. She supervised her own filmic presentation in detail, even to the point of having sets designed to permit her entrances from the side that flattered her. She was no pawn but a collaborator in producing an image of Cleopatra to seduce both men and women.[35]

The 1934 film was designed for viewing by a mixed audience, it is true, but its casting of Claudette Colbert in the title role and the sale of goods promoted by the film invited women in the audience to see and equip themselves as Cleopatra, while men were to recognize the identifi-cation too. There was only tentative encouragement for men to identify with Antony: they could buy a 'Chukka' shirt, as sported by the star who played him, Henry Wilcoxon.[36]

First, the matter of circulation. De Mille's Cleopatra is proposed as Everywoman, and not just inside America. The figure was created for an international market. Hollywood films linked communities world-wide at a democratic level quite independent of formalized association. As the film audience, societies across the globe were brought together in contemplation of Hollywood-produced fantasy. In the early thirties about half of all the cinema seats in the world were in America but a third of the profits from films came from overseas sales.[37] Hollywood studios set up offices and film exchanges overseas to secure the circulation of their own products. The history of Paramount, the studio that produced *Cleopatra*, is not unusual. As early as 1917 they had opened an office in Australia. In January 1922, having already arranged for the distribution of their products in a number of South American countries, they added six more. Central America and the Caribbean were already covered; now Mexico was also included. At the end of the year Paramount opened exchanges in the French provinces and new branches in Switzerland, Brussels, Cairo, Algiers, and Constantinople. Agents for Scandinavia were signed. At the beginning of 1925 they had up to forty-five international exchanges and agents, including new exchanges opened that year in Athens, Sofia, and Constantinople. That June Paramount SA was formed to serve most of South America except Brazil, with offices in Chile, Santiago, and Buenos Aires.[38] In principle, the distribution of Hollywood films was wide enough to cover any country in which women were campaigning, with or without success, for a share of work and public responsibility.

In Europe at least resistance to this hegemony was formalized. Attempts were made, in the first place in order to protect the home industry, to impose quota systems.[39] American films were a genuine threat to the native industries but there were other reasons to wish to limit their exposure.[40] They created desire: a yearning for motor cars and refrigerators, soft furnishings and soft drinks that could only be satisfied by American products and branded goods. Trade followed the films, as the American government recognized.[41] No less important was the colonization process to which audiences were subject: in 1926 it could already be recognized that 'American producers are now actively "Americanising" England, her dominions and colonies, and all of Europe.'[42] Not just frocks and sofas but attitudes, beliefs, and values were touched with magic by the way they were presented on screen. This included the understanding of the relation between women and political authority promoted in *Cleopatra* and its grounding in anatomical difference.

Attention has already been drawn to the importance of casting in this film: it established one of the modes in which the audience was to view the story, as a tale of modern times in fancy dress. At first sight it might have seemed that Mae West would have offered just the screen persona to embody an account of Cleopatra developed for a mass audience. In 1933 she had already appeared in a number of films and was established in the minds of audiences as a figure of buoyant female sexuality on the make. Instead, de Mille chose Claudette Colbert and, to support her, Henry Wilcoxon and Warren William. Wilcoxon was a newcomer, from

Britain, as his accent made very clear: sound had only come to films at the end of the previous decade and its imprint was still sharp.[43] Warren William was famous for playing sophisticated New Yorkers. Each brought an inescapable identity into the film and defined it as a comedy of contemporary manners, plus true love.

De Mille was clear from the outset, so the story goes, that Colbert was the one to play Cleopatra. In view of the fact that Everson, her most enthusiastic biographer, asserts that Colbert was never at ease in costume pictures, that is, in period dress, if this reported intuition was authentic it was also surprising. What Colbert excelled in was the presentation of lively, witty, contemporary women, in control of their lives. Immediately before *Cleopatra* she had made *It Happened One Night*, which won five Academy Awards and was the most celebrated Hollywood film of 1934. It is with this film, according to Stanley Cavell, that there begins a series of Hollywood explorations of what he has defined as the comedy of remarriage, whose heroine is the married woman.[44] In these too, the difference between the sexes was being re-examined, mainly in terms of questioning gendered behaviour by showing sassy women and sensitive men. Cavell argues, however, that in *It Happened One Night*, as in other examples of the genre, the more radical question of 'whether . . . we know how to think satisfactorily about the difference between male and female' is an essential feature.[45] Nevertheless, in these films the question is always posed within the terms of heterosexual marriage. Because it was not posed outside those terms, and the issue of power relations between the sexes was elided, no very disruptive moves were made by Cavell's comedies. In contrast, de Mille moved into a confrontational engagement with sexual difference when he proposed to tell the story of Cleopatra.

The presentation of Cleopatra's body was crucial. Colbert's sexuality, though undeniable, was not disturbing. In many ways, her biographer declares, Colbert offered a model of all that was 'tasteful and attractive' in contemporary female sexuality. She loved to wear make-up and, unlike other stars, was uneasy without it: a point whose significance will emerge later. Her body did not overwhelm by its opulence but was trim and neat. She conformed, in fact, to the demands of contemporary fashion in women's looks, without exceeding them. Her body bore the signs of discipline for the sake of health in its sporting slimness.[46] This physique was emphasized by the costumes, some of them unusually scanty for such a famous star, that Colbert was called upon to wear in *Cleopatra*.[47] All reference to the fullness or heaviness routinely developed in the bodies of mature women was excluded. It was a version of the feminine which, unlike the version produced by Curtius, specifically denied the maternal, even by association. Elegant, self-possessed, and able to stand up for herself, the screen persona of Claudette Colbert could be closely identified with the ideal companion and wife of the 1930s: but not, not on any account, with the mother.

As defined by Colbert, Cleopatra's personal sexuality was not a threat but an affirmation of the social order. This was because in the early twentieth century an active sexual appetite in women had begun to be identified with the achievement of maturity and the maintenance of health.[48] When it was noted that a lower than average proportion of the first generation of college women in the States chose to marry, it was feared that women might learn to reject marriage altogether. Such fears were behind the contemporary movement for Sex Reform, which campaigned to inform women about their sexuality and to make them able to enjoy it more freely. In fact, the notion of sexuality involved was restricted to a heterosexual desire for the husband: Cleopatra's serial monogamy, as presented by Colbert, could read as a blueprint for both personal and national welfare.

Somewhat surprisingly, then, cinema could make of Cleopatra a role model for the woman spectator. It was a possibility kept in circulation by reminding the audience of the conscious masquerade in which the actors were engaged, by keeping the stars' personalities outside the film paramount. Wilcoxon, as Antony, strides about with two large dogs on a leash, underlining his identity as the upper-class English man in a comedy of manners. Warren William, the professional New Yorker, cracks steely one-liners as Caesar: when Cleopatra urges, 'Together we could conquer the world,' he returns, 'Nice of you to include me.' Special trouble is taken to address a British audience and perhaps at the same time to invoke it, mockingly, for those of other nations. There is a taciturn retainer of giant dimensions wearing a Viking helmet and rough pelts, who admits in a grunt that he comes from 'Britain'. As Caesar goes off to bed with Cleopatra, he purrs, 'I found a flower in Britain once that was the colour of your eyes.' Such cues encouraged spectators to take pleasure in the knowledge that they were linked in an invisible international community of the film audience, sharing the language of Hollywood, tuned to its products. And adapted to its 'international' racism: when a Roman *ingénue* asks if Cleopatra is black she is greeted with peals of laughter. These cues also privileged the present moment of the film, inviting viewers to keep recognizing it as a romp of the smart set of their own day, or a costume charade put on by sophisticated contemporaries. The film's claim to represent a historical reality was carefully compromised and undercut.

The continuity between life on screen and off it was further emphasized by the elaborate publicity programme. Women were specifically invited to confirm their identification with Colbert in the film. The press-book sent out to cinema managers to orchestrate publicity for the film explained that provision had been made in advance for goods linked with *Cleopatra* to be available across the country wherever it was on show.[49] The motion picture industry had its own chain of 'Cinema Shops' where garments as seen in recent films, 'Hollywood Cinema Fashions', could be bought. These shops were subject to careful control; only one was allowed in each city and prices were deliberately kept up to foster a sense of exclusiveness.[50] 'Cleopatra' gowns and accessories had been prepared for these outlets and specially designed window-displays were available.

Special tie-ups had also been arranged with F.W. Woolworth, whose branches covered the country coast to coast, and R.H. Macy & Co. of New York. This meant that both ends of the market were covered. Those who bought at the Five and Ten Cent store would find a 'Cleopatra' perfume, 'alluring and lasting', at 10 cents. Macy's grand New York department store devoted big in-store promotions and four complete window-displays to goods associated with the film: it was the first time they had agreed to a tie-up of this kind.

Care was taken that no woman should be excluded: a permanent to give Cleopatra bangs at $10 was advertised next to aluminium end curlers at 5 cents for those who could only afford to do the job themselves (Plates 5.3 and 5.4). Both ads carried pictures of Colbert: in one she wore aluminium end curlers. Whether the goods were in fact purchased or not, an identity between the most anonymous woman in the street and Colbert/Cleopatra was proposed in shop windows and in ads right across the country. Commodities that had to be bought on a regular and repeated basis could also be a means of identifying with Cleopatra. There were tie-ups with Lux soap and with Old Gold cigarettes. In fact, the less money was available to be spent, the more intimate was the identification with Colbert and Cleopatra. It was through a remodelling of the body of what the press-book called 'feminine patrons' of the cinema – their hair, their smell, their skin, their lungs – that the ideal was to be acknowledged, however fleetingly.

Using stars to advertise merchandise was not in itself new, nor was the invitation that women should identify with them. It was not, however, merely a question of the democratization of luxury here. An imaginative levelling was taking place, to produce an equation between two different degrees of power, the power of the queen and the power of the enfranchised, voting, wage-earning woman with money to spend on herself. What was exceptional in this case was the way the film situated the star in relation to specifically political responsibility. It took, in Cleopatra, a woman who had been committed by the accident of her birth to a political role and demonstrated how that commitment might be placed in relation to the economy of a woman's life. The mass of women that were invited by the film to align themselves with her were also by implication invited to understand the economy of their own lives in similar terms. Any political rights and responsibilities they might be

Plate 5.3 Cleopatra bangs.

Plate 5.4 Aluminium end curlers as worn by Colbert in the photograph displayed towards the upper right of the image.

saddled with must be treated with caution as a threat to personal fulfilment.

In de Mille's treatment, Cleopatra's political responsibilities are presented as a source of confusion to her in the journey towards self-reali-
zation in true love. There is no question of seeing her doing any work.
Caesar is repeatedly shown with desk strewn with papers; he is sitting at
one when Cleopatra has herself brought in wrapped in a carpet, only to
find herself very much out of place in that busy office (Plate 5.5). When
she is officially queen, there are no papers for Cleopatra to read; called to
deliberate with a fellow-sovereign, Herod of Judaea, the only preparation
required is that she 'must go and dress'. Her public role is carefully
established from the start as at odds with her 'natural' desires. This
perspective is developed from the time of the opening sequences.
Although she is outraged at being stolen away from her palace by the
scheming Prime Minister, Pothinus, she is too hungry, because she has
had no breakfast, to listen to adjurations to 'think of Egypt'.

Politics are an abstraction to which a healthy woman should not give
first priority. That goes to love. And this love is a jealous god, for
Cleopatra finds that, when she tries to satisfy her political ambition at
the same time as her need for love, by her liaison with Caesar, she makes
a disastrous mistake. The great revelation that follows on the assassination
of Caesar, according to de Mille, is that Cleopatra realizes that Caesar
had never loved her. When she does find true love, in the person of
Antony, she nearly fails to appreciate it, because she has entered on the
affair as a matter of calculation, in the interests of Egyptian dominance,
and is persuaded by Herod that it would serve her country's interests
with Octavian for her to poison Antony. In fact, it is only at the moment
when Antony, stung by Octavian's challenge, determines to fight and
casts Cleopatra off, since he has 'no time for women now', that she
recognizes the authority of her feeling for him. Then she knocks over
the poisoned chalice she has prepared. But then of course it is too late:
they are both going to be destroyed by the political order in which
Cleopatra was so incapable of operating without disaster for herself and
everyone else.

The most important device by which the film constructs itself as political, however, is subliminal and operates in a register that is distinct from
comedy romance. It is matched by the opulent excess of the exotic settings
and accoutrements (Plates 5.5 and 5.6). The final part of this argument
will address the fact that the imagery of vagina and head that was earlier
identified with the medusa when Curtius brought it to bear also articulates
de Mille's film. How this works in the film and how it might be theorized
will close the account.

It is signalled at the very start of the film with a discreet image of the
vagina in the parting of stone walls. They slide apart from each other,

Plate 5.5 De Mille, *Cleopatra*: Colbert unrolled in Caesar's office.

Plate 5.6 De Mille, *Cleopatra*: blazing hoops in the carnival of desire.

opening to reveal the location of the film as 'the place between', the site of birth as Jungian terminology names it. The camera looks into and through this gap to discover the action of the film. One of the first scenes takes place in the empty desert and is located only by the proximity of a stone head standing isolated among the sand. The most important images of head and vagina occur at spectacular climaxes, the large-scale set pieces in the second and third reels, the cabaret and the battle. The finale of the cabaret staged by Cleopatra for Antony consists of three blazing hoops, held aloft while girls dressed as leopards tumble through them. By these the genital is mimed both as form – the flaming circles reproduce the fringed circle of the classical medusa – and as generative passage. It is specifically offered as a spectacle both for Antony and for the cinema audience. This is followed and completed in the third reel by the presentation of Cleopatra's head: this looms over the chaotic scenes of bodily damage in the final battle. This is a sight for the audience only.

The form of the medusa, the sign of genital difference, is used here as a means of identifying a scapegoat and assigning blame. It goes with making Cleopatra, and beyond her the enfranchised women in the audience with whom she is so closely identified, responsible for the disaster and dissolution that overtake Antony and other male bodies in the final reel. Their responsibility may extend even beyond this to the warfare that already threatened Europe in 1933, the year that Germany had rearmed. (De Mille's shots of Roman soldiers marching diagonally across the screen match and suggest contemporary newsreels.) The modish figure cut by Colbert earlier in the film gives way in this presentation to an image of unambiguous danger, a source of threat to be eliminated. When Cleopatra kills herself at the end of the film that demand is satisfied. It is not simply as a lover that she is seen to die but as a woman whose anomalous power undermines the social fabric.

The part played by the vision of the medusa in this economy is illumined by the work of Tobin Siebers, in his study of fascination.[51] Like Hertz and Gallagher, though working in his case transhistorically, Siebers understands the medusa as a term in social organization. Siebers starts by identifying it with its early use in antiquity as an amulet against the evil eye. He goes on to explore it as a sign of the attempt to control and channel the violence of envy within the community, which is particularly associated with the act of looking. The enterprise, as he argues, involves the social creation of difference, that is the creation of 'outcasts', 'outsiders', or 'scapegoats' that can be blamed for misfortunes and expelled in the interests of group cohesion. He concludes that the likely victim of this mechanism is 'a citizen who has become strange in the eyes of the community . . . He may be someone who has moved into the community and only recently joined it as a citizen.'[52] Siebers associates the form of the medusa and its occurrence with the regulation of access to formalized association.

The difference which must be identified before exclusion can take place has to be created out of what is essentially similar, however. It requires work. This account is helpful in explaining the redefinition of Cleopatra that takes place in the latter part of the film, once she has ceased to be presented as a potential wife for Caesar. From the time when Cleopatra gets Antony on her barge, the work of creating difference and locating it in Cleopatra can be seen in process. The narrative defines her as a witch, a form of designated outcast, while the imagery insists on genital difference. The difference which requires exclusion is here made identical with genital difference.

In line with Bernheimer's argument that 'sexual difference remains a focus of fantasmatic elaboration in the unconscious', it is around the representation of this difference that the register of fantasy becomes most evidently engaged in de Mille's film.[53] When Cleopatra lures Antony into boarding her barge and regales him there with her show of sophisticated pleasures, she is aligned with the witch who seduces children with elaborate delights only to trap and consume them in the end. What she shows him there is geared both to the adult and the child, a parade of polymorphous sexuality, where cruelty and greed figure as well as the pleasurable loss of differentiation. Whips, pearls, a real bull, and languid 'mermaids' figure multiple forms of desire. It is at this point that the sign of the vagina is raised, in the form of the leopard-girls' hoops: it is offered as the sign of difference and danger. Once Antony is fully in Cleopatra's power, the play on his status as both (feminized) child and adult continues. Like the young Cleopatra at the start of the film he is told to 'run along' by busy, socially engaged elders. The figuring of Cleopatra as witch is completed by her bid to poison Antony. The sequence of entrapment and attempted destruction has now been acted out in full and Antony appears to resume an active adult capacity.

The description of Antony, and by implication other men, as child in relation to Cleopatra is never entirely abandoned, however, and this understanding qualifies the battle scenes towards the film's close. Early in the film Caesar had been observed trying out model battering-rams and other war toys: now full-scale versions are seen in operation, flinging fiery shots and battering walls. Male bodies are hurled together, battered, pierced, transfixed. The fantasy of desire in the middle reel of the film is replaced by a fantasy of bodily damage. A fallen soldier sees the spiked wheel roll towards him: we glimpse him borne aloft on it as it revolves. Form itself gives way. Ships flame from stem to stern, break open like flowers under the water-line, scattering oars like twigs. A hand in the water grasps at a floating timber and slides off as the invisible body sinks into the depths. Over this disintegration looms the enigmatic face of

Cleopatra. A previous shot of her driving, alert, coiffed, and black-cloaked, into the fray first presented her at the battle as participant: it is as muse, signed not as royal but merely as female, by her long unbound hair, that she is held responsible for it.

It remains to consider how this fragmented representation was engaged by the film audience. What unconscious pleasures were solicited and satisfied by the spectator positions offered to men and to women by this focus on anatomical difference? Gaylyn Studlar has recently proposed that Deleuze's work on masochism offers a means to think through the representation in cinematic display of the powerful maternal body.[54] Deleuze, as she claims,

> regards masochism as an oral stage phenomenon in which the subject's sexuality is fixated at an infantile (i.e. pre-genital and therefore perverse) level . . . The masochist does not desire to despoil or destroy the woman, but to idealise her, to submit to her and to be punished by her so that the father (in himself) may be symbolically punished and denied. The unconscious fantasy underlying this masochistic disavowal of the father is the wish for a re-symbiosis with and fantastical rebirth from the powerful pre-Oedipal mother that will result in the 'new sexless man' who owes nothing to the father and phallic sexuality.[55]

There is, however, ambivalence towards the figure of this powerful mother, a fear of being overwhelmed which creates a tension between the pleasures of looking at the woman from a distance and of sinking into her in symbiotic identification.

There is a very close fit between this outline and the way Cleopatra is represented, seducing and dominating Antony on her barge. The play between a remote and distanced view and surrender to an abandoned oral intimacy is striking. For that reason I shall examine the sequence in detail. As he steps on to the barge, with the two mastiffs which accompany him throughout the film, he enters an enclosed world dedicated as the site of desire. Way ahead of him, as he gazes down through the exaggerated vista of banked oars, reclines the person of Cleopatra, beneath gently moving fans of ostrich-feathers. She is prepared, however, not only to entice but to confuse him: her first move is charmingly to admit to her own strategy. This destabilizes Antony's firm sense of antagonism and difference from her. By her far from artless confidence she has obliged him momentarily to share the position she has adopted for herself. Then she reflects his quandary back to him, offering herself as a mirror: 'If you could see your face, you'd know I'd have more chance with a stone wall.' In fact, he has already been stirred to giving signs of a reluctant, almost shamefaced, pleasure in the first spectacle she has called up for his entertainment. Pretending to be unaware of his incipient excitement, she repeats her act of spurious mirroring. Tucking a rose inside his helmet,

Cleopatra proposes they exchange identities, ostensibly so that he can see her guy his obdurate hostility. 'Do I look like that?' he exclaims. Of course he does not. She does not mirror his arousal. And she does not mirror his masculinity, already compromised by the rose in anticipation of what is to come.[56] By being taken back through the stage of misrecognition of the self, going backwards through the looking-glass, Antony is losing his grip on the post-Oedipal male identity he brought with him on to the barge. He is to find himself in the world of perverse and polymorphous sexuality, the imaginary world of undifferentiated union with the mother.

This is dramatized with the utmost opulence and freedom, by means of the cabaret that follows. The first turn had been a living, garlanded bull, round which female dancers undulated, caressingly. A dancer pressed her body to the beast's: it was wooed. It was to the depravity of this suggestion that Antony responded. But a yet more disturbing image of the abandoning of legitimated and containing forms for desire was close on its heels. In a net drawn up from the sea lay a troubling and undifferentiated mass of femininity. From it supine forms slithered to lie arms outstretched. Repulsion, at the loss both of individuation and of independent movement, contested with greed and wonder at the jewels cupped in oyster shells that they held up. The longing for what is natural is played off against a frank desire for the perversion of nature. If a dream of incestuous union is adumbrated here, it melts swiftly into images of humiliation, self-concerned appetite, and cruelty.

The servants are suddenly pressed into the service of the cabaret. Cleopatra manipulates their own greed to produce a spectacle of abasement: as she and Antony throw jewels among them, they scrabble dementedly for them on the floor. They are cleared from it only by the entrance of a troop of snarling leopard-girls, under their whip-cracking trainer. It is now, as the leopard-girls worry and snarl in vicious mimicry between themselves, that Antony's mastiffs are shown struggling to throw their collars and escape from the scene. They recognize, perhaps, that the final spectacle is the ultimate threat that the sight of the female body can offer to the male. Held aloft, three blazing hoops, the circus of the medusa, through which the cat-girls tumble, publicly declare the nature of the female genital (Plate 5.6)

Antony and Cleopatra's intimacy grows as they drink together. The full panoply of Antony's desire is being aroused and manipulated. She never loses her grip, though she mimes abandon, in a fit of hiccups that she clowns through. When finally Antony is ready to succumb to her, she lingeringly holds him off: as his lips begin to graze over her arms, in a display of frank orality, above his bowed head she sends a silent look to Appollodorus. This instructs him both to cast off, effectively taking Antony captive, and to curtain the lovers off from public gaze.

The magnificent veiling offers a visual token that Antony has made a full identification with a woman. The veil is associated in the psychoanalytic theory developed by Joan Rivière a few years before this film was made with the need to conceal the truth of the female genital.[57] The opulent veiling defines the scene behind it as the site of that genital.

This fantasy of a return to maternal plenitude, of course, is quickly shown to have been intolerably risky: Antony is feminized and infantilized. Cleopatra nearly succeeds in poisoning him. But although he attempts to regain his foothold in the world of male identity, with his resumption of authority as a commander, the lure of submission to the maternal is played out again in the fantasies of violence, bodily damage, and disintegration during the battle and in the fact of Antony's self-inflicted death. The fear of being overwhelmed and destroyed which is figured so graphically here can only be calmed by a secure view of the maternal figure from a distance. It is with such a scene that the film closes. The film moves directly from Antony's corpse to the preparations for the final tableau to be staged by Cleopatra. She is dressed and reaching calmly for the asp within moments. When she puts it to her breast, her thrill of anguish is transposed into a piercing vibrato on the sound-track, as she sits with eyes closed and head thrown back, in an image of ecstatic intensity. The sexual abandon she has never shown before is now achieved, as she takes the phallus-like snake, in her apotheosis as the phallic mother. Heavy-lidded and nearing death – a medusa who cannot return the look of those who gaze on her – she maintains a slightly sagging formal pose as the Romans batter at the doors. When they break through and stream into the suddenly cathedral-like space, they are silenced. They move up the audience chamber towards her but the camera makes her recede in front of them, a diminutive figure of hieratic authority, composed, remote. As they stand speechless at the sight, the stone blanks, which moved apart at the start of the picture, close up again. The enigma of the mother's body remains.

The ambition of this masochistic fantasy, as Deleuze defines it, is to obliterate the father and with him phallic sexuality. The film does go along with this – not least in its nomination of a proxy victim for Antony on whom Cleopatra's poisons may be tried out. She offers death by poison as an alternative to crucifixion to a man convicted of killing his wife and children in a drunken frenzy. First Cleopatra asks him how long it would take him to die by crucifixion and he explains that because he is so strong the process would take up to three days. He perfects the masochistic scenario by his humility and gratitude: he takes his punishment, the poison, with the words 'Majesty is kind'.

But the erasure of the father proceeds only up to a point: in the bearded elder figure of Enobarbas (whose performance de Mille thought both exceptional and unrecognized) the father confronts Mark Antony and survives him. Enobarbas, who had taught Mark Antony to speak disparagingly about women, withdraws his support towards the close of the film. The repeated gesture with which, one by one, he rips from his chest the medals of campaigns fought alongside Antony mimes the self-mutilation Antony has called down. In Shakespeare Enobarbas dies of a broken heart: in de Mille he survives, an elder statesman in Octavian's camp. He is the one who insists that Cleopatra must be allowed a safe conduct back to her own lines after she comes to plead with Octavian for Antony's life. She came under a white flag: the code must be honoured. Enobarbas and the symbolic order of the father outlive the fantasized depredations on them.

The film elicits a desire that precedes the Oedipal organization of sexuality: the mot important thing about this is the way it could temporarily abolish sexual difference in the spectators but ends by renewing it. Male and female viewers are equally subject to the fantasy of reunion with the phallic mother in the unconscious but the consequences for them of exploring this scenario are disparate. The unconscious identifications open to them are not the same. The male viewer watches his drive for identification with the mother acted out by a male proxy, Antony. It is not clear that a direct identification with Cleopatra is ever made: fantasy stops short, as it must. The fantasy reunion or identification with the mother carries the threat of dissolution and bodily damage: true identification could only be achieved by mutilating himself. This threat is not left unexplored in *Cleopatra*. Antony drives his sword into his own body. After his death, however, the fantasy is not destroyed. There are still two male subject positions available to the viewer. The phallic order, as I have indicated, is intact, in the person of Enobarbas, while the pre-Oedipal masochistic spectator has not disappeared with Antony. In the stream of Roman soldiers who burst in to view the dying Cleopatra, remote on her throne, the image of Mark Antony gazing from the threshold of her barge at Cleopatra enthroned at the end of a long perspective is replayed. For men, masochistic longing is both confirmed and inexorably placed.

It is open to women in the audience to identify both with Antony's longing and with Cleopatra's power. The identification with Antony involves the assumption of a male gaze which recognizes in the female a genital difference fraught with menace. It is a menace that from a female perspective may be equally acute: the woman's struggle to differentiate herself from the mother may charge the vagina with the threat of dissolution and loss of identity. On the other hand, identification with Cleopatra, so far as it can be separated from identification with the vagina, carries with it obvious narcissistic advantages for the female spectator. It is this identification that the film and its publicity will play up. Locked within it, however, is the designation of the female genital as alien. The subject positions available to the woman spectator place her at a distance from her own body.

As we have seen, women viewers were specifically invited to make a strong identification with Colbert, their living contemporary, who made her own way just by the force of her personality: an identification that would carry through to the terms and actions of their everyday lives.

Paradoxically, in spite of the central place allotted to the image of the female genital, as I observed earlier there was no invitation to see Colbert as a mother. Overwhelmingly, as the press-book advertisements attest, identification with her was solicited on the basis of the image of her head. From cigarettes to curlers, it is the head and shoulders of Colbert that endorse the products that are to be sold in the name of Cleopatra.

Although those products included jewellery and footwear, as well as books, I want to concentrate in conclusion on the range of cosmetic services offered, particularly the Solo aluminium end curlers and the permanent wave offered by Best's Beauty Salon. They are symptomatic of the demands of the new beauty culture for women that was developed after the First World War. It was only then that it became usual for women to visit hairdressers regularly: in the 1920s, among the increased percentage of women in the work-force, large numbers of women took up hairdressing as a profession. By 1922 the permanent wave was commonly available in America, although it could require spending up to twelve hours in the beauty parlour.[58] And of course the waves were not permanent, as James Stevens Cox shrewdly explained: the hair is fixed in a permanent curl and it is the hairdresser who sets the permanent curl into waves, which need resetting every time the hair is shampooed.[59]

Make-up too, formerly the mark of the courtesan or the actress, became more widely acceptable at this date: but only for women. In *Mrs Dalloway* (1925), Peter Walsh returning in 1923 from five years abroad comments on 'the delicious and apparently universal habit of paint'.[60] It was in the twenties that many of the now famous cosmetic houses were founded, to produce the lipsticks, creams, and powders that the up-to-date woman was wearing. Make-up also demanded a constantly renewed commitment: OED quotes *Punch* in 1930 to the effect that 'One make-up each morning, says Popkin, is plenty' – an indication that repeated repairs to the face were becoming a common feature.

In sum, the attention of women and their manual dexterity, even the professional aspirations of those employed in the industry, were trained on the maintenance of a specific appearance. It was a discipline without parallel. Margaret Lawrence, writing in 1937, recognized this and struggled to raise the question of its relation to the emancipation of women.

Women have now been in the professions and in business and industry for a period long enough to calculate effects. What do we see? A commercial world spinning on the buying power of women, if the setting of the advertising is a good basis for arriving at judgement! There must be, we gather from the advertising, a world of women profoundly interested in keeping up a feminine appearance, determined to hold their own against time and against other women, and their place in the feminine scheme with men. Fortunes have been made by corsetières and by cosmeticians. Women are groomed, in all countries where they have buying power and where manufacturing is at a zenith, as possibly they never were before, certainly on so general a scale.[61]

The demand for this feminine appearance, she uneasily concludes, is bound up with certain kinds of answer to 'the feminist issue', and with 'grouping women as a sex'; the arrangements are not felt to be satisfactory or necessarily permanent. Meanwhile, she can see that women are not enjoying that professional success that might have been anticipated: 'the feminist victory flickers on the screen and hesitates, preparatory, it may be, to a fade-out'.

In Lawrence's writing, film and the imposition of a new sense of themselves on women are brought together in the context of the failure of their hopes for success as public agents. Modelled and inculcated by film, the new grooming is associated with the old impotence. How can this be? The work of Paul Connerton offers a means of theorizing the relation between them. In *How Societies Remember*, Connerton argues for the role of incorporated knowledge, that is a knowledge of values that is taken into the body rather than written down or inscribed.[62] By means of such tacit but re-enacted knowledge, he claims, the transmission of social values is achieved and most efficiently preserved unchanged. 'Every group will entrust to bodily automatisms the values and categories they are most anxious to conserve.'[63] Connerton's favoured examples are the ritual of public events and the skills, such as typing or cycling, that have become so deeply internalized that the practitioner is unaware of them. In public ritual the disciplined body acts out its acquiescence to a social order.

Making up the face and fixing the hair require the acquisition of some of the dexterity and confident sense of the body in space involved in cycling or typing, though they are activities in which the body is bound reflexively back into itself, producing neither muscular work, as in cycling, nor a perceptible mark on the external world, as in typing. It reminds itself, through the necessary checking in the mirror, that it is an object to be viewed from the outside. Both making up and arranging the hair are also frequently described as rituals. They are performed in public, however, only in the sense that they are performed in the presence of other women: these are acknowledged to be the appropriate spectators, outside the home or not. Transgressions of this code, shameless making up in public places, used to be interpreted in terms of class – failure of discretion, taste, and so on – but are perhaps better understood as transgressive in so far as they demonstrate the fabricated nature of gender differentiation. The result rather than the process is for mixed viewing. What these rituals attest, what they commemorate, is sexual difference performed by women themselves, reinscribed on to their own heads and faces, displaced, in Ferenczi's words, 'from below upwards'.

Notes

INTRODUCTION

1 *Economist*, 14 September 1991, pp. 75–6.

1 LOOKING LIKE A QUEEN

1 Plutarch, *Life of Antony* 27, 11, 3.
2 In addition to the coin portraits and marble heads there survive a number of contemporary representations of Cleopatra from Egypt. These were not portraits but showed the queen according to formalized conventions. The most important image is the one on the outside rear wall of the temple at Dendera. They include an engraved stele at Armant and a reference on the funerary stele of a Memphite high priest; she is said to be shown on the wall of a chapel at Coptos, though this has not yet been published. A graffito from the fourth century AD at Philae makes reference to 'overlaying the [wooden] statue of Cleopatra with gold': it has been taken to refer to a posthumous cult of Cleopatra VII. In Rome it is said that Caesar placed a statue of Cleopatra in the temple of Venus Genetrix and that Octavian had an image of her made to be carried in his triumph after the taking of Egypt.

   See J. Quaegebeur, 'Cleopatra VII and the cults of the Ptolemaic queens', in R. Bianchi (ed.), *Cleopatra's Egypt: Age of the Ptolemies*, New York, Brooklyn Museum, 1988, pp. 41–54.
3 For the arguments by which they are related to the coins and to each other, see R.R.R. Smith, *Hellenistic Royal Portraits*, Oxford, Clarendon Press, 1988, pp. 97–8 and 132–5. There is no discussion, here or elsewhere, so far as I have been able to discover, of the claims of the three stone heads on exhibition in the museum at Alexandria under the name of Cleopatra. They are stylistically distinct from the ones accredited by Western scholarship and would not be amenable to identification by the same system. How the Alexandria museum has identified them is not explained.
4 In 1984 the Berlin head was featured on a 0.30 DM stamp. There were three other designs in the series, all showing objects from Berlin museums, a married pair, a goddess with pearl turban, and a majolica bowl. I am grateful to the Staatliche Museen Preussischerkulturbesitz for this information.
5 The head may also have played a part in the post-war rivalry for mastery of the past between East and West in the divided city of Berlin. The Berlin Museum was built in the West in 1962. The East's Pergamon Museum held

a very strong hand, in the processional way of Nebuchadnezzar and the Pergamon altar.

6 Bianchi, *op. cit.*, p. 25.

7 T. V. Buttrey, 'Pharaonic imitations of Athenian tetradrachms', *Proceedings of the 9th International Congress of Numismatics, Berne, 1979*, Louvain, 1982, and 'Seldom what they seem – the case of the Athenian tetradrachm', in W. Heckel and R. Sullivan (eds), *Ancient Coins of the Graeco-Roman World*, Calgary, Calgary Institute for the Humanities, 1984, pp. 292–4; Bianchi, *op. cit.*, p. 158.

8 Ibid., pp. 159–65; Smith, *op. cit.*, pp. 133–4.

9 Ibid., p. 94.

10 I am grateful to Kevin Butcher for bringing this to my attention and for the following information: if it is asked whether a coin should be seen as Antony's coin or Cleopatra's, the technology of minting offers tentative supplementary evidence. To strike a coin a blank was first placed between an obverse die, mounted on some device such as an anvil, and the reverse die, which was a punch. The punch was then hammered down on to the coin blank, impressing both sides and often slightly bowling the reverse. The constant hammering of the reverse punch meant that it tended to chip and wear out quickly and in consequence reverse dies tended to have a much shorter life than obverse dies. A die count on the existing tetradrachms of Cleopatra and Antony showed that there were more dies for Antony than for Cleopatra; add to this the fact that if there is any bowling on the coin it is always on the Antony side, and that those of the coins which bear letters or symbols (characteristic of reverse dies) always have those letters or symbols on the Antony side, and it appears fair to conclude that Antony's head was on the reverse. This would leave Cleopatra's head on the obverse, the side on which the person issuing the coin is regularly found.

11 Bianchi, *op. cit.*, pp. 161, 164. I have not been able to obtain a photograph of one of these coins.

12 S. Price, *Rituals and Power: the Roman Imperial Cult in Asia Minor*, Cambridge, Cambridge University Press, 1984, p. 204.

13 Ibid., pp. 22–30 and 51–2.

14 Quaegebeur, *op. cit.*, pp. 41–53.

15 Ibid., p. 43.

16 See, in antiquity, Apuleius, *The Golden Ass*, Plutarch, *De Iside et Osiride*; modern works include R. E. Witt, *Isis in the Graeco-Roman World*, London, Thames and Hudson, 1971; J. Stevens Curl, *The Egyptian Revival*, London, George Allen and Unwin, 1982; M. Garrard, *Artemisia Gentileschi*, Princeton, Princeton University Press, 1988; L. Hughes-Hallett, *Cleopatra: Histories, Dreams and Distortions*, London, Bloomsbury, 1989.

17 D. J. Thompson, *Memphis under the Ptolemies*, Princeton, Princeton University Press, 1988, pp. 124–5. See also Bianchi, *op. cit.*, pp. 213–14.

18 I should like to thank Eleni Vasiliki for allowing me to draw heavily on her expert knowledge of Ptolemaic wall-reliefs in the account which follows. The relief is reproduced in its entirety in the *Description de l'Egypte*, and the figures are identified in E. Chassinat, *Le Temple de Dendara*, Cairo, Institut français de l'Archéologie Orientale.

19 This interpretation of the strategy of representation and of the choice of Dendera as a site I owe to John Ray.

20 E. E. Rice, *The Grand Procession of Ptolemy Philadelphus*, Oxford, Oxford University Press, 1983, p. 13.

21 See H. Volkmann, *Cleopatra: a Study in Politics and Propaganda*, trans. T. J. Cadoux, London, Elek Books, 1958; also, more recently, Garrard, *op. cit.*, and Hughes-Hallett, *op. cit.*

22 It is true that the official Roman tradition favoured a frugal and hardy way of life and it is this ideology that endorses the rejection of the body in luxurious display. But, in fact, day-to-day life in Rome, quite apart from the life of pleasure, owed most of its refinements and graces to the skills imported from Hellenistic states. It could be seen in the city layout, the construction of baths, aqueducts, basilicas, and marble buildings; Rome was only now acquiring a library, while the one at Alexandria had been in existence for over 200 years. Alexandria itself was a city that was not only more beautiful and more cultured than Rome but also better policed. Scholars, doctors, poets, and scientists came from the East: it was on the calculations of one of the scholars who had accompanied Cleopatra to Rome that the establishment of the Julian calendar had been based. So Hellenistic culture, while it was undeniably associated with the life of pleasure, was also responsible for the most developed thinking and the best city management (J. Griffin, *Latin Poets and Roman Life*, London, Duckworth, 1985, pp. 1–31).

23 K. Hopkins, 'Brother–sister marriage in Roman Egypt', *Comparative Studies in Society and History*, 1980, vol. 22, pp. 340–2. Hopkins claims that brother/sister marriage had been widespread in the population at large for a very long time but D. J. Thompson, in conversation, pointed out that no trace of it is to be found in artisan family trees going back three hunded years.

24 Ibid., pp. 303–55.

25 M. R. Lefkowitz and M. B. Fant, *Women's Life in Greece and Rome*, London, Duckworth, 1982, p. 206.

26 C. Pelling, 'The triumviral period', in A. W. Lintott, A. K. Bowman and E. A. Champlin (eds), *Cambridge Ancient History*, vol. X, Cambridge, Cambridge University Press, 2nd edn forthcoming. M. Wyke has argued in an unpublished paper that terms were not available for the representation of Cleopatra's defeat on public monuments: there was no provision for showing a female enemy defeated in battle.

27 Propertius, 3, 11, 53–4.

28 For an ironic account of these, see R. Graves, *Claudius the God*, Harmondsworth, Penguin, 1954, p. 266.

29 Among these are Hughes-Hallet, *op. cit.* and Volkmann, *op. cit.*

30 He might have preferred 'Romulus': then we should have hoped for fine weather on Romul Bank Holiday and Augsburg would have been Romsburg. R. Syme, *The Roman Revolution*, Oxford, Clarendon Press, 1939, pp. 313–14.

31 Griffin, *op. cit.*, p. 12.

32 E. Buchner, *Die Sonnenuhr des Augustus*, Mainz am Rhein, Philipp von Zabern, 1982. I am grateful to Philip Pattenden for his help with this material. Two obelisks were in fact brought to Rome from Egypt at this time and both were engraved with identical inscriptions. The second was set up on the spina of the Circus Maximus, where races and public spectacles were held, a site which had close connections with the sun cult.

33 A. K. Bowman, *Egypt after the Pharaohs*, London, British Museum Publications, 1986, pp. 37–8.

34 Thompson, *op. cit.*, p. 266.

35 Stevens Curl, *op. cit.*, p. 11.

36 Bianchi, *op. cit.*, pp. 213–14.

37 This was made clear by the care taken to redefine the place of women in

public representation in Rome. When the Ara Pacis was built the emperor's wife and children were featured on a public monument for the first time. See British Museum exhibition, *The Image of Augustus*, 1989.

2 CLEOPATRA: HOUSEWIFE

1 Albert Blankert *et al.*, *Gods, Saints and Heroes: Dutch Painting in the Age of Rembrandt*, Washington, National Gallery of Art, 1980; see particularly pp. 22–3 and 224. The problem posed by this family portrait is also raised by Svetlana Alpers in *The Art of Describing*, London, Murray, 1983, p. 14.
2 For an illuminating discussion of seventeenth-century family images as ideological constructs, see Jonathan Goldberg, 'Fatherly authority: the politics of Stuart family images', in M. Ferguson, M. Quilligan and N. Vickers (eds), *Rewriting the Renaissance*, Chicago, Chicago University Press, 1986, pp. 3–32.
3 See D. Cherry and G. Pollock, 'Woman as sign in Pre-Raphaelite literature: a study of the representation of Elizabeth Siddall', *Art History*, 7, 2, 1984, pp. 206–27.
4 For full-scale biographies, see J. Lindsay, *Cleopatra*, New York, Coward McCann and Geoghan, 1971, and M. Grant, *Cleopatra*, London, Weidenfeld & Nicolson, 1972. See also E. Huzar, *Mark Antony: a Biography*, Minneapolis, University of Minnesota Press, 1978.
5 Joan Kelly-Gadol, 'Early feminism and the querelle des femmes', *Signs*, 8, 1, 1982, pp. 4–28.
6 In Ferguson *et al.*, *op. cit.*, pp. 191–224.
7 Lawrence Stone, *The Family, Sex and Marriage*, London, Weidenfeld, 1977.
8 Richard Halpern, 'Puritanism and maenadism in *A Mask*', in Ferguson *et al.*, *op. cit.*, p. 92.
9 Allison Heisch, 'Queen Elizabeth and the persistence of patriarchy', *Feminist Review*, 1, 4, 1980, pp. 45–56; Louis Montrose, '*A Midsummer Night's Dream* and the shaping fantasies of Elizabethan culture', in Ferguson *et al.*, *op. cit.*, pp. 65–87.
10 Sheila ffolliott, 'Catherine de Medici as Artemisia: figuring the powerful widow', in Ferguson *et al.*, *op. cit.*, pp. 227–41. See also Peter Stallybrass's account in the same volume of the problematic relation between Elizabeth's and family rule, ibid., p. 131.
11 For an account of the popularity of the story of Antony and Cleopatra in sixteenth-century literature, see Marilyn Williamson, *Infinite Variety: Antony and Cleopatra in Renaissance Drama and Earlier Tradition*, New Haven, Conn., Mystic, 1974. Jean Guillaume's article, 'Cleopatra Nova Pandora', *Gazette des Beaux Arts*, 80, 1972, pp. 185–94, gives an indication of the reworking of the figure of Cleopatra in the visual arts during the same period.
12 Elizabeth Eisenstein, *The Printing Press as an Agent of Change*, Cambridge, Cambridge University Press, 1979.
13 There was before 1506 no Italian edition of this text available in either Latin or the vernacular. The Ulm Boccaccio may also have been the first work of Boccaccio's to be published in German. See Clifton Olds, Ralph Williams, and William Levin, *Images of Love and Death*, Michigan, Museum of Art, 1976, p. 44.
14 Ibid.
15 Vittore Branca, *Boccaccio: the Man and his Works*, New York, New York University Press, 1975, pp. 109–11.
16 Bacchi della Lega, *Serie delle edizioni delle opere di G. Boccaccio*, Bologna, 1875.

17 Charles Trinkaus, *The Poet as Philosopher*, New Haven, Conn., Yale University Press, 1979, p. 120; W. Fiske, *Petrarch's Treatise De Remediis utriusque fortunae*, Florence, 1888, p. 2.

18 Most notably, John Gould, in 'Law, custom and myth: aspects of the social position of women in classical Athens', *Journal of Hellenic Studies*, 100, 1980, pp. 38–59; Mary Lefkowitz and Maureen Fant, *Images of Women in Antiquity*, Bromley, Croom Helm, 1983.

19 Mary Lefkowitz and Maureen Fant, *Women in Greece and Rome*, Toronto, Samuel-Stevens, 1977, pp. 104–6.

20 The equation of moral integrity in women with monogamy and its relation to the protection of inheritance rights is too familiar to require further commentary. The process by which a woman who offends against gender patterns in her society and in consequence is imputed to be promiscuous or unreliable in her primary role as the bearer of legitimate heirs merits some attention in the context of the present argument (see Gould, *op. cit.*, pp. 44–5).

21 W. W. Tarn, 'The war of the East against the West', in S. A. Cook, F. E. Adcock and M. P. Charlesworth (eds), *Cambridge Ancient History*, Cambridge, Cambridge University Press, 1934, vol. X, p. 111, claims, in a frequently quoted passage, that Cleopatra was the only human being apart from Hannibal that Rome, who had feared no people and no other nation, did condescend to fear. Williamson, *op. cit.*, however, is sceptical of the terror expressed by the poets on behalf of the Roman people: they might more realistically be described as adopting attitudes of extreme ideological severity.

22 See P. W. Pestman, *Marriage and Matrimonial Property in Ancient Egypt*, Leiden, Brill, 1961. He claims that 'under the influence of Greek law the woman loses gradually but [with] inexorable certainty her prominent position', p. 184.

23 Sarah B. Pomeroy, *Goddesses, Whores, Wives and Slaves*, New York, Schocken Books, 1975, pp. 124, 187.

24 Edward Said, *Orientalism*, London, Routledge & Kegan Paul, 1978, p. 56.

25 See Tarn, *op. cit.*

26 Quoted by Constance Jordan (her own translation), 'Feminism and the humanists', in Ferguson *et al.*, *op. cit.*, pp. 243–4.

27 Ibid., p. 242.

28 Kelly-Gadol, *op. cit.*

29 It is also relevant that the work was undertaken 'almost as a "pendant", a companion, to Petrarch's *De Viris Illustribus*' (Branca, *op. cit.*, p. 110). Initiated in 1361, it was revised nine times, the last in 1375.

30 Boccaccio, *Concerning Famous Women*, trans. G. Guarino, London, Allen and Unwin, 1964, pp. 192–7.

31 Pliny, *Historia Naturalis*, IX, lviii.

32 M. Scott, *The History of Dress Series, Late Gothic Europe 1400–1500*, London, Mills and Boon, 1980, pp. 62, 87, 108, 126, 157. I am grateful to Penelope Kenrick for bringing this material to my attention.

33 For a discussion of comparable images of dominating women, see Natalie Zemon Davis, 'Women on top', in *Society and Culture in Early Modern France*, London, Duckworth, 1975.

34 See Goldberg, *op. cit.*

35 For a discussion of the status of the home and the housewife in seventeenth-century Holland, see S. Schama, *The Embarrassment of Riches*, London, Collins, 1987, pp. 375–481. Schama argues that both idealization of domestic order and satires of its disruption exist in tension together, often in the same work (see pp. 156–7). He suggests that at the mid-century marriage portraits become

more dynamic and companionable, showing a degree of equality within the home, with wives interrupting their husbands, for instance: he quotes in evidence de Braij's own pair portrait, *Abraham Casteleyn and Margareta van Bancken* of 1663 (p. 426). A wife's limited challenge to the absolute authority of her husband within the domestic space, made while emphasizing her religious and sexual orthodoxy, may be what is at stake in the de Braij family portrait. Svetlana Alpers points out in correspondence that Dutch culture has never made a separation between the sexual and the domestic, so that mapping the figure of Cleopatra on to the ordinary mistress of the household would not involve the same intrusion of the profane (Cleopatra) into the sacred (domestic space) that it might in other cultures.

36 E. de Jongh, 'Pearls of virtue and pearls of vice', *Simiolus*, 8, 1975–7, pp. 69–97. See also by the same author 'Grape symbolism in paintings of the 16th and 17th centuries', *Simiolus*, 7, 1974, pp. 166–91, where he argues that the presence of many children in a family portrait may also be an indication of the sexual restraint within marriage exercised by the parents: over-frequent cohabitation was said to lead to sterility.

37 See R. H. Bainton, *Women of the Reformation in Germany and Italy*, Minneapolis, Augsburg Publishing House, 1971.

38 See R. Bridenthal and C. Koonz, *Becoming Visible: Women in European History*, Boston, Mass., Houghton Mifflin, 1977, pp. 174–6.

39 See Morris Bishop, *Petrarch and his World*, London, Chatto and Windus, 1964.

40 Quotations are taken from Thomas Twyne's translation of *Physicke against Fortune*, London, 1579; I have modernized the spelling.

41 See Lyndal Roper's brilliant article 'Prostitution and the Reformation in Augsburg', *History Workshop Journal*, 19, 1985, pp. 3–28.

42 Bridenthal and Koonz, *op. cit.*, p. 172.

43 See Michel Foucault, *The History of Sexuality*, Harmondsworth, Penguin, 1976, vol. I, pp. 115–16.

44 Quoted in S. Ozment, *When Fathers Ruled: Family Life in Reformation Europe*, Cambridge, Mass., Harvard University Press, 1983, p. 22.

45 Alison Stewart, *Unequal Lovers*, New York, Abaris, 1978, p. 60.

46 W. Scheidig (ed.), *Die Holzschnitte des Petrarca-Meisters: zu Petrarcas Werk von der Artzney bayder Glück des guten und widerwärtigen, Augsburg 1532*, Berlin, Akad. d. Künste, 1955, p. 123.

47 Charlotte Brontë, *Villette*, London, 1853. I am grateful to Catherine Pearce for bringing this material to my attention.

3 NEWTON AND CLEOPATRA

1 S. Schaffer, 'Natural philosophy and public spectacle', *History of Science*, 21, 1, 51, 1983, pp. 1–43, especially pp. 3–5. The role allotted to visual evidence in the work of rational analysis at the period is an important study in itself. In her work on the theory of illusion in eighteenth-century France, *The Object of Art*, Cambridge, Cambridge University Press, 1982, Marian Hobson observes that baroque art sharpens the opposition between illusion and truth by the way it both foregrounds appearances and insists on their fragility (p. 45). This emphasizes the strain put on looking by Cartesian thought, the rationality in which the European Enlightenment is grounded. 'In the movement of the Cartesian *Cogito*, absolute doubt, the suspicion that all may be appearance, was powerless against one certainty, that of consciousness: appear-

ance led on to truth' (p. 28). See also L. Jordanova, *Sexual Visions*, Madison, University of Wisconsin Press, 1989.

2 Naples, 1737. The place of publication was misrepresented for reasons of prudence. In fact the book came out with the title *Il Newtonianismo per le dame* at Milan; see E. Bonora (ed.), *Illuministi Italiani, Tomo II: Opere di Francesco Algarotti e di Saverio Bettinelli*, Ricciardi, Milan and Naples, 1970, p. 10. For a discussion of *Newtonianismo* and its relation to the practice of both science and philosophy by women, see C. Merchant, *The Death of Nature: Women, Ecology and the Scientific Revolution*, San Francisco, Harper & Row, 1980, pp. 269–74.

3 S. Schaffer, 'Newtonianism', in R. Olby, G. N. Cantor, J. R. R. Christie and M. J. S. Hodges (eds), *Companion to the History of Modern Science*, New York and London, Routledge, 1990, pp. 605–16.

4 For an account of the emblematic use of the prism experiment in the *Traité d'Optique*, see H. Guerlac, *Newton on the Continent*, Ithaca, NY, and London, Cornell University Press, 1981, pp. 154–63. The painting is now in the Fitzwilliam Museum, Cambridge.

5 S. Schaffer, 'Glassworks', in D. Gooding, T. Pinch and S. Schaffer (eds), *The Uses of Experiment*, Cambridge, Cambridge University Press, 1989, pp. 67–104, especially p. 91.

6 P. Casini, *Newton e la Coscienza Europea*, Bologna, Il Mulino, 1983, pp. 173–227.

7 O. Chadwick, 'The Italian Enlightenment', in R. Porter and M. Teich (eds), *The Enlightenment in National Context*, Cambridge, Cambridge University Press, 1981, p. 91. This assertion should probably be treated with scepticism, since attempts by the University of Bologna to document it have failed.

8 Merchant, *op. cit.*, pp. 268–74.

9 Ibid., pp. 268–70.

10 See G. D. Meyer, *The Scientific Lady in England 1650–1760*, Berkeley and Los Angeles, University of California Press, 1955, pp. 17–48.

11 F. Algarotti, *Sir Isaac Newton's Philosophy Explained for the Use of the Ladies*, London, 1739, vol. II, p. 30.

12 Ibid., vol. I, p. 67.

13 Ibid., p. v.

14 Ibid., p. 78.

15 Ibid., vol. II, p. 40.

16 Ibid., vol. I, pp. 79–80.

17 Ibid., p. 80.

18 For an account of Algarotti see F. Haskell, *Patrons and Painters: a Study in the Relations between Art and Society in the Age of the Baroque*, New Haven and London, Yale University Press, 1980, pp. 347–60.

19 M. Kemp, *The Science of Art*, New Haven and London, Yale University Press, 1990, p. 131.

20 Algarotti, *op. cit.*, vol. II, p. 28.

21 Ibid., vol. I, p. 210.

22 Ibid., vol. II, p. 43.

23 N. Bryson, *Looking at the Overlooked: Four Essays on Still Life Painting*, London, Reaktion, 1990, p. 119.

24 D. Rosand, *Painting in Cinquecento Venice*, New Haven and London, Yale University Press, 1982, pp. 15–26.

25 M. Levey, *Giambattista Tiepolo*, New Haven and London, Yale University Press, 1986, pp. 125–33 and 143–66.

26 A. Pigler, *Barockthemen*, Budapest, Akadémiai Kiadó, 1974, vol. II, p. 366 and pp. 395–403.

27 Haskell, *op. cit.*, p. 195; Levey, *op. cit.*, p. 21; Pigler, *op. cit.*, p. 396; P. Maecius, *Emblemata*, Bologna, 1628.

28 F. DiFederico, *Francesco Trevisani: Eighteenth-century Painter in Rome*, Washington, DC, Decatur House Press, 1977, pp. 47–8.

29 This very unusual theme is taken from the biblical tale of Abigail, the wife of David. She was first married to a ruler called Nabal, who brought his own life and his kingdom's safety into danger by offering gratuitous insults to David. His wife was wiser and intervened to placate David, an occasion often represented by painters. She returned from her diplomatic mission to find Nabal feasting carelessly: apprised of his near escape he had a stroke and died shortly afterwards (Samuel, i, 25). It is thus a story which offers scope for the image of a central oriental male figure and one which incidentally turns on the theme of a failure of perception which leads to disaster. See also Levey, *op. cit.*, p. 132.

30 Kemp, *op. cit.*, p. 143. For his account of the history of perspective in Italy see pp. 69–98 and 131–48.

31 The classic account of illusionism in fresco decoration remains S. Sandström, *Levels of Unreality*, Uppsala, Acta Universitatis Uppsaliensis, 1963.

32 Kemp, *op. cit.*, p. 104.

33 T. Pignatti *et al.*, *Palazzo Labia a Venezia*, Turin, Eri, 1982, p. 268.

34 Jean Baudrillard, 'The trompe l'oeil', reprinted in N. Bryson (ed.), *Calligram: Essays in New Art History from France*, Cambridge, Cambridge University Press, 1988, pp. 53–62.

35 H. Janson, *Apes and Ape-lore in the Middle Ages and the Renaissance*, London, Warburg Institute, 1952, pp. 287–314. Janson also notes that the figure was sufficiently vital in the eighteenth century for Watteau, Tiepolo's French contemporary, to employ it. He made use of the figure of the artist as ape to pour scorn on painters who put undue reliance on academic theory (p. 311).

36 A. Barzaghi, *Donne o cortegiane? La prostituzione a Venezia documenti di costume dal XVI al XVIII secolo*, Verona, Bertani, 1980; C. Santore, 'Julia Lombardo, "Somtuosa meretrize": a portrait by property', *Renaissance Quarterly*, xli, i, 1988, pp. 44–83.

37 J. Georgelin, *Venise au siècle des lumières*, Paris-La Haye, Mouton, 1978, p. 730. The ambiguity of the image extends to arranging the figure of Cleopatra so that only one of her breasts is within the compass of the gaze: it is for the viewer to construct the sight of the other.

38 See, however, *Visit of Cleopatra to Antony*, manner of Francesco di Giorgio, National Gallery of America, Kress Collection, which I have not been able to examine. Pliny, *Historia Naturalis*, IX, lviii.

39 Meyer, *op. cit.*, p. vii.

4 SPACED OUT: CLEOPATRA AND THE CITIZEN-KING

1 Kevin Lynch, *The Image of the City*, Cambridge, Mass., MIT Press, 1960, pp. 126–7.

2 Fredric Jameson, 'Cognitive mapping', in Cary Nelson and Lawrence Grossberg (eds), *Marxism and the Interpretation of Culture*, Basingstoke, Macmillan, 1988, pp. 347–57.

3 *Guardian*, 22 January 1989.

4 Marie-Hélène Huet, *Rehearsing the Revolution: the Staging of Marat's Death*

1793–1797, Berkeley, University of California Press, 1982; Neil Hertz, 'Medusa's head: male hysteria under political pressure' and 'Response from Catherine Gallagher', in *The End of the Line: Essays on Psychoanalysis and the Sublime*, New York, Columbia University Press, 1985, pp. 160–96. Marie-Hélène Huet offers a psychoanalytic interpretation of the necessity for the repeated theatrical restagings of the trial and execution of Robespierre; Neil Hertz investigates the imagery of the medusa, which was often to be found representing revolutionary violence. Catherine Gallagher relates the imaging of the female genital to the fear of a disrupted succession of name and property rights.

5 Desmond Seward, *Marie-Antoinette*, London, Constable, 1981, pp. 81–2, 85, and 261–6.

6 Before this point, mother and child had been forcibly divided and the Dauphin removed to live in separate apartments: an engraving of this scene illustrates Claude Langlois, 'Les dérives vendéennes de l'imaginaire révolutionnaire', *Annales*, 43, 3, 1988, pp. 771–97. Langlois argues that there was considerable counter-revolutionary play with Marie-Antoinette as a figure of threatened domesticity.

7 M. Agulhon (ed.), *Histoire de la France urbaine*, Paris, Seuil, 1983, vol. IV, pp. 74–5.

8 Ibid., p. 575.

9 Quoted in Maurice Agulhon, *Marianne into Battle*, Cambridge, Cambridge University Press, 1981, p. 61.

10 In this context it is appropriate to note that the endpapers chosen for *Histoire de la France urbaine* display an aerial view of the centre of Paris, in which the obelisk takes a central place, pointing up the centrefold via the Champs Elysées to the Arc de Triomphe.

11 This can be seen by considering the history of the column in the Place Vendôme. Designed at the end of the seventeenth century by Hardouin-Mansart to enclose a monumental statue of Louis XIV, the space of the Place Vendôme was to be surrounded by the edifices of national authority: the Mint, the National Library, academies. At first called Place des Conquêtes, its nomination became contested between the two male potentates who might claim to dominate the space; it was variously known as Louis-le-Grand after the statue, or Place Vendôme, after the Duke of Vendôme whose mansion originally stood there. At the Revolution both name and monument were discarded. Girardon's statue of the Sun-King was destroyed and the square renamed, temporarily, Place des Piques. Into this literal power vacuum, but drawing on its historically accumulated charge, Napoleon later inserted himself to celebrate his own conquests, erecting a stone column clad in the bronze of 1,200 cannon captured at Austerlitz in 1805. At its summit stood a representation of himself, togaed, imperial. If this was not to last, for at his deposition in 1814 it was replaced by Henri IV, sign of reasserted continuity with an acceptable and historically remote monarchy, it was eventually to be re-established. For in its turn the statue of Henri IV was removed for the Hundred Days and Louis XVIII elected to crown the column with the monarchist fleur-de-lis. The figure of Napoleon, however, as restored by the citizen-king, Louis-Philippe, on his accession in 1830, was clad in contemporary rather than imperial style. When the Third Republic put the column up again, Napoleon was dressed as Caesar once more. (Topographical information available in the *Michelin Guide to Paris*.)

12 Agulhon, 1983, *op. cit.*, p. 563. After the revolution of 1848, when these

celebrations ceased, the column became a memorial to the Parisians killed in the fighting of 1830 and 1848.

13 Population figure quoted from Richard Terdiman, *Discourse/Counter Discourse: the Theory and Practice of Symbolic Resistance in Nineteenth-century France*, Ithaca, NY, Cornell University Press, 1985, p. 129.

14 M. Warner discusses the revised layout in *Monuments and Maidens: the Allegory of the Female Form*, London, Weidenfeld, 1985, pp. 30–1.

15 It is hardly too much to say that in early nineteenth-century France Egypt functioned as a signifier of the cultural superiority of the French nation. Between 1808 and 1829 were published the twenty-three volumes of the *Description de l'Egypte*, a monumental work of cultural inscription, incorporating the systematic study of the country authorized by Napoleon after the conquest of Egypt. For its significance see Edward Said, *Orientalism*, London, Penguin reprint, 1987, pp. 84ff. To celebrate this event the Baron Vivant Denon, as Directeur de la Monnaie des Médailles, had a medal struck showing a Roman soldier in the act of unveiling an Egyptian queen: it is illustrated on the jacket of James Stevens Curl, *The Egyptian Revival*, London, Allen & Unwin, 1982. At the same time, it was in fact the case that by the 1830s Egypt was second only to England in its modern industrial capacity and was active in creating its own overseas empire. It was European commercial penetration that weakened and finally destroyed successful Egyptian industry after the settlement of 1839. See Martin Bernal, *Black Athena*, London, Free Association, 1987, pp. 247–9. It was also under the July Monarchy that Egypt became virtually a cultural province of France.

16 Paris, Poulet-Malassis, 1856. Martin Bernal points out, however, in a private communication, that an obelisk was *de rigueur* as an item of urban furniture throughout Europe in the nineteenth century and that it may have been perceived as classical as much as Egyptian. This can hardly be the case, however, in the case of the Paris obelisk, since its journey from Egypt was a matter of popular interest. See B. Menu, *L'Obélisque de la Concorde*, Paris, Lunx, 1986.

17 The first part appeared in the issue of 29 November 1838, the day before subscriptions, which could be dated from the first or the fifteenth of the month, were due for renewal. Newspapers were not sold by the issue but by subscription and the timing of the publication of Gautier's story was part of the journal's marketing strategy. The other parts appeared in the days immediately following, with two interruptions.

18 In September 1835 a new press law was passed, prohibiting criticism of the regime and stipulating that offences against this law should be tried outside the jury system. See Terdiman, *op. cit.*, pp. 160–2.

19 Ibid., p. 130.

20 Ibid., p. 125.

21 Ibid., pp. 129–35.

22 Ibid., p. 137. See also Michael B. Miller, *The Bon Marché: Bourgeois Culture and the Department Store, 1869–1920*, Princeton, Princeton University Press, 1981, pp. 21–6, and R. Bowlby, *Just Looking*, New York and London, Methuen, 1985.

23 Sextus Aurelius Victor, *De Viris Illustribus*, 86.

24 In his paper 'A special type of object-choice made by men', Standard Edition, vol. 11, pp. 165–75, Freud discusses the relation between early love for the mother and a subsequent choice by some men of women perceived as promiscuous or even as prostitutes. This choice marks a particular form of resol-

ution of the Oedipus complex. Freud's account makes it possible to understand the tale of Cleopatra the 'prostitute' as also satisfying fantasies of the maternal, related in this case to the dead queen. Freud suggests that in the fantasies of such sons the mother's lover 'almost always exhibits the features of the boy's own ego, or more accurately of his own idealised personality' (ibid., p. 171). Gautier's deployment of the figure of Hercules, ideal representative of the people, in this role fits well with this. See pp. 93–8.

25 Théophile Gautier, 'Une nuit de Cléopâtre', in *Le Roman de la Momie*, Paris, Garnier, 1960, p. 7.

26 Ibid.

27 V. Vatsuro, quoted in Leslie O'Bell, *Pushkin's Egyptian Nights*, Ann Arbor, Ardis, 1984, p. 92.

28 Jean-Marie Carré, in *Voyageurs et écrivains français en Egypte*, Cairo, L'Institut français de l'Archéologie Orientale, 1956, suggests as principal sources Champollion's *Lettres écrites d'Egypte et de Nubie* and *Monuments de l'Egypte et de la Nubie*, with possibly some reference to the *Description de l'Egypte*. Carré does not believe that Gautier was attempting an effect of documentary authenticity: he gives a detailed analysis of his borrowings, including an analysis of inaccuracies, describing Gautier's Egyptology, in this tale, as 'a mixture of the unreliable and the fantastic' ('aussi incertaine que fantaisiste'). Interestingly, Carré lays special emphasis on the inappropriateness of the massive and monumental architecture described by Gautier. It may have been wrong for Ptolemaic Egypt, but in the 1830s, when Gautier was writing, massive architecture had specifically revolutionary and populist associations. Other sources may have included Vivant Denon, *Voyages dans la Basse et la Haute Egypte, pendant les campagnes du général Bonaparte*, 2 vols, Paris, 1802. Since the 1780s, fired by the neo-classical movement, and in particular by the tragedian Francois-Joseph Talma, a pioneer of historical accuracy in stage costume, costume books devoted to classical dress had been published with the aim of securing authenticity on stage. A collection of these was made by the Baron Joseph von Lipperheide. Examples include P. S. Maréchal, *Costumes civils actuels de tous les peuples connus*, 4 vols, Paris, 1788, and J. Grasset de S. Sauveur, *Encyclopédie des voyages, contenant l'abrégé historique des moeurs . . . de tous les peuples: Et la collection complette de leurs habillemens civils, militaires, religieux et dignitaires*, 5 vols, Paris, 1796. I am grateful to Dr Aileen Ribeiro of the Courtauld Institute for advice here and elsewhere on matters of costume history.

29 Gautier, *op. cit.*, p. 24.

30 Agulhon, 1981, *op. cit.*, pp. 15, 16; Hertz, *op. cit.*, pp. 179–93.

31 It is clear that the relation between the female figure of Liberty and female figures bearing the gendered signifiers of class power was inherently unstable and required constant redefinition: Liberty could be represented holding a sceptre. The lines from 'La Curée' ('The Spoils'), published in the *Iambes* of Auguste Barbier and written in August 1830, are quoted in Agulhon, 1981, *op. cit.*, p. 40:

> C'est que la Liberté n'est pas une comtesse
> Du noble faubourg Saint-Germain,
> Une femme qu'un cri fait tomber en faiblesse,
> Qui met du blanc et du carmin.
> C'est une forte femme aux puissantes mamelles,
> A la voix rauque, aux durs appas,
> Qui, du brun sur la peau, du feu dans les prunelles,
> [. . .]

Qui ne prend ses amours que dans la populace.
(The truth is that Liberty is not a countess
From the noble faubourg Saint-Germain,
A woman who swoons away at the slightest cry
And who wears powder and rouge.
She is a strong woman with thrusting breasts,
A harsh voice and a hard charm,
Who, with her bronzed skin and her flashing eyes
[. . .]
Takes her lovers only from among the people.)

The aristocratic woman constructed in terms of lack – no authentic colour, no resilience – is rejected. The object of desire is constructed as the transgressive woman: the woman who by her class position would previously have fallen outside the category 'woman'. She repudiates gender prescriptions by choosing her own lovers (in the plural); although the harsh voice and hard charm define her as non-aristocratic, her authority in taking lovers from among the people seems to reimpose a different power structure. The overthrow of aristocracy implies a disturbance of gender significations and gender relations too.

32 Gautier, *op. cit.*, p. 25.
33 Ibid., p. 14.
34 Ibid., pp. 21–2.
35 Lynn Hunt, *Politics, Culture, and Class in the French Revolution*, Berkeley, University of California Press, 1984, pp. 94–116.
36 Gautier, *op. cit.*, p. 16.
37 Ibid., p. 17.
38 The very invocation of Dionysus, never a popularized figure, makes the representation less democratic in tone, even though it appeals to the power to recognize Hercules as a figure of the people.
39 *Antony and Cleopatra* was not a regular item in the Shakespearean repertoire in England in the early nineteenth century; it was revived briefly in 1813 and again in 1833. See G. C. Odell, *Shakespeare from Betterton to Irving*, 2 vols, New York, Scribner, 1920. Hence it is also unlikely that Delacroix could have seen a production when he visited England in 1825 and saw Kean as Othello. Mérimée's reference to the performance tradition of Cleopatra is puzzling. (Quoted Lee Johnson, *The Paintings of Eugène Delacroix*, Oxford, Clarendon Press, 1986, vol. III, p. 81.)
40 There is some indication that the theme, if not Shakespeare's play, was more resonant in France, just prior to the Revolution. Marmontel's *Cléopâtre* was played in 1784 and in 1788 Garnier's tragedy of the same name was put on, while a ballet *Cléopâtre et Marc Antoine*, was staged at the Théâtre de Varsovie in 1789. A second ballet, *Les Amours d'Antoine et de Cléopâtre*, was staged in 1808. See C. D. Brenter, *Bibliography of French Plays, 1700–89*, Berkeley, 1947.
41 See note 28; see also Stevens Curl, *op. cit.*, pp. 110–19 for an account of Egyptianizing furniture in the period. I would like to thank Clive Wainwright of the Victoria and Albert Museum for his generous help in dealing with this material.
42 For all information concerning jewellery I am indebted to Mrs Diana Scarisbrick; for further details of the jewels of Frances Ann, Lady Londonderry, see her article 'Blazing like the sun', *Country Life*, 14 June 1984, pp. 1728–31. The Lawrence portrait referred to in my text is illustrated in this article.
43 See M. Sérullaz, *Les Peintures murales de Delacroix*, Paris, Temps, 1963, pp. 27–49, especially pp. 31ff. Graphic images of Cleopatra in France appear to

be more freely produced about the period of the Revolution. Twelve Cleopatra pieces are recorded between 1700 and 1787, and then ten in the next decade: two in 1787, three in 1789, one each in 1793, 1795, and 1796, and two in 1798, after which there is a gap of twenty years before the next. The first three deal with the death of Antony, while the five following dwell on the circumstances surrounding the death of Cleopatra. The drawing dated 1793, the year of Marie-Antoinette's death, however, holds back from a reference to the finality of death and is entitled *Cléopâtre endormie*. The two Guillaume Martin images of 1798 strike a less evidently equivocal note. They show the encounter of Cleopatra and Mark Antony at Tarsus and the scene of Cleopatra's banquet. (I am grateful to Dr Jon Whiteley of the Ashmolean Museum, Oxford, for permission to consult his index of French paintings.)

44 *La Presse*, 29 November 1838, p. 2.
45 E. Marks and I. de Courtivron (eds), *New French Feminisms*, Brighton, Harvester, 1981, p. 16.
46 Quoted in S. Voilquin, 'Variétés', *La Tribune des femmes*, 1832 volume, p. 167.
47 Marks and de Courtivron, *op. cit.*, p. 17.
48 Voilquin, *op. cit.*, p. 166.
49 Ibid., p. 167.
50 Ibid.

5 A BODY FOR CLEOPATRA

1 The world première of *Cleopatra* was on 18 August 1934 and it was released in London on 5 November that year. L. Curtius, 'Ikonographische Beiträge zum Porträt der römischen Republik und der julisch-claudischen Familie, IV. Kleopatra VII. Philopator', *Mitteilungen des Deutschen Archäologischen Instituts, Abteilung Rom*, 48, 1933, 182–92.
2 N. Hertz, *The End of the Line: Essays on Psycho-analysis and the Sublime*, New York, Columbia University Press, 1985, pp. 161–93; C. Gallagher, ibid., pp. 194–6; T. Siebers, *The Mirror of Medusa*, Berkeley, Los Angeles, and London, University of California Press, 1983.
3 See F. Mort, *Dangerous Sexualities*, London, Routledge, 1987; S. Jeffreys, *The Spinster and her Enemies*, London, Pandora, 1985, see also S. Jeffreys (ed.), *The Sexuality Debates*, London, Routledge, 1987; J. Weeks, *Sex, Politics and Society*, London, Routledge, 1985. For the first time, too, sexuality was brought within the domain of legislation, with the Contagious Diseases Acts of the 1860s.
4 E. Boulding, S. Nuss, D. Carson and M. Greenstein, *Handbook of International Data on Women*, New York, Sage, 1976, pp. 250–1. For a history of the struggle for women's rights in Egypt, Iran, China, and Japan, see K. Jayawardena, *Feminism and Nationalism in the Third World*, London and Totowa, New Jersey, Zed Books, 1986; for the campaigns in France, M. Albistur and D. Armogathe, *Histoire du féminisme français du moyen-âge à nos jours*, Paris, des femmes, 1977; E. Marks and I. de Courtivron (eds), *New French Feminisms*, Brighton, Harvester, 1981, pp. 10–27; F. Gordon, *The Integral Feminist: Madeleine Pelletier 1874–1939*, Cambridge, Polity, 1990; S. Hause, *Hubertine Auclert: the French Suffragette*, New Haven and London, Yale University Press, 1987.
5 Even activists often shied at the full implications of the demand for the suffrage, preferring to play down what would now be understood as its revolutionary character. This was both strategic, in order to make it more likely they would avoid arousing an opposition that would hinder their success,

and self-preserving. Few could endorse actual revolution with a good conscience and still call for recognition as responsible citizens.

6 For an investigation of the terms on which women are incorporated into civil society and their obligations within it, see C. Pateman, *The Sexual Contract*, Cambridge, Polity, 1988. I am obliged to Emily Hamer for this reference.

7 *The New Encyclopaedia Britannica*, 15th edn, vol. 12, pp. 733–4.

8 Ibid. The years quoted are the earliest dates when women actually took part in national elections.

9 L. Tickner, *The Spectacle of Women*, London, Chatto and Windus, 1987.

10 Ibid., pp. 55–151, particularly pp. 80–104.

11 Ibid., pp. 100–4.

12 Ibid., pp. 266–7.

13 C. Koonz, *Mothers in the Fatherland*, London, Methuen, 1988, p. 32.

14 Ibid., p. 55.

15 Ibid., *passim*, and K. Millett, *Sexual Politics*, London, Virago, 1977, pp. 159–68, particularly pp. 161–2.

16 M.-A. Macciocchi, 'Female sexuality in fascist ideology', *Feminist Review*, 1, 1, pp. 67–82.

17 See, for example, the discussion of Charles Nodier's arguments against extending the franchise to women, above, Chapter 4, pp. 101–2; also Tickner, *passim*.

18 See, for instance, the title of a contemporary work: *Cleopatra – a Royal Voluptuary* (see below, n. 19).

19 The Dictionary Catalogue of the Research Libraries of the New York Public Libraries lists half a dozen plays about Cleopatra published at the period; two at least were Italian and an Italian account of *Cleopatra contra Roma*, published in Florence by Mattio Mattii, was in its third edition by 1939. Among the entries in the British Library catalogue are four studies in German, dated 1931, 1936, 1937, and 1938, including W. Goerlitz, *Kleopatra: Bildnis einer dämonischer Frau (Cleopatra: Portrait of a Demonic Woman)*, Hamburg, Sieben, Stäbeverlag, 1936; three in French, one in 1932 and two in 1934; and one in Italian, also published in 1934. Maurice Baring's play of 1934, 'Three minutes', in *The London Magazine*, vol. xxx, was particularly forceful in bringing the figure of Cleopatra into a new form determined by the technological experience of the twentieth century: the action took place over the telephone. When Mary Butts's novel, *Scenes from the Life of Cleopatra*, London, Heinemann, 1935, was reviewed, the reviewer complained of the recent spate of books on the same topic. The five translations, all published in London, were as follows: C. Ferval, *The Life and Death of Cleopatra*, 1924, translated from the French by H. Wilson; H. Stadelmann, *Cleopatra, Egypt's Last Queen*, Routledge, 1931, translated from the German by M. M. Green; O. von Wertheimer, *Cleopatra – a Royal Voluptuary*, Harrap, 1931, translated from the German by H. Paterson; G. Delayen, *Cleopatra*, New York, E. P. Dutton, 1934, translated from the French by F. Symons; E. Ludwig, *Cleopatra, the Story of a Queen*, London, Viking Press, 1937, translated from the German by B. Miall. Ferval's and von Wertheimer's books were brought out in the United States in special editions to coincide with the release of the de Mille film. (See press-book, p. 12.) Also specially reprinted for the occasion was E. Barrington, *Cleopatra, the Laughing Queen*, originally published in 1929.

20 W. W. Tarn, 'The war of the East against the West', in S. A. Cook, F. E. Adcock and M. P. Charlesworth (eds), *Cambridge Ancient History*, Cambridge, Cambridge University Press, 1934, vol. X, p. 111.

21 P. Harvey, *The Oxford Companion to Classical Literature*, Oxford, Clarendon Press, 1937, p. 445.

22 For an account of some classical redactions of the myth, see Siebers, *op. cit.*, pp. 1–11.

23 S. Freud, 'Medusa's head', Standard Edition, vol. 18, pp. 273–4.

24 S. Ferenczi, 'On the symbolism of the head of Medusa', in *Further Contributions to the Theory and Technique of Psychoanalysis*, London, Hogarth Press, 1926, p. 360.

25 S. Freud, 'The infantile genital organisation', Standard Edition, vol. 19, p. 144 and fn. 3; 'New introductory lectures on psycho-analysis', Standard Edition, vol. 22, p. 24.

26 C. Bernheimer, 'Castration as fetish', *Paragraph*, 14, 1, 1991, pp. 1–9.

27 Ibid., p. 3.

28 Quoted in Siebers, *op. cit.*, p. 110.

29 Hertz, *op. cit.*, pp. 194–6.

30 Curtius, *op. cit.*, p. 187.

31 Reproduced in Koonz, *op. cit.*, second sheet of unpaginated illustrations.

32 See Hans F. K. Günther, *The Racial Elements of European History*, translated from the second German edition by G. C. Wheeler, London, Methuen, 1927, p. 3. As Günther explains it, 'race shows itself in a human group which is marked off from every other human group through its own proper combination of bodily and mental characteristics, and in turn produces only its like' (ibid.). I am grateful to Catherine Sutherland for bringing this work to my attention and for her translation of the passage from Curtius which follows.

33 Curtius, *op. cit.*, p. 189.

34 Ibid.

35 D. Bordwell, J. Staiger, and K. Thompson (eds), *The Classical Hollywood Cinema*, London, Routledge, 1985, pp. 139–40 and 224–5 for de Mille's innovations in production and lighting. See also W. Everson, *Claudette Colbert*, New York, Pyramid, 1976.

36 'Chukka' is a term from polo, a sport exclusive since the nineteenth century to men of the ruling class. Derived from Hindi 'chakar' and Sanskrit 'cakra', 'to circle', it is used to name the periods into which the game is divided. It is a word associated with empire, that is the rule of one race over another, and particularly with British rule in India, where the British learned to play the game; it was only then that it was taken up by Indian princes. OED qutoes 'chukka boot' as a fashion term from 1948, as in 'the Eton Clubman chukka boot'.

There is evidence that Wilcoxon's 'upper-class' English accent was an important marker for identification in the film. De Mille was arrested by the mere sound of his voice, before setting eyes on him. Publicity materials, as reproduced in the press-book, quoted de Mille's belief in the importance of 'pure' English: he linked the decay in standards of spoken and written language with a loss of national self-esteem in Americans and a diminishing sense of America's political authority abroad. It was claimed in publicity that de Mille had exchanged letters with the president of Yale on the subject.

37 T. Guback, 'Hollywood's international market', in T. Balio, *The American Film Industry*, Wisconsin and London, University of Wisconsin Press, revised edition, 1985, pp. 465 and 470.

38 K. Thompson, *Exporting Entertainment: America in the World Film Market, 1907–34*, London, British Film Institute, 1985, pp. 206–9.

39 Guback, *op. cit.*, pp. 468–9.

40 The American market remained effectively closed to films made outside the country: this was much resented (Guback, *op. cit.*, p. 467). There was also the question of the perceived racism of film presentation: in 1922 the Mexican government banned the import of films by companies that portrayed Mexicans unfavourably.

41 The wittiest account of film and consumer culture remains C. Eckert, 'The Carole Lombard in Macy's window', reprinted in J. Gaines and C. Herzog (eds), *Fabrications: Costume and the Female Body*, London, Routledge, 1991, pp. 100–24. See also J. Allen, 'The film viewer as consumer', *Quarterly Review of Film Studies*, 5, 4, 1980, pp. 481–99.

42 Guback, *op. cit.*, pp. 465–8, especially p. 468.

43 D. Bordwell *et al.*, *op. cit.*, pp. 298–308.

44 S. Cavell, *Pursuits of Happiness: The Hollywood Comedy of Remarriage*, Cambridge, Mass. and London, Harvard University Press, 1981.

45 Ibid., p. 82.

46 Everson, *op. cit.*, pp. 9–31.

47 Ibid., pp. 69–70.

48 C. Simmons, 'Companionate marriage and the lesbian threat', *Frontiers*, 4, 3, 1979, pp. 54–9. Also Jeffreys, 1985, *op. cit.*

49 It was not the making of films that produced wealth for the studios but their ability to control the means of exhibiting them. This is where the investment was made. In the early 1930s the industry nearly went bankrupt because so many cinemas had been bought and the Depression reduced the number of seats sold, so the loans taken out for buying the cinemas could not be serviced. When the banks stepped in to save Paramount they instituted a regime of tight financial control and accountability. This included daily reports from local managers and instruction from head office, by means of 'press-books', in ways of maximizing local interest in individual films. Film-going was deliberately linked with the pleasures of shopping. See J. Izod, *Hollywood and the Box-Office, 1895–1986*, London, Macmillan, 1988, pp. 95–110, and Eckert, *op. cit.*

50 Izod, *op. cit.*, p. 102. See also Gaines and Herzog, *op. cit.*

51 See n. 2 above.

52 Siebers, *op. cit.*, p. 40.

53 Bernheimer, *op. cit.*, p. 8.

54 G. Studlar, 'Masochism, masquerade, and the erotic metamorphoses of Marlene Dietrich', in Gaines and Herzog, op. cit., pp. 229–49. See also G. Deleuze, *Masochism: an Interpretation of Coldness and Cruelty*, New York, George Braziller, 1971.

55 Studlar, *op. cit.*, pp. 233–4. Studlar makes a careful distinction in a footnote, modifying the pathological aspect implied by Deleuze. She points out that Freud regarded polymorphous sexuality as the normal mode of childhood sexuality and one that persisted into adult life: it became pathological only when it replaced instead of coexisting with genital sexuality. See S. Freud, 'Three essays on the theory of sexuality', Standard Edition, 1905, vol. 7, p. 231.

56 A feminized Gary Cooper wore a rose behind his ear and carried a fan in von Sternberg's *Morocco* (1930), in a similar confusion of sexual identities, as Studlar, *op. cit.*, points out, p. 245.

57 J. Rivière, 'Womanliness as masquerade', 1929, reprinted in V. Burgin, J. Donald and C. Kaplan (eds), *Formations of Fantasy*, London, Methuen, 1986.

58 *Chambers's Encyclopaedia*, Oxford, Pergamon, 1966, vol. 6, pp. 699–700; G.

Durbin, *Wig, Hairdressing and Shaving Bygones*, Aylesbury, Shire Publications, 1984, p. 29.

59 J. Stevens Cox, *An Illustrated Dictionary of Hairdressing and Wigmaking*, London, Batsford, 1966, p. 110.

60 V. Woolf, *Mrs Dalloway*, London, Hogarth Press, 1925, Grafton paperback edition, p. 64. I am obliged to Camilla Hamer for this reference.

61 M. Lawrence, *We Write as Women*, London, Michael Joseph, 1937, p. 162.

62 P. Connerton, *How Societies Remember*, Cambridge, Cambridge University Press, 1989.

63 Ibid., p. 102.

Bibliography

Agulhon, M. (1981) *Marianne into Battle*, Cambridge: Cambridge University Press.
—— (ed.) (1983) *Histoire de la France urbaine*, vol. IV, Paris: Seuil.
Albistur, M. and Armogathe, D. (1977) *Histoire du féminisme français du moyen-âge à nos jours*, Paris, des femmes.
Algarotti, F. (1737) *Il Newtonianismo per le dame ovvero dialoghi sopra la luce e i colori*, Naples.
—— (1739) *Sir Isaac Newton's Philosophy Explained for the Use of the Ladies*, London.
Allen, J. (1980) 'The film viewer as consumer', *Quarterly Review of Film Studies*, 5, 4.
Alpers, S. (1983) *The Art of Describing*, London: Murray.
Bacchi della Lega (1875) *Serie delle edizioni delle opere di G. Boccaccio*, Bologna.
Bainton, R. H. (1971) *Women of the Reformation in Germany and Italy*, Minneapolis: Augsburg Publishing House.
Balio, T. (ed.) (1985) *The American Film Industry*, Wisconsin and London: University of Wisconsin Press.
Bann, S. (1989) *The True Vine: Visual Representation in Western Art*, Cambridge: Cambridge University Press.
Barcham, W. (1984) 'Patriarchy and politics: Tiepolo's "galleria patriarcale" in Udine revisited', in D. Rosand (ed.), *Interpretazione Veneziane*, Venice: Arsenale.
Baring, M. (1934) 'Three minutes', *The London Magazine*, xxx.
Barrington, E. (1929) *Cleopatra, the Laughing Queen*, New York: Grossnet and Dunlap.
Barzaghi, A. (1980) *Donne o cortegiane? La prostituzione a Venezia documenti di costume dal XVI al XVIII secolo*, Verona: Bertani.
Baudrillard, J. (1988) 'The trompe l'oeil', in N. Bryson (ed.), *Calligram: Essays in New Art History from France*, Cambridge: Cambridge University Press.
Baxandall, M. (1985) *Patterns of Intention*, New Haven: Yale University Press.
Bechler, Z. (ed.) (1981) *Contemporary Newtonian Research*, Dordrecht: Reidel.
Bernal, M. (1987) *Black Athena*, London: Free Association.
Bernheimer, C. (1991) 'Castration as fetish', *Paragraph*, 14, 1.
Bianchi, R. (ed.) (1988) *Cleopatra's Egypt: Age of the Ptolemies*, New York: Brooklyn Museum.
Bishop, M. (1964) *Petrarch and his World*, London: Chatto & Windus.
Blankert, A. *et al.* (1980) *Gods, Saints and Heroes: Dutch Painting in the Age of Rembrandt*, Washington: National Gallery of Art.
Boccaccio, G. (1964) *Concerning Famous Women*, trans. G. Guarino, London: Allen and Unwin.

Bonora, E. (ed.) (1970) *Illuministi Italiani, Tomo II: Opere di Francesco Algarotti e di Saverio Bettinelli*, Milan and Naples: Ricciardi.

Bordwell, D., Staiger, J., and Thompson, K. (1985) *The Classical Hollywood Cinema*, London: Routledge.

Bottari, G. (1822–5) *Raccolta di lettere sulla pittura*, Milan: Silvestri.

Boulding, E., Nuss, S., Carson, D., and Greenstein, M. (1976) *Handbook of International Data on Women*, New York: Sage.

Bowlby, R. (1985) *Just Looking*, New York and London: Methuen.

Bowman, A. K. (1986) *Egypt after the Pharaohs*, London: British Museum Publications.

Branca, V. (1975) *Boccaccio: the Man and his Works*, New York: New York University Press.

Brenter, C. D. (1947) *Bibliography of French Plays, 1700–89*, Berkeley.

Bridenthal, R. and Koonz, C. (1977) *Becoming Visible: Women in European History*, Boston, Mass.: Houghton Mifflin.

Bronte, C. (1853) *Villette*, London.

Bryson, N. (1983) *Vision and Painting: the Logic of the Gaze*, London: Macmillan.

—— (ed.) (1988) *Calligram: Essays in New Art History from France*, Cambridge: Cambridge University Press.

—— (1990) *Looking at the Overlooked: Four Essays on Still Life Painting*, London: Reaktion.

Buchner, E. (1982) *Die Sonnenuhr des Augustus*, Mainz am Rhein: Philipp von Zabern.

Buttrey, T. V. (1982) 'Pharaonic imitations of Athenian tetradrachms', in *Proceedings of the 9th International Congress of Numismatics, Berne, 1979*, Louvain.

—— (1984) 'Seldom what they seem – the case of the Athenian tetradrachm', in W. Heckel and R. Sullivan (eds), *Ancient Coins of the Graeco-Roman World*, Calgary: Calgary Institute for the Humanities.

Butts, M. (1935) *Scenes from the Life of Cleopatra*, London: Heinemann.

Caizzi, B. (1965) *Industria e commercio della repubblica veneta nel XVIII secolo*, Milan: Banca Commerciale Italiana.

Carré, J.-M. (1956) *Voyageurs et écrivains français en Egypte*, Cairo: Institut français de l'Archéologie Orientale.

Casini, P. (1983) *Newton e la coscienza Europea*, Bologna: Il Mulino.

Cavell, S. (1981) *Pursuits of Happiness: the Hollywood Comedy of Remarriage*, Cambridge, Mass., and London: Harvard University Press.

Chadwick, O. (1981) 'The Italian Enlightenment', in R. Porter and M. Teich (eds), *The Enlightenment in National Context*, Cambridge: Cambridge University Press.

Champollion, J.-F. (1833) *Lettres écrites d'Egypte et de Nubie*, Paris.

—— (1835–45) *Monuments de l'Egypte et la Nubie*, Paris.

Chassinat, E. (1965) *Le Temple de Dendara*, Cairo: Institut français de l'Archéologie Orientale.

Cherry, D. and Harris, J. (1982) 'Gainsborough and Van Dyck', *Art History*, 5, 3.

Cherry, D. and Pollock, G. (1984) 'Woman as sign in Pre-Raphaelite literature: a study of the representation of Elizabeth Siddall', *Art History*, 7, 2: 206–27.

Ciriacono, S. (1985) 'Echecs et réussites de la proto-industrialisation dans la Vénétie: le cas du haut-vicentin', *Revue d'histoire moderne et contemporaine* 32: 311–23.

—— (1988) 'Mass-consumption goods and luxury goods: the de-industrialisation of the republic of Venice from the sixteenth to the eighteenth century', in H.

Van der Wee (ed.), *The Rise and Decline of Urban Industries in Italy and the Low Countries*, Louvain: Louvain University Press.

Connerton, P. (1989) *How Societies Remember*, Cambridge: Cambridge University Press.

Cox, J. Stevens (1966) *An Illustrated Dictionary of Hairdressing and Wigmaking*, London: Batsford.

Curtius, L. (1933) 'Ikonographische Beiträge zum Porträt der römischen Republik und der julisch-claudischen Familie, IV. Kleopatra VII. Philopator', *Mitteilungen des Deutschen Archäologischen Instituts, Abteilung Rom*, 48: 182–92.

Davis, N. Z. (1975) 'Women on top', in *Society and Culture in Early Modern France*, London: Duckworth.

Debord, G. (1972) *Society of the Spectacle*, Detroit: Black and Red.

DeJean, J. (1989) *Fictions of Sappho, 1546–1937*, Chicago: Chicago University Press.

de Jongh, E. (1974) 'Grape symbolism in paintings of the 16th and 17th centuries', *Simiolus*, 7.

—— (1975) 'Pearls of virtue and pearls of vice', *Simiolus*, 8.

de Lauretis, T. (1989) *Technologies of Gender*, Basingstoke: Macmillan.

Delayen, G. (1934) *Cleopatra*, trans. F. Symons, New York: E. P. Dutton.

Deleuze, G. (1971) *Masochism: an Interpretation of Coldness and Cruelty*, New York: George Braziller.

Denon, V. (1802) *Voyages dans la Basse et la Haute Egypte, pendant les campagnes du général Bonaparte*, 2 vols, Paris.

Description de l'Egypte (1809–28), 23 vols, Paris: Imprimerie imperiale.

DiFederico, F. (1977) *Francesco Trevisani: Eighteenth-century Painter in Rome*, Washington, DC: Decatur House Press.

Durbin, G. (1984) *Wig, Hairdressing and Shaving Bygones*, Aylesbury: Shire Publications.

Durgnat, R. (1972) *Sexual Alienation in the Cinema*, London: Studio Vista.

Eckert, C. (1978) 'The Carole Lombard in Macy's window', *Quarterly Review of Film Studies*, 3, 1.

Eisenstein, E. (1979) *The Printing Press as an Agent of Change*, Cambridge: Cambridge University Press.

Everson, W. (1976) *Claudette Colbert*, New York: Pyramid.

Ferenczi, S. (1926) 'On the symbolism of the head of Medusa', in *Further Contributions to the Theory and Technique of Psychoanalysis*, London: Hogarth Press.

Ferguson, M., Quilligan, M., and Vickers, N. (eds) (1986) *Rewriting the Renaissance: the Discourses of Sexual Difference in Early Modern Europe*, Chicago: Chicago University Press.

Ferval, C. (1924) *The Life and Death of Cleopatra*, trans. H. Wilson, London.

ffolliott, S. (1986) 'Catherine de Medici as Artemisia: figuring the powerful widow', in M. Ferguson, M. Quilligan, and N. Vickers (eds), *Rewriting the Renaissance: the Discourses of Sexual Difference in Early Modern Europe*, Chicago: Chicago University Press.

Fiske, W. (1888) *Petrarch's Treatise De Remediis utriusque Fortunae*, Florence.

Foucault, M. (1970) *The Order of Things: an Archaeology of the Human Sciences*, London: Tavistock.

—— (1976) *The History of Sexuality*, vol. I, Harmondsworth: Penguin.

Freud, S. (1955) *The Complete Psychological Works of Sigmund Freud*, trans. J. Strachey, 24 vols, London: Hogarth. (Hereafter referred to as Standard Edition.)

—— 'Three essays on the theory of sexuality', Standard Edition, vol. 7.

—— 'A special type of object-choice made by men', Standard Edition, vol. 11.

―― 'Medusa's head', Standard Edition, vol. 18.
―― 'The infantile genital organisation', Standard Edition, vol. 19.
―― 'Female sexuality', Standard Edition, vol. 21.
―― 'New introductory lectures on psycho-analysis', Standard Edition, vol. 22.
Fried, M. (1980) *Absorption and Theatricality: Painting and the Beholder in the Age of Diderot*, Berkeley: University of California Press.
Gage, J. (1983) 'Newton and painting', in M. Pollock (ed.), *Common Denominators between Arts and Sciences*, Aberdeen: Aberdeen University Press.
Gaines, J. and Herzog, C. (eds) (1991) *Fabrications: Costume and the Female Body*, London: Routledge.
Gallagher, C. (1985) 'Response from Catherine Gallagher', in N. Hertz, *The End of the Line: Essays on Psycho-Analysis and the Sublime*, New York: Columbia University Press.
Garrard, M. (1988) *Artemisia Gentileschi*, Princeton: Princeton University Press.
Gautier, T. (1960) 'Une nuit de Cléopâtre', in *Le Roman de la Momie*, Paris: Garnier.
Georgelin, J. (1978) *Venise au siècle des lumières*, Paris-La Haye: Mouton.
Goerlitz, W. (1936) *Kleopatra: Bildnis einer dämonischer Frau (Cleopatra: Portrait of a Demonic Woman)*, Hamburg: Sieben Stabeverlag.
Goffen, R. (1986) *Piety and Patronage in Renaissance Venice*, New Haven and London: Yale University Press.
Goldberg, J. (1986) 'Fatherly authority: the politics of Stuart family images', in M. Ferguson, M. Quilligan, and N. Vickers (eds), *Rewriting the Renaissance: the Discourses of Sexual Difference in Early Modern Europe*, Chicago: Chicago University Press.
Gömery, D. (1986) *The Hollywood Studio System*, New York: St Martin's Press.
Gordon, F. (1990) *The Integral Feminist: Madeleine Pelletier 1874–1939*, Cambridge: Polity.
Gould, J. (1980) 'Law, custom and myth: aspects of the social position of women in classical Athens', *Journal of Hellenic Studies*, 100.
Grant, M. (1972) *Cleopatra*, London: Weidenfeld & Nicolson.
Grasset de S. Sauveur, J. (1796) *Encyclopédie des voyages, contenant l'abrégé historique des moeurs . . . de tous les peuples: Et la collection complette de leurs habillemens civils, militaires, religieux et dignitaires*, 5 vols, Paris.
Graves, R. (1954) *Claudius the God*, Harmondsworth: Penguin.
Griffin, J. (1985) *Latin Poets and Roman Life*, London: Duckworth.
Guback, T. (1985) 'Hollywood's international market', in T. Balio (ed.), *The American Film Industry*, Wisconsin and London: University of Wisconsin Press.
Guerlac, H. (1981) *Newton on the Continent*, Ithaca, and London: Cornell University Press.
Guillaume, J. (1972) 'Cleopatra Nova Pandora', *Gazette des Beaux Arts*, 80: 185–94.
Günther, H. F. K. (1927) *The Racial Elements of European History*, London: Methuen.
Guthmuller, B. (1986) *Studien zur antiken Mythologie in der italienischen Renaissance*, Weinheim: Acta Humaniora.
Hakfoort, C. (1988) *Let Newton Be*, Oxford: Oxford University Press.
Hall, C. (1984) *Vogue in the Thirties*, London: Octopus.
Halpern, R. (1986) 'Puritanism and maenadism in *A Mask*', in M. Ferguson, M. Quilligan, and N. Vickers (eds), *Rewriting the Renaissance: the Discourses of Sexual Difference in Early Modern Europe*, Chicago: Chicago University Press.
Harvey, P. (1937) *The Oxford Companion to Classical Literature*, Oxford: Clarendon Press.

Haskell, F. (1980) *Patrons and Painters: a Study in the Relations between Art and Society in the Age of the Baroque*, New Haven and London: Yale University Press.

Hause, S. (1987) *Hubertine Auclert: the French Suffragette*, New Haven and London: Yale University Press.

H.D. (1956) *Tribute to Freud*, New York: Pantheon.

Heath, S. (1978) 'Difference', *Screen*, 19, 3.

—— (1981) *Questions of Cinema*, Bloomington: Indiana University Press.

Heilbron, J. (1980) 'Experimental natural philosophy', in G. S. Rousseau and R. Porter (eds), *The Ferment of Knowledge*, Cambridge: Cambridge University Press.

Heisch, A. (1986) 'Queen Elizabeth and the persistence of patriarchy', in M. Ferguson, M. Quilligan, and N. Vickers (eds), *Rewriting the Renaissance: the Discourses of Sexual Difference in Early Modern Europe*, Chicago: Chicago University Press.

Hertz, N. (1985) *The End of the Line: Essays on Psycho-analysis and the Sublime*, New York: Columbia University Press.

Hobson, M. (1982) *The Object of Art*, Cambridge: Cambridge University Press.

Holdsworth, A. (1988) *Out of the Doll's House*, London: BBC Books.

Hopkins, K. (1980) 'Brother–sister marriage in Roman Egypt', *Comparative Studies in Society and History*, 22.

Huet, M.-H. (1982) *Rehearsing the Revolution: the Staging of Marat's Death 1793–1797*, Berkeley: University of California Press.

Hughes, D. (1986) 'Distinguishing signs: ear-rings, jews and franciscan rhetoric in the Italian Renaissance city', *Past and Present*, 112: 3–59.

Hughes-Hallett, L. (1989) *Cleopatra: Histories, Dreams and Distortions*, London: Bloomsbury.

Hunt, L. (1984) *Politics, Culture, and Class in the French Revolution*, Berkeley: University of California Press.

Huzar, E. (1978) *Mark Antony: a Biography*, Minneapolis: University of Minnesota Press.

Izod, J. (1988) *Hollywood and the Box-Office, 1895–1986*, London: Macmillan.

Jameson, F. (1988) 'Cognitive mapping', in C. Nelson and L. Grossberg (eds), *Marxism and the Interpretation of Culture*, Basingstoke: Macmillan.

Janson, H. (1952) *Apes and Ape-lore in the Middle Ages and the Renaissance*, London: Warburg Institute.

Jardine, A. (1985) *Gynesis: Configurations of Woman and Modernity*, Ithaca, NY, and London: Cornell University Press.

Jayawardena, K. (1986) *Feminism and Nationalism in the Third World*, London: Zed Books.

Jeffreys, S. (1985) *The Spinster and her Enemies*, London: Pandora.

—— (ed.) (1987) *The Sexuality Debates*, London: Routledge.

Johnson, L. (1986) *The Paintings of Eugène Delacroix*, 3 vols, Oxford: Clarendon Press.

Jordan, C. (1986) 'Feminism and the humanists', in M. Ferguson, M. Quilligan, and N. Vickers (eds), *Rewriting the Renaissance: the Discourses of Sexual Difference in Early Modern Europe*, Chicago: Chicago University Press.

Jordanova, L. (1989) *Sexual Visions*, Madison: University of Wisconsin Press.

Kaplan, E. (ed.) (1990) *Psychoanalysis and Cinema*, New York and London: Routledge.

Kelly-Gadol, J. (1982) 'Early feminism and the querelle des femmes', *Signs*, 8, 1: 4–28.

Kemp, M. (1990) *The Science of Art*, New Haven and London: Yale University Press.

Koonz, C. (1988) *Mothers in the Fatherland*, London: Methuen.

Kuhn, A. (1982) *Women's Pictures: Feminism and Cinema*, London and Boston: Routledge.

—— (1985) *The Power of the Image: Essays on Representation and Sexuality*, London and Boston: Routledge.

Kyrieleis, H. (1975) *Die Bildnisse der Ptolemaer*, Berlin: Mann.

Lacan, J. (1977) *Ecrits: a Selection*, New York: Norton.

Lane, F. (1973) *Venice, a Maritime Republic*, Baltimore and London: Johns Hopkins University Press.

Langlois, C. (1988) 'Les dérives vendéennes de l'imaginaire révolutionnaire', *Annales*, 43, 3.

Lawrence, M. (1937) *We Write as Women*, London: Michael Joseph.

Lefkowitz, M. R. and Fant, M. B. (1982) *Women's Life in Greece and Rome*, London: Duckworth.

—— (1983) *Images of Women in Antiquity*, Bromley: Croom Helm.

Levey, M. (1986) *Giambattista Tiepolo*, New Haven and London: Yale University Press.

Libby, L. (1973) 'Venetian history and political thought after 1509', *Studies in the Renaissance*, 20: 7–45.

Lindsay, J. (1971) *Cleopatra*, New York: Coward, McCann and Geoghan.

Lloyd, A. (ed.) (1983) *Movies of the Thirties*, London: Orbis.

Ludwig, E. (1937) *Cleopatra, the Story of a Queen*, trans. B. Miall, London: Viking Press.

Lunardini, C. (1986) *From Equal Suffrage to Equal Rights*, New York and London: New York University Press.

Lynch, K. (1960) *The Image of the City*, Cambridge, Mass.: MIT Press.

Macciocchi, M.-A. (1979) 'Female sexuality in Fascist ideology', *Feminist Review*, 1, 1: 67–82.

Maecius, P. (1628) *Emblemata*, Bologna.

Maréchal, P. S. (1788) *Costumes civils actuels de tous les peuples connus*, 4 vols, Paris.

Marini, R. (1981) *L'Opera completa di Veronese*, Milan: Rizzoli.

Marks, E. and de Courtivron, I. (eds) (1981) *New French Feminisms*, Brighton: Harvester.

Mattii, M. (1939) *Cleopatra contra Roma*, Florence.

Menu, B. (1986) *L'Obélisque de la Concorde*, Paris: Lunx.

Merchant, C. (1980) *The Death of Nature: Women, Ecology and the Scientific Revolution*, San Francisco: Harper & Row.

Meyer, G. D. (1955) *The Scientific Lady in England 1650–1760*, Berkeley and Los Angeles: University of California Press.

Millar, F. and Segal, E. (1984) *Caesar Augustus: Seven Aspects*, Oxford: Oxford University Press.

Miller, M. B. (1981) *The Bon Marché: Bourgeois Culture and the Department Store, 1869–1920*, Princeton: Princeton University Press.

Millett, K. (1977) *Sexual Politics*, London: Virago.

Molmenti, P. (1880) *La storia di Venezia*, Turin.

Montrose, L. (1986) '*A Midsummer Night's Dream* and the shaping fantasies of Elizabethan culture', in M. Ferguson, M. Quilligan, and N. Vickers (eds), *Rewriting the Renaissance: the Discourses of Sexual Difference in Early Modern Europe*, Chicago: Chicago University Press.

Mort, F. (1987) *Dangerous Sexualties*, London: Routledge.

Muir, E. (1981) *Civic Ritual in Renaissance Venice*, Princeton: Princeton University Press.

Mulvey, L. (1975) 'Visual pleasure and narrative cinema', *Screen*, 16, 1.

—— (1989) *Visual and Other Pleasures*, Basingstoke: Macmillan.

Nelson, C. and Grossberg, L. (eds) (1988) *Marxism and the Interpretation of Culture*, Basingstoke: Macmillan.

Newton, I. (1952) *Opticks*, New York: Dover Publications reprint.

Newton, S. M. (1988) *The Dress of the Venetians 1495–1525*, Aldershot: Scolar.

O'Bell, L. (1984) *Pushkin's Egyptian Nights*, Ann Arbor: Ardis.

Odell, G. C. (1920) *Shakespeare from Betterton to Irving*, 2 vols, New York: Scribner.

Olds, C., Williams, R., and Levin, W. (1976) *Images of Love and Death*, Michigan: Museum of Art.

Ozment, S. (1983) *When Fathers Ruled: Family Life in Reformation Europe*, Cambridge, Mass.: Harvard University Press.

Parish, J. (1972) *The Paramount Pretties*, New York: Arlington House.

Pateman, C. (1988) *The Sexual Contract*, Cambridge: Polity.

Pelling, C. (forthcoming) 'The triumviral period', in A. W. Lintott, A. K. Bowman, and E. A. Chapman (eds), *Cambridge Ancient History*, vol. X, 2nd edn, Cambridge: Cambridge University Press.

Pestman P. (1961) *Marriage and Matrimonial Property in Ancient Egypt*, Leiden: Brill.

Pigler, A. (1974) *Barockthemen*, 3 vols, Budapest: Akadémiai Kiadó.

Pignatti, T., Pedrocco, F., and Pedrocco, E. (1982) *Palazzo Labia a Venezia*, Turin: Eri.

Pliny, *Historia Naturalis*, IX, lviii.

Plutarch, *Life of Antony*.

Pomeroy, S. B. (1975) *Goddesses, Whores, Wives and Slaves*, New York: Schocken Books.

Porter, R. and Teich, M. (eds) (1981) *The Enlightenment in National Context*, Cambridge: Cambridge University Press.

Price, S. (1984) *Rituals and Power: the Roman Imperial Cult in Asia Minor*, Cambridge: Cambridge University Press.

Propertius, 3, 11, 53–4.

Quaegebeur, J. (1988) 'Cleopatra VII and the cults of the Ptolemaic queens', in R. Bianchi (ed.), *Cleopatra's Egypt: Age of the Ptolemies*, New York: Brooklyn Museum.

Quirk, J. (1985) *Claudette Colbert*, New York: Crown.

Ravoux-Rallo, E. (1984) *La Femme à Venise aux temps de Casanova*, Paris: Stock.

Ribeiro, A. (1983) *A Visual History of Costume: the Eighteenth Century*, London: Batsford.

Rice, E. E. (1983) *The Grand Procession of Ptolemy Philadelphus*, Oxford: Oxford University Press.

Ricketts, L. (1980) 'The administration of Ptolemaic Egypt under Cleopatra VII', unpublished PhD thesis, Ann Arbor.

Rivière, J. (1986) 'Womanliness as masquerade', in V. Burgin, J. Donald, and C. Kaplan (eds), *Formations of Fantasy*, London: Methuen.

Roper, L. (1985) 'Prostitution and the Reformation in Augsburg', *History Workshop Journal*, 19.

Rosand, D. (1982) *Painting in Cinquecento Venice*, New Haven and London: Yale University Press.

—— (1984) 'Venetia figurata: the iconography of a myth', in D. Rosand (ed.), *Interpretazione Veneziane*, Venice: Arsenale.

Rousseau, G. S. and Porter, R. (1980) *The Ferment of Knowledge: Studies in the Historiography of Eighteenth-Century Science*, Cambridge: Cambridge University Press.

Sabra, A. (1981) *Theories of Light from Descartes to Newton*, Cambridge and New York: Cambridge University Press.

Said, E. (1978) *Orientalism*, London, Routledge & Kegan Paul.

Sandström, S. (1963) *Levels of Unreality*, Uppsala: Acta Universitatis Uppsaliensis, Figura N.S. 4.

Santore, C. (1988) 'Julia Lombardo, "Somtuosa meretrize": a portrait by property', *Renaissance Quarterly*, xli, i.

Scarisbrick, D. (1984) 'Shining like the sun', *Country Life*, 14 June.

Schaffer, S. (1983) 'Natural philosophy and public spectacle', *History of Science*, 21, 1.

—— (1989) 'Glassworks', in D. Gooding, T. Pinch, and S. Schaffer (eds), *The Uses of Experiment*, Cambridge: Cambridge University Press.

—— (1990) 'Newtonianism', in R. Olby, G. N. Cantor, J. R. R. Christie, and M. J. S. Hodges (eds), *Companion to the History of Modern Science*, New York and London: Routledge.

Schama, S. (1987) *The Embarrassment of Riches*, London: Collins.

Scheidig, W. (ed.) (1955) *Die Holzschnitte des Petrarca-Meisters: zu Petrarcas Werk von der Artzney bayder Glück des guten und widerwärtigen, Augsburg 1532*, Berlin: Akad. d. Künste.

Scott, M. (1980) *The History of Dress Series, Late Gothic Europe 1400–1500*, London: Mills and Boon.

Sella, D. (1961) *Commerci e industrie a Venezia nel secolo XVII*, Venice: Istituo per la collaborazione culturale.

Sérullaz, M. (1963) *Les Peintures murales de Delacroix*, Paris: Temps.

Seward, D. (1981) *Marie-Antoinette*, London: Constable.

Shapin, S. (1980) 'Social uses of science', in G. Rousseau and R. Porter (eds), *The Ferment of Knowledge: Studies in the Historiography of Eighteenth-Century Science*, Cambridge: Cambridge University Press.

Siebers, T. (1983) *The Mirror of Medusa*, Berkeley: University of California Press.

Simmons, C. (1979) 'Companionate marriage and the lesbian threat', *Frontiers*, 4, 3.

Sinding-Larssen, S. (1974) *Christ in the Council-Hall: Studies in the Religious Iconography of the Venetian Republic*, Rome: Spoleto.

Smith, R. R. R. (1988) *Hellenistic Royal Portraits*, Oxford: Clarendon Press.

Stadelmann, H. (1931) *Cleopatra, Egypt's Last Queen*, trans. M. M. Green, London: Routledge.

Stallybrass, P. (1986) 'Patriarchal territories: the body enclosed', in M. Ferguson, M. Quilligan, and N. Vickers (eds), *Rewriting the Renaissance: the Discourses of Sexual Difference in Early Modern Europe*, Chicago: Chicago University Press.

Stevens Curl, J. (1982) *The Egyptian Revival*, London: George Allen and Unwin.

Stewart, A. (1978) *Unequal Lovers*, New York: Abaris.

Stone, L. (1977) *The Family, Sex and Marriage*, London: Weidenfeld.

Straker, S. (1985) 'What is the history of theories of perception the history of?' in M. Osler and P. Farber (eds), *Religion, Science and World View: Essays in Honour of Richard S. Westfall*, Cambridge: Cambridge University Press.

Studlar, G. (1991) 'Masochism, masquerade and the erotic metamorphoses of Marlene Dietrich', in J. Gaines and C. Herzog (eds), *Fabrications: Costume and the Female Body*, London: Routledge.

Syme, R. (1939) *The Roman Revolution*, Oxford: Clarendon Press.

Tarn, W. W. (1934) 'The war of the East against the West', in S. A. Cook, F. E. Adcock, and M. P. Charlesworth (eds), *Cambridge Ancient History*, vol X, Cambridge: Cambridge University Press.

Terdiman, R. (1985) *Discourse/Counter Discourse: the Theory and Practice of Symbolic Resistance in Nineteenth-century France*, Ithaca: Cornell University Press.

Thompson, D. J. (1988) *Memphis under the Ptolemies*, Princeton: Princeton University Press.

Thompson, K. (1985) *Exporting Entertainment: America in the World Film Market, 1907–34*, London: British Film Institute.

Tickner, L. (1987) *The Spectacle of Women*, London: Chatto & Windus.

Toffolo, S. (1987) *Antichi strumenti Veneziani*, Venice: Arsenale.

Trinkaus, C. (1979) *The Poet as Philosopher*, New Haven: Yale University Press.

Turner, V. (1975) *Dramas, Fields and Metaphors*, Ithaca and London: Cornell University Press.

Twyne, T. (1579) *Physicke against Fortune*, London.

Urban, L. P. (1968) 'La festa della Sensa', *Studi Veneziani*, 10: 291–353.

Victor, Sextus Aurelius, *De viris illustribus*, 86.

Voilquin, S. (1832) 'Variétés', *La Tribune des femmes*, Paris.

Volkmann, H. (1958) *Cleopatra: a Study in Politics and Propaganda*, trans. T. J. Cadoux, London: Elek Books.

von Wertheimer, O. (1931) *Cleopatra – a Royal Voluptuary*, trans. H. Paterson, London: Harrap.

Warner, M. (1985) *Monuments and Maidens: the Allegory of the Female Form*, London: Weidenfeld.

Webster, C. (1982) *From Paracelsus to Newton*, Cambridge: Cambridge University Press.

Weeks, J. (1985) *Sex, Politics and Society*, London: Routledge.

Weir, A. and Jerman, J. (1986) *Images of Lust: Sexual Carvings on Medieval Churches*, London: Batsford.

Williamson, M. (1974) *Infinite Variety: Antony and Cleopatra in Renaissance Drama and Earlier Tradition*, New Haven: Mystic.

Witt, R. E. (1971) *Isis in the Graeco-Roman World*, London: Thames & Hudson.

Woolf, V. (1925) *Mrs Dalloway*, London: Hogarth Press.

Index

This is an index of topics referred to in the text. For names of critics, historians, and theorists cited, see Notes, pp. 135–51